HAIL OF FIRE

HAIL OF FIRE

A Man and His Family Face Natural Disaster

RANDY FRITZ

Trinity University Press
San Antonio

Published by Trinity University Press
San Antonio, Texas 78212
Copyright © 2015 by Randy Fritz

Jacket and book design by Pinafore Press / Janice Shay

Cover photograph: Bastrop wildfire, courtesy of Alexey Sergeev
Author portraits and interior images: Amanda Hartfield

Author's note: This book is a memoir about my family's experience with a historic natural disaster and its aftermath. To the extent that memory and notes can be trusted, it is an accurate description of what happened. While I didn't keep a journal, I did make voice and written notes on my smartphone about critical events immediately after they happened, and I have an e-mail and text message archive to remind me of my thoughts and activities on specific days. There are no composite or imagined characters or events. I haven't changed anyone's name, although in some cases I chose not to identify particular individuals.

Trinity University Press strives to produce its books using methods and materials in an environmentally sensitive manner. We favor working with manufacturers that practice sustainable management of all natural resources, produce paper using recycled stock, and manage forests with the best possible practices for people, biodiversity, and sustainability. The press is a member of the Green Press Initiative, a nonprofit program dedicated to supporting publishers in their efforts to reduce their impacts on endangered forests, climate change, and forest-dependent communities.

The paper used in this publication meets the minimum requirements of the American National Standard for Information Sciences—Permanence of Paper for Printed Library Materials, ANSI 39.48–1992.

ISBN 978-1-59534-259-1 hardcover
ISBN 978-1-59534-260-7 ebook
CIP data on file at the Library of Congress

19 18 17 16 15 | 5 4 3 2 1

To my beloved family,
my never-ending seed of gratitude

PROLOGUE

At least seventy thousand wildfires happen every year in America, and most regenerate healthy forests, culling underbrush, improving the soil, and unspooling the life resting inside pinecones.

Some of them shed their better natures, mutating into something dangerous enough that heavy equipment and elite firefighters must be called in. Of those, only a few turn into criminals, taking lives and destroying homes.

But in the modern era, there have been only two wildfires, both in California, more vicious and pitiless than the one that changed my life after nearly killing me.

With the tag-team help of a malicious sun that baked Central Texas dry for months and a tropical storm that uncoiled from the Gulf of Mexico with a hateful wind instead of rain, the fire that ravaged Bastrop County—my home for more than thirty years—on a holiday weekend in 2011 left behind a scorched and violated landscape shaped like a giant teardrop.

The fire started in two separate locations as people were returning home from church or finishing their lunches. In each case, a dead tree on private property blew into a power line, and the resulting sparks lit the bounty of fuel on the ground—a desiccated carpet of pine needles and twigs that were like gasoline vapor waiting for a match.

The wind curling off Tropical Storm Lee's dry side energized the embryonic flames. In short order, as they skittered along the ground, vaulted from tree to tree, and sprinted from house to house, the fires began shooting off flaming pieces of bark or wood, like the sparks of a campfire, except the embers weren't innocent or nostalgic.

As these fiery hailstones prepped the drought-stricken forest for the arrival of each fire, yet another one began five miles southwest of the first two before the event was an hour old. By the time the conflagration crossed Highway 71—one of the major arterials connecting two of the nation's largest cities—they had merged into a colossus, and a thousand homes were burning or about to be.

The teardrop-shaped fire destroyed more homes, and upended more lives, than any other fire in Texas history. It reached a level of intensity that fire experts have scientifically confirmed only a handful of times before.

One of them—the 1980 Mack Lake Fire in the northern region of Lower Michigan—released as much energy as ten Hiroshima-sized atomic bombs and destroyed almost forty square miles of remote forest. That inferno had horizontal roll vortices, which are like twisters of fire spinning on their sides.

For the vortices to form, a wildfire has to create its own unspeakable environment, a violent and unstoppable combination of flames, heat, smoke, convection, and wind. At that point, the fire's hellish ecosystem curls the flames near the treetops and spins them parallel to the doomed ground below.

The flipped-on-their-side twisters are like a conveyor belt that allows the fire to glide across the forest's ceiling. They are also a catastrophic fire's unmistakable "I was here" inscription, signifying a power and force that can be described with over-the-top metaphors or, conversely, with an utter lack of poetry: "uncontrollable by any means under human manipulation," in the words of an expert who has studied the effect.

The Bastrop wildfire spawned dozens of horizontal roll vortices that left their long and narrow tattoos on almost fifty-five square miles of seared landscape, much more forestland than the ten-H-bomb Mack Lake Fire wiped out. Some of them were in the neighborhood where my children were born and grew into strong, confident, and beautiful young women, and where my wife and I planned to live out our remaining days.

My story is about what this hail of fire did to the iconic pine forest I cherished and revered, and the creatures that lived in it, including our three dogs. It is about what happened to my wife and our three daughters, one of whom turned twenty-one on the day the fire reached its climax. Most of all, it is the story of what fire—my former friend and artistic collaborator—brought about as it ripped me from my comfortable and self-satisfied life and brought me to a place both strangely familiar and utterly new.

In America, but especially in Texas, there is a mythology of what a man is supposed to be like. A man figures out what he wants and goes after it. He knows what he believes, and a little trouble isn't going to talk him out of it. When circumstances knock him down, he gets up, brushes himself off, and gets going again, possibly with a laugh and definitely not with tears. If things really go haywire, he doesn't waste time complaining about it or begging for help. With a clear head and steely resolve, he fixes it.

Before the fire, I modeled myself after that myth. Then, as often happens with a natural disaster or some other event that is as shocking as it is unforeseeable, I involuntarily turned into something different. As my new self replaced the old one, I didn't need a feel-good story or inspirational blog or self-help book to prop me up and show me the way back to how things were. I needed something or someone to help me understand what was happening to me and why it was irreversible. I needed strength and knowledge from the community of shared experience.

I needed a book like this one.

PART I
A LIFE
IN THE PINES

CHAPTER 1

September 6, 2011, 6 a.m. It was still dark when I gave up on the nearly worthless sleep that finally came to me an hour or two earlier. As I put my feet on the floor, my head throbbed, my neck was stiff, and my stomach felt acidy and tight. During the middle-of-the-night hours that I stared at the low motel ceiling or fidgeted on the bed, I had won and lost a dozen debates with myself about whether our home and property had escaped again.

"The answer machine doesn't pick up. The house is gone."

"No, it just means the electricity is out."

"The thermal maps on the Internet say it never got to our neighborhood."

"Nobody in their right mind would believe anything online at this point."

"It's impossible that we've lost everything. It simply can't have happened."

"Oh, really? What about our friends who got burned out in the first hour?"

"The wind never shifted in our direction."

"How would you know?"

Enough was enough. I couldn't wait any longer. I needed to go back one more time, even though the fire continued to rage and grim-faced law enforcement officers were ready to thwart me at every entry point.

After I put the toilet seat back down—the reflex of a man who lives only with females—I caught a glimpse of myself in the small, rectangular mirror over the bathroom sink. The half-moon flesh under my bloodshot eyes was wrinkled and loose. My hair was unpresentable, not that I cared.

I tried to slip out without waking my wife, Holly, or my youngest daughter and birthday girl, Miranda, who were sleeping side by side on the other bed. But my bed squeaked as I sat on its edge to lace up my tennis shoes, and Holly lifted up her head, her voice quiet and scratchy.

Her objections didn't work. I was too determined and she was too groggy. A minute later, I was walking across the overflowing parking lot. It was very dark except in the east, where a thin wash of light painted the sky dark gray.

Highway 71 was closed a mile away, and vehicles from the direction of

Houston were being rerouted northwest. It was too early for traffic to be backed up, and I quickly faced a young officer with a flashlight in his hand.

"Good morning sir," he said. "Where are you going today?"

"To Austin," I lied.

"Follow this road. You'll come to Highway 290 in a half hour. Turn left and you'll be there before you know it."

"That's what I figured from my phone's GPS," I said. "Any idea what's happening with the fire? Can't see anything except for that orange glow."

"It's been like that since my shift started. I dunno any more than you. Our job is to keep people safe, and that's what we're doing."

"God's work, I guess."

"You got it," he said and nodded to his uniformed companion, who waved me through.

It was hard to believe that they would watch where I went, but I wasn't taking any chances. I drove out of their sightline. Then I shut off my lights, made a U-turn, and turned west on the county road that eventually intersected with Park Road 1C, the narrow and curvy ribbon of asphalt connecting the two state parks that form the eastern and western boundaries of the Lost Pines.

I kept my lights off for about a mile. The western firelight and the increasingly pale eastern sky were enough for me to keep my car on the road.

My business was urgent. But I stopped at an overlook several hundred feet above the highway. I needed to know if I was about to drive into the fire's maw.

The last time I was here—early afternoon the previous day—cars and pickups were parked at cockeyed angles. The conversations I joined or overheard over the wind's moan were a mixture of resignation and threadbare hope. Nobody knew for sure what was happening on the ground, but there were a lot of theories.

I was certain some of my overlook companions were already wiped out, like my friends at the motel, or about to be. Others would be fine by the time it was all over. I couldn't imagine how the lucky, including me, would fight back their guilt, or the unlucky their anger and bitterness.

From our vantage point, the fire took on two forms. The main one was a vast and heaving cloud of smoke towering many thousands of feet above us. It filled our entire western and southern visual horizon. While it was mainly white, there were dark streaks and blotches in it and lighter spots where the blue sky behind it was almost visible.

The other form was a yellow curtain of flame hanging and writhing over the ground. Within it, sharp bursts of light appeared and almost immediately vanished. Each one was like a tweet from the fire informing us that another home had been claimed and the secure future of another family forfeited.

While we were a small community of collective ignorance, there was one thing we knew: this fire was vastly more dangerous and destructive than the one two and a half years earlier that took three helicopters, two airplanes, and twenty-two fire departments to contain.

That one worried us. This one terrified us.

That one threatened dozens of families. This one was a predator of hundreds, if not thousands.

That one surrendered in a week. This one looked like it might never give up until its gluttony expired for lack of food.

Labor Day 2011 was the first day of a new era in Bastrop County, one in which its most prominent and beloved feature—the Lost Pines—would be ugly and desolate for many years. For those of us in middle age or beyond, our deaths would precede the rejuvenation of the forest into the bounty of life it was when we built our homes and started our families.

Eighteen hours later, with dawn breaking, I was alone at the overlook. Perhaps I was the only person sneaky or defiant enough to go where the highway patrol and sheriff's office insisted I shouldn't. Or maybe my fellow scofflaws were just getting dressed and plotting their way in.

Just as the weather forecasters had predicted, the hysterical wind had died down overnight. A mild breeze made the 80-degree temperature pleasant, almost balmy. I leaned against one of the large circular wooden barriers at the edge of the bluff and stared at the fire.

Low, clean eastern light illuminated the smoke cloud, giving it an ethereal, almost hypnotic quality. It was beautiful and humbling.

But it was also awful and confounding. As a matter of science, the fire was easily explained: a record-breaking drought, tropical-force winds, and decades of fuel untouched by the natural fire events that keep a forest healthy. But physics and biology couldn't explain why the rules of normal life could be repealed in such an arbitrary and irrevocable way. Or why so many loblolly pines at the zenith of their slender elegance had to come to such a terrible end.

My eyes followed the line of the highway into the pale, yellowish, billowing wall. There were no more flares, perhaps because there were no more structures left in the neighborhoods west and south of mine.

While the fire was far from contained, the entire scene felt like the last stages of a great battle, the smoke signifying immense destruction and a future reckoning of sorrow and despair. I was heartbroken for the forest and sad for the friends and acquaintances that were already starting to hunker down in the face of a bleak future. But I didn't count myself among them. I had won the nighttime debate with myself because there was clear sky in the direction of my home, trees, and land. In less than a quarter hour, I would confirm what my gut already knew.

Suddenly I noticed a man standing in the middle of the road, facing me. I didn't recognize him. He was calm and almost smiling.

"Morning," he said.

"Howdy," I said. "Where are you coming from?"

"Down the park road a bit."

"I was just getting ready to go that way myself. Any reason I shouldn't?"

"Not really."

"So it's safe?" I asked.

"You're looking at me, aren't you?"

I described where I lived. "You know where I'm talking about?"

He nodded.

"Well, how does it look?"

FINDING THE LOST PINES

In 1979, my new wife Holly and I relocated from Chicago after gutting it out through one of the worst winters on record. We chose Central Texas because rumor had it the Austin area was one of the most promising places in America for a young couple with artistic ambitions (I a potter, Holly a dance teacher), a tiny budget, and a desire for beautiful, open spaces.

Many people who move to Central Texas to live a self-sufficient life default to the area west of Austin. So that is where we started driving around, looking for cheap land and pleasant surroundings.

But having spent all of my childhood in a Wisconsin community where it is usually green or white, I didn't know what to think about rocky and brown landscapes with scrubby trees and gnarled undergrowth. The charms of the Texas Hill Country, which are considerable for those who take the time to see them, were lost on my eyes, accustomed as they were to tall trees and lavishly green alfalfa fields. With each day, the sense that we had made a big mistake grew a little larger until my sister-in-law, Laura, suggested we try our luck east of Austin.

We drove for almost an hour and saw nothing to calm our anxious minds. And then, true to its name and reputation, the Lost Pines appeared out of nowhere and without warning, like a dream that couldn't possibly be real. Twelve miles later, it abruptly disappeared.

Within hours, the decision practically made itself. This is where Holly and I would live, because it felt like home. With the help of my father-in-law, we bought five acres in the heart of the Lost Pines, where we intended to build a small pottery studio and equally modest house.

The Lost Pines circa 1979—when the highway between Austin and Houston was undivided and development was spotty and primitive—was a dense forest of mature loblolly pines, some of which soared nearly a hundred feet, with four-foot diameters. Along the highway on the southern edge of the Lost Pines, the land went up and down like a low-grade roller coaster. While there were oaks sprinkled among the pines, the dominant image from the high point where the Lost Pines began was an overpopulated city of loblollies: impenetrable, and as green as a major-league outfield.

As I grew to love this beguiling forest, I savored a fanciful idea of how it came to be. Eons ago, I imagined, a group of East Texas loblolly pines skipped out on their siblings, made a wrong turn to the West, and decided to stay put in a place where they didn't really belong. Over time, they grew stronger and more resilient than their eastern ancestors, facing down periods of drought and excessive heat by drilling taproots deep into Bastrop County sand and clay.

There is a haunting image from the Terrence Malick movie *Tree of Life* that looks steeply upward through several large loblollies in what was, before the fire destroyed it, Bastrop State Park. It is easy to see why Malick wove this view into a movie about the biggest themes imaginable. The trees that tower over Jessica Chastain are primordial and spiritual.

The Lost Pines are—or were—almost everything the popular, Wild West image of Texas isn't. Before the fire, I could drive Park Road 1C—the barely two-lane road connecting Bastrop and Buescher State Parks—and crane my head upward and wonder how I could be in the middle of Texas while feeling like I was nearing the much-loved redwood and giant sequoia forests of Northern California.

On cloudless and crisp fall or winter days, with windows and sunroof open, I felt like an actor in a car commercial in my revved-up five-speed, fighting the urge to look around and upward rather straight ahead. Summer days brought trips to the Bastrop State Park pool, a lovely artifact of the Civilian Conservation Corps, my girls strapped in and their stomachs sloshing about with every hairpin curve.

The road insinuated itself through mile after mile of mature pines and oaks. It rose and fell, dipping over low-water crossings, and almost kissing the edge of ephemeral ponds that would overflow with heavy spring rains and then fade to nothingness in the summer.

Park Road 1C was where, like many other biking enthusiasts in Central Texas, I would go for rides on hills whose verticality injected fire into my lungs, surrounded by trees that provided shade throughout the day, with part of my ride hugging a cliff with vistas that stretched for miles to the south.

Over more than thirty years, as our family grew to include three daughters, my wife Holly and I occupied four houses within a three-mile radius, deep in the forest and a brisk walk from the park road. Each was much more than the sum of its foundation, studs, roof, plumbing, and electrical wires. Our family took root in these homes and grew strong like the trees that surrounded them. Then the fire came.

February 28, 2009, 1:30 p.m. So this was what a wildfire looked like from ground level as it shot through a narrow strip of the Lost Pines: a crackling and sparking comet flying along the ground with a tail of orange flame and black smoke. As it rammed into a pine tree, there was a deep hiss or *whoosh* as the needles evaporated in a flare. Waves of heat shimmered over the fire. It was like a viscous compound was being mixed with the air, giving it mass and weight.

When the Red Flag warning was posted that morning, I paid no attention to it. Surely this would be the latest in a series of false alarms that had been issued on other gusty days that winter in Bastrop County and a dozen other counties in south-central Texas where the drought was worse than any other place in America. The wind whipping in from the north was typical for a late-season cold front. The pine needles on the forest floor were as deep and brittle as they'd been for years. Why would this day be different?

Just after lunch, Holly called me outside. "You smell that?" she said as we stood on our deck and scanned the blue sky, our hands cupped over our eyebrows.

"Smoke," I said.

"I know that," she said. "I'm talking about how strong it is."

"I hope nobody around here is stupid enough to be burning trash in these conditions," I said.

"That's not the smell of trash," she said.

"I better take a quick drive to see what's happening."

"Just please be careful," she said.

As I drove uphill to the intersection with Cottletown Road—the county road that dead-ended into the state highway two miles away—an elongated pillar of off-white smoke rose over the forest to the northwest. A minute later I was at the electrical highline, an easement cut into the forest that would expose the fire as the wind blew it south. I didn't have to wait long as I leaned against the edge of my car's hood.

One second I was looking over the crest of a hill; the next second the hill disappeared as the fiery comet crossed the easement. Several people soon joined me at the highline. I kept quiet and they returned the favor.

The fire was less than a half mile to the west of our little group, but I felt safe because the wind was pushing it perpendicular to us. While I felt bad for what was about to slam into the homes and businesses of people we knew or occasionally acknowledged with a wave or nod of the head, I was also mesmerized and dazzled.

Unlike the hatefulness of intentional man-made destruction, this kind of natural forest devastation demanded respect. If it was going to happen, I was grateful to see it. After this brief spectacle was over, there was little chance I'd encounter such raw and unapologetic power ever again.

My phone rang, and I had to answer it because it was Walter, my friend and building partner. He was about to claim a moral victory.

"For years you've been saying it would happen," I said. "Well, you're finally right."

"I wish I'd been wrong," he said.

"I assume your place is OK."

"For now. But we're about to pack and leave, and I think you should too."

"I'm staring at it right now from the road, and I'm almost positive we'll be fine."

"You're assuming it won't change direction," he said.

"I don't see how it could at this point."

"I don't think you should take any chances. I already told Holly that when I called your house a minute ago."

If Walter had set something in motion back at the house, I knew I couldn't keep watching as the fire ate through the forest. Holly was carrying a load of clothes out to her SUV as I pulled into the garage.

With the smoke plume barely visible over the trees, I couldn't accept even the theoretical possibility that something very bad could soon happen to the house where I had lived for longer than any other in my life, or the one nearby that Walter and I were about to finish—the one where Holly and I would live out our remaining days, possibly with Miranda.

For over fourteen years, we had lived in a capacious red-brick house with matching bay windows nestled into a knoll near the back of our sixteen acres bordering Long Trail. Surrounded by mature pines, it was completely hidden. We had a twenty-two-foot-high living room—floating on a lake of solid oak—into which we could have fit the rudimentary house Holly and I built in 1980 when our aspirations and optimism exceeded our common sense. Fireplaces with intricately trimmed mantels anchored the north and south sides of the house, one in the living room and the other in my oak-paneled office.

Every room, with the possible exceptions of the laundry and kitchen, was bigger than it needed to be. Through my mother-in-law's generosity, and the legacy of Holly's father, who died in 2004, we filled that space with artwork—including a signed Marc Chagall lithograph—and large Oriental and Navajo rugs. Most of the art we hung was the work of Holly's maternal grandfather, a painter trained in Paris and at the Art Institute of Chicago at the turn of the century. His understated and quietly beautiful pastels and oil paintings were of landscapes, mainly in the desert Southwest. One of them, however, was an oil painting of the Lake Michigan dunes. This reminder of where I grew up hung above the fireplace in my study.

Except for the bathrooms and laundry, every room had at least one of my pots, with my most prized wood-fired pots in the places of greatest prominence.

Our furniture and art were surrounded by memories of what had happened there since the hot July day in 1994 when we moved in. As Holly and I stood on our bedroom balcony on the first night, Miranda was about to turn four years old, Amelia was six, and Hillary had just celebrated her twelfth birthday.

Now we were less than a month from leaving the house we no longer needed, with two daughters living on their own. Instead of "good-bye," we were about to say "see you later" to the place where our frightened intuitions for Miranda had turned into despair and finally hope.

A long-occupied home records, celebrates, and sometimes mourns a family's history. Because we were friends with the couple who bought it, we could recharge, through occasional visits, our thankfulness for what Miranda had become by remembering what might have been.

"I know you've already talked to Walter," I said to Holly as we both walked toward the house. "Is your mind made up?"

"First tell me what you saw up there," she said.

"It's the sort of thing you have to see for yourself to fully appreciate. It was awe-inspiring and dreadful."

"Are we in danger?"

"Not now and probably not at all."

"But what's the harm in leaving for a day or two? Think of how our daughters would feel if we didn't and then something awful happened to us."

"I suppose you're right that we shouldn't sleep here if the fire is still going," I said.

"And if we're going to stay with Hillary, do you really think we should go empty-handed?"

"Point taken," I said. "I'll wrap my pots in newspaper and spread them on my seats. We can stuff whatever clothes we can't fit into your car around the pots to keep them from jiggling around. I'll put our photos and videos in my trunk."

With Miranda helping, we were packed and on our way in less than an hour. It was hard to know what to say or think as I locked the door with our feather pillows squeezed between my elbows and ribcage. You don't wish a large inanimate object "Good luck" or "Be safe." But was our house really inanimate with all those memories inside it? And how does one properly soak up a moment that may, in hindsight, reveal itself as the gyre around which everything now spins?

CLOSE FRIENDS

Walter and his wife, Jeri Nell, were among the first people we befriended when we moved to Bastrop County. They were a little older than us and lived less than a mile away. Jeri Nell was medium height, thin and lithe, with short light-brown hair and a warm smile. Walter and I shared a similar physique: around six feet tall, slender, and skinny-faced. While I had a mop of long, blondish hair, his was brown, shorter, and thicker. His laugh was full-throated.

Walter had designed and built their new home and workshop. It was a cedar-clad and metal-roofed multilevel affair, with a sprawling workshop on the bottom, the main wood-heated living area in the middle, and a hideaway bedroom at the top. It was utilitarian and beautifully sited. It bore the hallmarks of a very particular set of values: for one, the lack of air-conditioning.

"It's hard to be self-sufficient with an energy hog like that," said Walter. I tried to console myself with his argument as we followed their example through six Central Texas summers.

Walter and Jeri Nell ate vegetables from their garden and fruit from their trees. They supported themselves with their artwork—Walter made custom furniture with a style that was uniquely his, and Jeri Nell etched nature-themed windows and mirrors.

They were the embodiment of what we wanted to become.

Practically everything I needed to know about Walter was in plain sight the day we first met. An architect by training, he wasn't the type to work behind a desk for someone else. He was creative, found unique and sometimes counter-intuitive solutions to practical problems, didn't cut corners, had quiet but strong opinions, and was even more self-taught than me.

Walter's intellectual and personal interests and curiosities didn't seem to have any obvious boundaries. He was a walking compendium of factoids and useful tips. Between his skill and knowledge, he quickly became indispensable to us, given our meager resources and the gap between our aspirations and what we could do on our own.

He was also a volunteer fireman, a man who had constructively channeled his respect for the natural cycles of life in a pine forest. He positioned his balcony as a lookout in case a fire broke out. With only a narrow dirt road leading to his home, they'd have to get out fast if danger was coming, and the balcony gave him a wide horizon to search for trouble.

The possibility of a fire was never far from his mind. With annoying regularity, he would speculate about it and I would brush him off.

"A wildfire would probably come from that direction," he said as we stood on his balcony one afternoon with beers in our hands, looking toward the sunset. "Straight up the back of that ridge."

"If you say so."

"Once it got going, it'd be lights out. Too much fuel and no way for heavy equipment to get in."

"I'm sorry, but I just can't get worked up about this," I said. "If I really thought a fire could come through like you're talking about, how could I bear to live around here?"

"Fires happen in forests. You need to plan for it."

"You just said that it would be hopeless," I said. "If it happens, it happens, and then we'll all wonder why we ever wanted to live here."

There was another reason his speculations landed flat with me: fire was my friend, and friends don't betray each other.

The vehicle for our friendship was the wood-fired kiln I built halfway between my studio and our large vegetable garden in the middle of an open field. Like my other construction projects, my wood kiln demonstrated questionable skill and an inattention to detail. I dutifully rebuilt the arch each time it started to sag, and the fireboxes and primary chamber survived dozens of firings over five years, apparently through sheer force of will.

Most modern potters fire their pots in electric or gas kilns. Wood kilns are rare because the fuel has to be gathered, stacked, split, and then hand-fed into the kiln for the entire time it takes to reach the prescribed temperature, which for me was 2,500 degrees. Although burning oak and mesquite smells sweet, the work required to bring the interior chamber to the color of the noonday sun quickly becomes hot and exhausting. The moment when a potter wants to quit is the moment when the fire's artistry takes over.

During the years I made my living as a potter, wood-fueled fire was my companion, muse, and inspiration. Its graceful and subtle spirit lived inside my kiln, revealing a propensity for surprise that overshadowed the labor it demanded of me.

While the poetry was obvious, science was also at work.

When wood burns in a closed environment, most of the fire's energy is released as heat and light. But a tiny amount remains in the ash that circulates through the kiln and alights on any surface where it can take hold, such as the inside of a bowl or the shoulder of an urn. As the peak temperature is reached, the ash melts, creating colors, sheens, and surfaces that don't happen any other way.

My creative partner's other artistic palette came from reduction, which happens when the atmosphere inside a kiln runs low on oxygen. As the wood burns, and oxygen becomes scarce, the flames suck in oxygen molecules anywhere they can be found, including inside the clay itself. The fire inhales clay-trapped oxygen and exhales sublime hues of rust, red, and dark orange on the clay's glowing surface. Burning wood gave me colors I could never come up with on my own.

In a way, I only created the canvas. The true artist was fire.

It felt like Christmas morning every time I dismantled the bricks that served as a makeshift door into the primary firing chamber. I never knew what surprises the fire had in store for me following a night in which my sleep was fidgety and impatient. But I was rarely disappointed, and sometimes I was thrilled.

MY MOST DEMANDING CUSTOMER

In 1982, I read *The Path to Power*, Robert Caro's initial installment of his multivolume biography of Lyndon Johnson, a man who had a palpable and permanent effect on the area where I lived. Each time I floated down the Colorado River, I was on water that came from the bottom of dams that Johnson got built for dual reasons that embodied his approach to public life. The public and laudable reason was flood control, with the side benefits of hydroelectric power and recreation. The private and queasy reason was a lucrative contract to reward political benefactors.

Lyndon Johnson represented Bastrop County through every phase of his political career, first as a member of Congress, then as a US senator, and finally as president. As I read the book, I saw his imprint everywhere in my community, especially the stark difference in how the old-timers thought about race compared to my children and their classmates in the local schools.

His example planted in me a seed that germinated several years later. While I continued to make my living as a potter, I began to think about bigger horizons and more important opportunities.

Our first daughter, Hillary, was born halfway through this period of our lives. We gave her the middle name Lucie in honor of Lucie Rie, one of the greatest potters of the twentieth century and someone I nominally knew through our correspondence and two personal visits to her London studio. She was a

tiny woman with a full head of wavy white hair, the face of a European aris-
tocrat, and large, expressive hands. During our first visit, she shared with me
several of her most famous glaze recipes.

My admiration of her work bordered on idolatry, and I wasn't the least bit
embarrassed to demonstrate it through my pots, especially my thin porcelain
bowls.

I sold everything I made, but I was not as productive or disciplined as
other potters I knew. Plus, while I enjoyed making pots, marketing and selling
them was a hard and psychologically wearying slog.

My musings about the public sector, and my growing impatience with
a standard of living that had become increasingly indefensible for two new
parents about to turn thirty, came to a head one afternoon as I listened to the
radio in my studio. At the end of an NPR interview, Barbara Jordan was identified as being a professor at the University of Texas LBJ School.

I had an epiphany as life changing as seeing the Lost Pines for the first
time. With financial aid and a forty-five-minute drive, I could attend a graduate
school bearing the name of someone I unreservedly admired, with a curriculum
and degree that could lead to steady income and a chance to improve the world.

Less than a year later, I was splitting my time between graduate school
and a fading pottery career, driving back and forth to school several days a
week and doing my homework on a Macintosh computer that I bought soon
after the iconic and underpowered contraptions went on sale. Shortly before
the summer internship that would mark the midpoint of my graduate school
studies, I embarked on one last round of pottery making, this time for a very
particular and picky customer: myself.

These would be the pots that I would sell to no one. Several of them might
be reserved as future gifts for very special occasions.

I decided to make a group of pots that would be random in size and shape
but that would collectively embody my ideas, colors, and designs. I made a set
of thin porcelain bowls, some with a metallic surface and others with Lucie's
glassy white glaze.

The stoneware pots would be bare clay except for a splash of glaze near
their rims. I wanted to give the ash flying around the kiln lots of opportunities
to settle on and fuse with the clay. I wanted to give my friend one last chance
to prove its devotion to me.

As I loaded my wood kiln for the last time, I was anxious and filled with
anticipation. While I hoped that it would be the best firing ever, I also knew
that the opposite result was equally possible. Like all intimate friendships, my
relationship with fire was sometimes strained.

The firing began on a warm and humid spring afternoon. As the kiln was starting to develop a dull glow, I was stunned when it unexpectedly started raining and then turned into a downpour with no sign of letting up.

I was faced with two equally disagreeable options. I could soldier on in the hope that I could reach the necessary temperature with soaked wood and an atmosphere that was drenched with humidity. Or I could abort with no idea of where I could get replacement wood before the person who had purchased my kiln arrived to haul it off.

I kept going. What would normally have taken five hours took seven. While stoking wood was never easy, it was much harder in a storm. The rain turned to steam as it neared the kiln, producing a halo that made me think of a demented angel.

The ceramic cones that signified the desired temperature finally drooped and then swooned, meaning I could stagger into bed, numb with exhaustion.

The next morning, as I unbricked the kiln and pointed my flashlight inside, I was engulfed by exhilaration and wonderment. The water-soaked wood and the humidity the atmosphere ladled into the kiln had unleashed an explosion of beauty. Whatever those flames were up to as they hunted for oxygen molecules, the final result was color and sheen like I had never seen on my own work.

The pots I made for myself were the best of my potting career. Unlike the overwrought and self-involved relics of youth that become an embarrassment later in life, the pots I made for myself were a source of pleasure from the day I unloaded them.

I prized one pot above all the others. The urn's shoulder shimmered with an ash film of unusual depth and luster. It had a thin stripe of ochre glaze splashed across bare clay that looked like a sunset in the desert. If someone had told me that I would be forced one day to sacrifice all but one, this was the pot I would have chosen for posterity.

A quarter century after I unloaded that urn from my kiln, my some-time-friend fire showed me that I wasn't alone in thinking this.

February 28, 2009, 5:30 p.m. "The original Fritz family together again," said Hillary, as we piled into her cozy north Austin home.

"Plus a son-in-law and baby grandson," I said.

I nodded at the TV, which was tuned to a local news station. "What's the latest?" I said.

"I guess you know the fire jumped the highway," said Hillary's husband, Jared, a tall man with hair a little darker than mine.

"That's why we had to take the long way out of Bastrop," I said. "They were redirecting traffic, and we didn't want to get stuck in the middle of it."

"They're saying that everyone in the fire's vicinity should have evacuated by now, so I guess it's still dangerous," said Jared.

"But no information about whether it's spreading?"

"They're not really saying. Nothing online either."

"Well, at least I have a crude way of finding out if we're OK," I said as I dialed our home phone.

"You've reached the Fritz family," I heard my voice say from our old-fashioned answering machine. If our machine worked, the house was still there.

As we ate dinner, we channeled our nervousness by retelling some of our favorite family tales. Each story had the same unspoken punch line: there's no way the place where this happened could be taken from us. As I would have predicted, my daughters kicked things off with a snarky one.

"My friends never let me live down the slumber party when Dad came down in the middle of the night in his whitey-tighties," said Amelia.

"You always say that happened, but I don't quite remember it that way," I said.

"Because you can't bring yourself to admit that you did it," said Hillary, the daughter with the most experience picking arguments with me.

"You freaked them out," said Amelia, "complaining about the noise we were making in the middle of the night while you stood in the doorway in nothing but your undies."

"Even if that happened—and I'm not admitting that it did—at least I gave you a story that you've been able to milk at my expense for years now."

"At who knows what psychological damage to us girls," said Amelia.

"You've survived up to this point," I said.

I evened the score with a couple of groaners from their high school days when my two oldest daughters briefly and spectacularly parted ways with sensible thinking.

Then we warmed our collective insides by working our way through other birthdays; the annual day-after-Thanksgiving trek to the Christmas tree farm owned by some of our longtime acquaintances; prom dresses and graduation gowns; and the small parade of canines that finally brought us to our current trio of two wieners and an English bulldog.

Our Long Trail house reminiscences fizzled after dinner. After a game of Scrabble, we spread a sheet and blanket on Hillary's futon and laid out our pillows, and I made the evening's final call to our answering machine. It picked up on the third ring and I heard my voice.

In the minutes before I fell asleep, I replayed in my mind some of the stories we had told and one that we hadn't.

It was a long and agonizing experience that my mind recapitulated with a single image that one of my friends had captured in pencil drawing: five-year-old and shirtless Miranda sitting in my bespectacled grandfather's lap on a spring day in our living room, her right hand encased in his left, her left elbow propped on his shoulder, their faces calm and loving, the air around them thick with the grim possibilities of Miranda's future.

MIRANDA'S JOURNEY

My grandfather was holding my youngest daughter because of something that happened during a summer trip to the Rocky Mountains in Colorado during my third year as Bastrop County's top elected official.

We had barely arrived at a vacation home in Breckenridge when Miranda developed a severe lung infection. She began coughing and wheezing in a way that couldn't be blamed on the thin mountain air.

Our clothes were still in our suitcases when Holly said to me: "She's turning blue. We have to do something now. It's not open to discussion."

It was after 9 p.m., so we drove to the emergency room in the nearby town of Frisco. The doctor would allow only one parent to join him, so I stayed in the waiting room with Miranda's sisters.

"What's wrong with Miranda?" said Hillary.

"I don't know," I said.

"Why not?" said Amelia.

"Because I don't."

"When will you?" said Hillary.

"I don't know that either."

"Are we going to sleep here?" said Amelia.

"I hope not."

"Can we go now? I'm tired."

Like the cranky passengers on an airplane stuck on the tarmac who are told nothing about why their plane isn't moving, I stewed at the lack of information while I tried to be patient with my daughters. Why couldn't someone say something to me?

Amelia eventually wore herself out and laid her body across my lap, her sleeping head resting on my stomach and her legs stretched across the chair next to her. Hillary fought to stay awake by paging through magazines bulging with tales of celebrity indiscretions and make-believe heartbreak.

I was about to storm the examining room when Holly came out, her skin pale and her face taut. "One of us has to stay here tonight."

"Why?"

"They're not releasing her. She needs to be on oxygen and in a place where they can observe her vitals."

"What's wrong with her?"

"They don't know."

"You've been in there all this time and that's all they can tell us?"

"If they know something, they're not letting on."

"I'll stay here," I said.

"You sure?"

"The girls are better off with you. I don't know how to fix their ponytails in the morning."

"OK," she said. "I'll bring all of our stuff when I come back with them."

Miranda insisted that I stay next to her in a bed that was barely wide enough for me alone. Each time I tried to creep off the bed, she woke with a scream. Sleep was long in coming and pointless when it did. Each time one of the nurses came in to check on her, I woke to the sound of my daughter's wheezing and hacking.

Miranda's condition worsened during the night, and we were sent to Denver the next morning with an oxygen mask strapped to her face and a tank rattling around the floor of Holly's SUV. All of us knew something terrible was happening. Amelia didn't yack and Hillary stared out the window. Holly and I were nearly incapacitated with worry by worst-case scenarios our fevered imaginations concocted.

A team of nurses was waiting for us at the Denver Children's Hospital. Holly announced that she would be staying with Miranda around the clock. I knew better than to argue. I asked the woman at the intake desk for the phone numbers of hotels near the hospital.

"You won't be able to get a room," she said. "The pope is in town."

"That can't possibly be true."

"It is."

"What for?"

"International Youth Day. Every room in Denver has been booked for months."

"And there's literally no place for us to stay anywhere?"

"I doubt it. But if you want, I'll see if someone can call around to some of the places on the outskirts of town."

A room was finally found on the farthest perimeter of the city, but we had to check in immediately or risk losing it. Except for two fast-food meals, we spent the rest of the day in the motel room, with the girls watching TV. When I called the hospital to find out what was happening, they put me through to Holly.

"How's she doing?"

"Not well."

"Do they know what's wrong?"

"They're still waiting for the test results."

"But she's going to be OK, right?"

Silence. Finally, sniffling, she said, "I hope so."

We had to check out of our motel room the next morning and move to another one even farther out. With hundreds of thousands of Catholic pilgrims in town, the traffic to the hospital was unbearable. We were exhausted and sweaty when we trudged into Miranda's room. It was as dark and uninviting as a crypt. Holly sat on the edge of the bed, stroking Miranda's sleeping face. Our youngest daughter was hooked up to multiple IVs. Various machines clicked and whirred.

"She has a bad case of pneumonia," said Holly. "They're pumping her full of antibiotics. And they're fighting to keep her from getting dehydrated."

Hillary and Amelia gaped at their helpless sister. I didn't know whether to sit or stand.

"What are they telling you?"

"What I just said. Her lungs are filling up. Our daughter's life is in danger."

Silence.

"I know you're going to want to talk to someone about this," she said, "but please don't. They've already told me everything there is to know at this point. You don't need to be badgering them with questions."

I stared at my wife, frustrated and anxious.

"There's nothing here you can fix," she said.

I sat down.

"Did you get any sleep?" I said.

"Not much."

"How do you feel?"

"I'm worried sick. As you should be." She looked at the girls. "As we all should be."

It went on like this for two more days. Holly maintained her vigil while I shuttled Hillary and Amelia and tried not to hate Pope John Paul II and the massive crowd he had drawn to Denver. Our visits to Miranda's room were drenched with anxious and fearful silence.

On one of our slogs through the miserable traffic, a thought occurred to me: God was so busy basking in the company of the pope and his flock, riled up as they were with singing and prayers and exaltations, that he failed to notice little Miranda in her bleak hospital room. Our wordless prayers went unnoticed in the din and glare of the rapturous uproar.

Our youngest daughter was still sick when we began our drive back to Texas, but she was no longer in mortal danger. Several weeks later, her body was rid of the infection.

We will never know for certain what happened to her in Colorado and whether there was anything we could have done to prevent it. But she returned to Texas a different girl.

In the years to come, we would learn how malleable and profound the brain's capacity for hurt and recovery is. We would also learn not to take for granted the things that most schoolchildren do almost automatically as their brains rewire themselves into engines of learning and independence at the behest of teachers and the community of their classmates.

Soon after her third birthday, Miranda started behaving in ways that were very different from her siblings at that age. Her interactions with other children at her preschool became increasingly awkward and grating, and her motor skills lagged. Simple cognitive tasks that her sisters had easily mastered were difficult for Miranda. She had a hard time going to sleep.

We knew Miranda was "special." But this knowledge made us more bewildered than alarmed.

Almost a year after our Colorado trip, we learned that one of our friends was selling her large brick home a half mile from Walter and Jeri Nell's place and close to our original homestead.

We toyed with the idea of selling our place and buying hers, because our gorgeous but small house was bursting its walls with five people.

Holly and I decided to try an experiment. We would put our house on the market for a price we thought was unreasonable and offer to buy our friend's house at a similarly implausible price. If our property attracted any interest, the inevitable negotiations would buy the time we needed to make the final decision. We could bail out at any point.

Less than two weeks later, both offers were accepted "as is." Our experiment had escaped our grip. But there was no way to reverse course without going back on our word.

With hearts constricted by second-guessing, we left the first home Walter and I built together, the home all of us loved, for one that, while beautiful in its own way, was designed for the needs and tastes of another family.

During our first fall and winter in the Long Trail house, Miranda's specialness intensified. One evening, after the girls were asleep, Holly and I tried to make sense of it.

"All of this started after we got back from Denver," Holly said.

"That's when we noticed it. Maybe it was there all along."

"All those antibiotics they pumped into her," said Holly. "I hated it."

"I don't really see the point of rehashing what happened over a year ago," I said.

"Maybe. But it's hard not to think about."

"How bad do you think it is?"

"Miranda's condition?"

I nodded.

"She's going to have to work a lot harder at almost everything. And you'll have to be more patient. That may be the hardest thing of all."

"Thanks for the encouragement."

"I'm just saying."

"I keep wondering if we should do something about it."

"I know what you mean," said Holly.

"Maybe she'll grow out of it."

Our unease morphed into full-blown horror when—as the wildflowers bloomed and the weather turned warm—Miranda lost most of her speech. Holly and I were swamped by feelings of disbelief and helplessness. Day by day, her vocabulary leaked away. When she managed to form a coherent sentence, no matter how rudimentary, it was cause for rejoicing. One afternoon, with a self-awareness that was like a knife to the heart, she forlornly turned to Holly, as they were out running an errand, and said, "I don't talk so good."

The situation deteriorated to the point where Holly had to set aside her mistrust of traditional medicine so we could take Miranda to several neurologists.

She was diagnosed with a rare form of acquired aphasia, at that time considered to be on the autism spectrum. Then—as if to put an exclamation point on an increasingly desperate situation—she had a life-threatening seizure. During a routine bath, her eyes suddenly looked like two white marbles with small blue insets, her affect went vacant, and she began to compulsively snap her fingers. We raced to the emergency room in Austin, where her neurologist ordered an IV with a mixture of chemicals that, we were told, could save her life but that also had the same effect on her body as sticking a finger in an electrical socket.

She made it through the seizure and another smaller one that followed. In time we learned that she had been having tiny seizures for several years. These had perhaps created the perforations in her mind that finally culminated in her near total loss of language.

Over the next several years, we went through serial phases of hope and despair, improvement and lapses, conventional pharmaceuticals and holistic therapies and nutritional adjustments. Regardless of the eventual outcome, we knew Miranda's future life would be very different than those of her sisters and parents.

Nobody could ever tell us how or why she acquired her disabilities. While Holly and I had our suspicions, there was no way to meaningfully connect the dots between her condition and what happened during the pope's visit. It was hard to trust any of Miranda's doctor-prescribed treatments, and we had no faith in a long-term prognosis.

Holly and I struggled to find a way to be optimistic but not deluded, accepting without giving up. Our Long Trail house became an oversized symbol of Miranda's precipitous decline and slow recovery.

Seated around the green-tiled kitchen island, we forced medicines down her throat, including an evil-tasting oral steroid that affected her body like a balloon attached to a pump. We ground up pills and tried to mix them with food or sweets, a tactic that Miranda usually rejected with a retch. We changed our family diet to eliminate gluten and other foods that might be making a bad situation worse.

The kitchen also became the place where Holly increasingly took charge of Miranda's condition with a combination of compassion and defiance.

Amelia and Miranda's bedroom evolved from a nightly battlefield, in which she screamed herself to sleep, to a calm and safe place where the same music she needed to hear each night drifted over her and brought her peace.

The living room is where she began reading, one hard-won sounded-out word at a time, and where my grandfather held her during the terrifying time when her speech faded like a flashlight about to go dead.

In my home office, with a dial-up modem, I compulsively and fruitlessly searched the embryonic World Wide Web for anything that might explain what had happened, or was happening, to our youngest daughter.

When Miranda entered the public school system, I had only one goal for her: I wanted her to become an independent reader.

Her ability to communicate verbally gradually returned, although her vocabulary and sentence construction never caught up to her age. The goals we set for her in annual discussions with the school district put a high priority on reading, and this focus was rewarded by steady progress as she benefited from a series of attentive teachers and a wonderful therapist Miranda saw outside of school. As she entered secondary schools, she was integrated into "regular" classrooms with assignments and tests that were modified to accommodate her limitations, particularly those related to math and logical thinking.

By the time she graduated from high school in 2010—with me handing her the diploma, along with a ferocious hug, in my capacity as a former school board member—she could slowly and doggedly get through any of the Harry Potter and Chronicles of Narnia books.

Miranda has grown into the most resilient and contented person I have ever known. No one could have less guile or cynicism. No one could have more patience with very young children or greater self-acceptance. While she lacks what many people take for granted, she also possesses what many people yearn for and never attain. She has an old soul in a young, skinny body.

In looking back on her childhood, I am most proud of the time I spent with her on our brown leather couch, holding back my impatience. In the time it took one of her sisters to read a children's book, she would read a couple of paragraphs with my encouragement and help.

Little did I know—as I finally fell into a deep sleep on Hillary's futon—that when Miranda officially became an adult, she'd have a chance to even the score.

CHAPTER 2

March 1, 2009, 8:30 a.m. I didn't wake up during the night or get up early. When I did, my neck wasn't sore and my head didn't pound. My unconscious mind's apparent disinterest in the fire was validated when I heard my voice on the answering machine.

The TV reports and the online version of the Austin newspaper were vague about where the fire had been and where it was still burning. We decided that Holly and Miranda would stay in Austin until I confirmed that it was safe to go home and put everything back.

While March may start with slush, mud, and biting winds in much of the country, where I live it's usually as soft and irresistible as a newborn's cheek. It was that kind of a Sunday morning, with a pleasant breeze and the sky the pure blue of a crayon. It was hard to be worried or anxious about anything as I drove toward Bastrop with my car top open.

As I crested the last tall hill west of Bastrop, there was a funnel of smoke, with the stem hovering over an area that probably didn't include our neighborhood. The closer I got, the more certain I felt that another call to our answering machine was unnecessary.

The county's emergency operations center was set up in a nondescript gray building that most recently had been a gathering place for Alcoholics Anonymous meetings and, before that, a nondenominational church. In the dirt parking lot, backhoes, bulldozers, and a few fire trucks were lined up next to law enforcement vehicles, the cars and pickups of volunteer firemen and first responders, and an SUV with a county judge license plate. Its owner was the man in charge, and I had a pretty good idea what he was doing and thinking at this moment.

"Judge Fritz," said a sheriff's deputy in a light brown uniform whom I recognized by face but not name.

"It's been a while since someone's called me that."

We shook hands as he said, "I haven't see you in ages, it seems."

THE UPSTART VS. THE VETERAN

In fact, he probably hadn't laid eyes on me for at least fifteen years. That's how long it had been since I held the county's top elective office with a title that was a misnomer for my duties and theoretical span of influence. County government in Texas is a humdrum mix of public functions on a typical day, but during a disaster everything changes. When a fire or flood hits, the county judge—who is the county chief executive in most other states—takes center stage.

My first job out of graduate school was in the Texas legislature. I quickly learned that state lawmaking has a lot more to do with the Seven Deadly Sins than the Declaration of Independence. But it was also obvious that elected officials had the power to do good things, a lesson that Barbara Jordan frequently hammered home in the class I took from her. I decided to become a part of that elite group. I was elected to the Smithville School Board in 1988 on my second try and then decided to run for county judge.

When word started getting out late in 1989 that I intended to file against the incumbent, the courthouse regulars and local government hangers-on couldn't stop laughing. The list of charges against my campaign was long: I was too young, I wasn't a local, I was a Yankee (never mind that I hailed from the Midwest), I lived in the woods and did God-knows-what in my spare time, and—most important—the self-appointed county kingmakers would never bless my candidacy because I didn't come before them with a pleading look in my eye.

But I didn't care about any of that. Besides the hubris that any candidate for office must have, I also had a computer, a database of likely voters that I was tediously building, and a message.

The first week of January 1990 brought two pieces of very big news to the Fritz family: Holly was pregnant for the third time; and the most prominent and well-known local politician had decided to join the incumbent and me in the race. Neither was expected, and one was as good as the other was bad.

Jack was the closest thing Bastrop County had to a local political legend. He began his career as president of the Bastrop School Board when I was in first grade. He moved up to mayor and then spent eighteen years as county judge, retiring (or so I thought) in 1987. He was known and liked by almost everyone.

It was too late for me to change my mind. I had already invested too much time and emotional energy to give up. But now the odds were decidedly against me. Still, as I had proven by building a house with no prior experience, a challenge usually riled me up rather than discouraging me.

Mine was the first modern political campaign in Bastrop County history. I combined old-fashioned shoe leather with targeted direct mail and advertising zingers. But even my shoe leather took a new path: I printed out walking lists of people who voted in the most recent election so that I wouldn't waste my time knocking on the doors of nonvoters.

I saved my main direct-mail piece for the weekend prior to the early March primary election. I hand-signed every letter and then let the missiles fly. By the time the traditionalists got over their disbelief at what I had done, I led a five-person field.

But I didn't get enough votes to avoid a runoff with the former judge.

A week before the second election, I found myself face-to-face with a prominent community leader in the northern part of the county. He leaned back with his feet on his desk. I sat in a chair, rigid, my feet flat on the floor and my back straight.

"While I hope and expect you'll lose," he said, "I'll give you this. You ran the best campaign I've ever seen, probably the best ever around here."

I shrugged.

"I've had more than a bellyful of your 'out with the old' crap. But my hat is off to you for how you handled your business."

"Well, if things go my way, I won't owe anyone anything," I said. "Maybe even you can see the benefit of that."

He didn't.

"Look, if I win, there's no reason we can't see eye to eye on some things. We both want to serve the public, right?"

"First things first," he said.

The runoff was on the second Tuesday of April. Jack invited a horde of his friends and supporters to a party at his furniture store on the highway, where they would pop the champagne corks and toast his much-deserved comeback. I hung out at the courthouse with a couple of friends, hoping for the best and bracing for the worst.

Two hours after the polls closed, a grim-faced and elderly election judge walked up to me, tightened his jaw, shook my hand, and said, "Congratulations, Judge."

"So I won?" I could barely get the words out.

"You did. And even though I didn't support you, I have to say you earned it, fair and square."

I went outside the courthouse, shared a victory hug with Holly, and let loose with a whoop. Six months of hard work had paid off in the only way that mattered.

While my victory was unexpected, it was not entirely unexplainable. The county was growing and changing. The newcomers and younger people were ready for someone like me, and I was ready to lead. As the swearing-in date neared, I had big plans for my four-year term. If things went well, I would make my community a better place and could think about moving up the political ladder. Depending on what the future held, there might come a difficult time when I could help people in an immediate and tangible way: something like a natural disaster.

March 1, 2009, 11 a.m. All of that seemed very long ago as I shook hands with the deputy just inside the makeshift command center. The paint was peeling on the doorframe, and the screen door was coming apart at the edges. "The judge is probably too busy to spare a few minutes for me, right?" I said.

"I 'spect so. But maybe I can help. What can I do you for?"

I described where we lived. "Are we going to be OK?" I said. "And the people who live near us?" I was thinking of Walter and Jeri Nell.

"At this point, probably. It's going to take a few days to put this thing out, but the worst is over or fixing to be."

"So it's safe to go back?"

"I can't really give you that kind of advice."

"Fair enough. But are you going to try to stop me if I point my car in that direction?"

He smiled faintly.

"Roger that," I said.

"Just don't quote me."

"Nothing to quote," I said. "So what's it been like around here?"

"Pretty big deal. Lots of state people running around plus a few feds."

"No lack of equipment, I see."

"We've even had helicopters and a plane dumping water. I think they're getting it from the river."

"I saw the fire up close when it first broke out yesterday afternoon," I said. "Quite a sight. Almost impossible to describe, really."

"Yup. No matter what's been happening around here, it doesn't take long for the talk to come around to that."

"How much damage?"

"Some folks are saying at least twenty houses and businesses are gone. The flea market got it pretty bad."

"Anybody hurt?"

"That's the good thing. Nobody told us to get lost when we were trying to clear out the area yesterday afternoon."

"Including me," I said.

"Nobody would ever take you for a knucklehead, Judge."

He didn't need to know what I had been thinking twenty-two hours earlier, at the highline.

"Considering how dry it's been, I'd say we're getting off easy," I said.

"Maybe for most. But I wouldn't talk like that around those folks over there." He pointed to a small group, huddled and intense. "They've really suffered a shock."

He looked at me and I knew what he was thinking.

"I should be grateful and I am," I said. "Give my regards to the rest of the county gang in there."

I tried not to gawk at the fire victims as I walked back to my car. I felt bad for them, as much as I could for people who were strangers to me. But now that the danger seemed to be dying down, I couldn't put myself in their shoes.

Instead, I wondered how devastating the destruction of a house or small business would actually be if everyone is safe and the initial shock has worn off. With insurance, most or all of it could be replaced. Some of them might even end up with something better than what they lost.

"I just talked to a county cop who clued me in," I said to Holly. "We're OK to go back."

"He said that?"

"Pretty much."

"What does that mean?"

"It means I'm heading home and I hope the both of you join me in a few hours. You need to take the park road. I'm near the convenience store, and the smoke is thick just east of here."

I took my own advice and turned north on the first county road past the makeshift emergency operations center. Moments later, I briefly stopped to admire a striking cedar-clad and metal-roofed house set back about a football field from the road.

Anyone with a copy of *Time* magazine's 1985 end-of-the-year "best of" list would have recognized it as a marvel of intersecting rooflines and compressed space that won first prize in an architectural design contest sponsored that year by *House Beautiful* magazine.

THE BREAK-UP

The house set back from North Alum Creek Road was the first one Walter and I built together. On the surface, we were an odd couple. But our strengths meshed, even if our temperaments sometimes didn't. His intuition and creativity were a natural match for my organizational and budgeting skills, his innovative spirit a good fit with my managerial side.

In 1985, Holly and I put the handmade house, pottery studio, and pole barn we built together on the market. With a three-year-old daughter, our lack of privacy, air-conditioning, and kitchen space had gone from idiosyncratic to intolerable.

Our glorious pine trees, a bountiful raised-bed garden, and a front-door window into which Jeri Nell had etched the branch of a pine tree were enough for us to attract a buyer and turn six years of sweat equity into cold hard cash, giving us the ability to build something much more spacious and attractive.

The award-winning plans Holly and I bought from *House Beautiful* were complicated and far too risky for me to tackle by myself. I needed someone with the tools, engineering know-how, and construction savvy to build it. I asked Walter to take a time-out from his furniture building to lead a small, ragtag team I assembled. He agreed, and the framing began right after New Year's, 1986.

I spent my last semester at the LBJ School wearing the multiple hats of student, general contractor, framing assistant, and subcontractor on the finishing work. Holly's younger brother Kevin joined the crew, working by day and sleeping on a mattress in the other loft by night.

As the framing progressed, the design's complexity came to life as a series of problems that tested Walter but never defeated him. Some of his solutions were obvious, while others were counterintuitive and destined to fail until they worked.

During spring break, I strapped on goggles and sprayed two coats of white paint onto the interior walls of our new house during one long day. When I was done, I looked like an emaciated version of the Abominable Snowman. I tiled the bathroom showers and vanities and laid the kitchen and bathroom floors. Kevin and I worked as a team to install, sand, and seal a white pine tongue-and-groove floor in the living and dining rooms.

On the afternoon we moved into the house where Hillary's sisters would be born, I called my parents and exclaimed, without a trace of irony: "Never in my life did I think I would live in a house like this."

A month before I graduated, and almost a year before he died, Professor Wilbur Cohen and his pixie-like wife accepted my invitation for dinner at our brand-new house. He was a fellow Cheese-head, short of stature and immense of impact. Like any government bureaucrat in charge of implementing what politicians cook up, he remains anonymous to the tens of millions of Americans who have directly benefited from what he did during the four years he stood alongside LBJ as one of the unseen architects and builders of Medicare and Medicaid.

This cheerful and openhearted man was the model of a government technician in charge of complex programs that would bring his face to the public only if things went badly. He could expect no praise or adulation if he performed well; he would face public humiliation and disgrace if he didn't.

One afternoon, after my classmates had dispersed, he explained to me how the country's most visible and important public health insurance programs came to be. "The president gathered us in the Oval Office and told us what he expected and when it had to happen."

"Were you scared?"

"Let me put it this way: he had a way with words that sort of made you shiver. But the fear he put into us was nothing like the pride we felt in what we were doing. President Truman tried to do something about medical care for old folks, but he couldn't get Congress to go along. When President Johnson got the chance, he did it. Then it fell on me to make it work. It was one of the great honors of my life."

"What was that like?"

"Nonstop work. I also got yelled and cussed at by the president more than once."

"But it was worth it, right?"

The answer came in the form of a knowing grin set off by the round, geeky glasses he wore. In my eyes, he was a giant, a person whose imperfections were hidden in the glare of his accomplishments and bountiful spirit.

In the same way I asked him how he helped build the Great Society, he asked me that spring evening—as we ate the wonderful meal Holly had prepared—how I managed to build a house while I was finishing grad school. Like him, I felt proud of what I had done, with Walter and Kevin's help. Also, like him, I felt I had created something that would outlive me.

Shortly after her first birthday, Miranda outgrew her crib, and we moved her into Amelia's bedroom after converting my office into a room suitable for a four-year-old with girlie-girl tastes. As seen from the road, Amelia's bedroom window was one of the house's most prominent and distinctive features, four feet wide, eight feet high, capped by an arch, and centered under a steeple-like roofline.

One balmy late fall evening I was outside with the girls while Holly was teaching at her dance studio. We were wearing light jackets and enjoying the wooden playscape I had built for my daughters. Turning toward the house, we happened to glance toward the window of Amelia's darkened bedroom. It was bathed in the color of a pale tangerine. Just to the right of the window, something flickered. As I dashed inside, my heart racing, the smoke alarm began to screech.

In the corner of Amelia's bedroom, a very orange and somewhat serene fire was just starting to enjoy the first course of its meal: carpet and sheetrock paper. A frayed cord had burned away from Amelia's desk lamp and was still sparking.

The girls' shrieks and shouts almost drowned out the smoke alarm. I beat out the fire with a towel and my sneaker-clad feet. Then I unplugged the cord, opened the windows, and gaped in amazement at the charred corner of carpet and the raven-stained wall.

Finally, I said to Hillary: "I hope we don't have to rip up all this carpet and pull off the sheetrock that's still OK. That would really suck."

The headache of repair was something I could grasp. What would have happened if the cord had shorted out when nobody was at home was not. The idea that the fire could have started at night with a dead smoke alarm battery—a yardstick away from our middle daughter and two dozen feet from the other two—was entirely off-limits.

Eight years had passed since I had dismantled and sold my wood kiln. The pots that were a daily blessing to me left me with the feeling that fire and I had parted company on a high note. Apparently, my former artistic partner had other ideas and was finally ready to sever our ties with an acrimonious break-up message. I received it loud and clear. There wouldn't be any need to repeat it.

March 1, 2009, 12 p.m. My drive from the emergency operations center to our house wrapped around three sides of the fire. Judging from the smoke and what the sheriff's deputy had told me, the fire was uncontained in at least several sectors of a bloblike area that stretched from the highway to the forest catty-corner behind Walter's house.

Walter and Jeri Nell's property was just outside the skinny blob's boundary. With an unfavorable wind shift, they could lose everything, including the bookshelves, loveseats, and office furniture that Walter was creating for the house he had designed and I had built—the house into which Holly, Miranda, and I would move in less than three weeks.

"Where you at right now?" I said after Walter answered his cell.

He and his family had spent the night with friends, but he was on his way back.

"I'm parked next to your mailbox," I said. "How long before you're here?"

"Thirty minutes max. Why?"

"I don't want to make a bigger deal out of the situation than it is," I said. "But I'm thinking we might want to be safe and temporarily move the things you're making for us over to the new house. We could store it in the carport."

"That's probably not a bad idea. Let's talk about it when I get there."

To kill time, I drove back to the intersection with Park Road 1C, where some of our neighbors were gathered. They were comparing notes about what they knew and had heard. One of them, a forty-something man with a some-times rough demeanor, was matter-of-factly describing the incineration of his handmade house. He assured us that despite all this trouble, he was still stand-ing strong. It would take a helluva lot more than a wildfire to knock him out. His bravado was rewarded with pats on the back, handshakes, and a couple of hugs from women in the crowd.

I wanted to interrogate him—a person I had known for many years—about the mismatch between his lamentable situation and his defiant mood. Where was the shock and self-pity? But I also didn't want to get face-slapped, so I kept quiet.

As this was going on, I noticed Walter coming up the road and turning in the direction of his land. I got in my car and followed him up the narrow and winding road—it was more like a path—he had carved out of the forest to the relatively flat spot he had cleared for their house and garden.

There was almost no space between the loblolly pines and the helter-skelter ground-floor space filled with our furniture, other projects in various stages of completion, and an assortment of commercial and jury-rigged tools he had fab-ricated to solve tricky problems or standardize certain tasks. I couldn't imagine Walter exercising his artistic gifts and unimpeachable craftsmanship from any other place.

Even though we were about to move for the fourth time since we met them, Walter and Jeri Nell's house had been a constant in our lives. The life they had built with their two sons felt inseparable from their rambling and one-of-a-kind home. It echoed with what they had done for their son Jess, who was born with cerebral palsy.

Over the years, Walter had made adjustments to their house as their oldest son grew from a child to a man, including an elevator adjacent to the work-shop that opened into their living room. Where else but here could Walter and Jeri Nell continue to care for him?

Walter seemed calm, but I had enough anxiety for both of us. "I have to say it feels very uncomfortable for me to suggest that we move this stuff," I said.

"We're here and we should do it. I don't want to lose what I've been working on for many weeks any more than you do."

After the first piece was loaded and secured, we took a short break, and I gave it all a closer look. Everything was done except for the finishes. He would apply many thin layers of stain to our bookshelves and my desk and finish them with stencils, stamped patterns, or freehand lines and patterns of subtly contrasting paint. This was the first time I had seen any of it. I didn't need to approve or check on anything in progress, because I had total faith in his skill and artistry.

"What do you think?" he said.

"Beautiful, of course. No other result from you would be possible."

He flashed his trademark closed-mouth smile, and we got back to work.

While the furniture was wonderful, Walter's biggest contribution to our new house was his architectural vision. The prior spring, he and I discussed and debated our options with Holly's input, finally settling on a unique floor plan in which the bedrooms, living room, kitchen, and family room circled around the bathrooms and laundry that occupied the center of the house. A curved walkway would gradually rise almost four feet from the driveway, making stairs unnecessary, and a curved masonry wall would envelop the woodstove from the southeast corner of the living room. The deck would hug the house at its highest point, perched eight feet above ground level by massive aromatic cedar posts we planned to custom-order from a local sawmill.

The single-story house's most striking feature would be a complicated roof of silvery galvanized steel, a wonder of intersecting peaks and valleys, with the highest portion of the roof towering thirty feet above the foundation. More than most houses, the standing-seam roof would visually define the house for good or ill. Now that we were less than a month from moving day, the verdict was decisively in: the roof was much more than good. It was gorgeous.

The fact that I didn't expect to ever again go through this kind of project for myself meant I was the opposite of jaded and nonchalant. I brought an enthusiasm that on many days crossed the line into giddiness. The proximity of the project to the Long Trail house meant it was hard to stay away and leave the subs to do their work, unmolested by my inquisitive hovering.

Being on the northern side of middle age, I deferred most of the physical labor to the subs. But Walter, Holly, a neighbor, and I decided to lay the wood floor in the family and living rooms ourselves. In about a week, we would start by attaching flat pine boards to the foundation by bludgeoning curved nails into the concrete with miniature sledgehammers. Then we'd screw a plywood subfloor to the boards. The last step would be nailing tongue-and-groove strips of prefinished white ash to the plywood. This backbreaking but satisfying labor would create a kind of bond between our final house and the other two that I built with my own hands.

Before we unloaded the furniture onto the concrete carport pad, Walter and I took a walk around the inside of the house. With the sun high in the early afternoon sky, natural light was everywhere. The tubular skylights flooded the almost-finished kitchen and master bathroom. The clerestories in the living and family rooms distributed light from windows floating two stories above the floor. Like in every new house, the newly painted ceilings and walls were as clean and free of defects as they'd ever be.

Walter and I walked mostly in silence, because almost everything about the house worth saying had already been said. While each of the subs had been conscientious and diligent, special praise was due to the man who led the framing crew and solved the problems that inevitably crawl from the gap between the architect's ideas and the unyielding laws of structural mechanics. Jeff had the leathery skin, calloused hands, and no-nonsense disposition of a man who made his living outdoors and could see exactly what he had accomplished each day. By the time he clocked out of the project for good, he had won me over with his honesty, work ethic, and attention to detail.

With its high ceilings and flowing design, the house felt bigger than its actual square footage. It hadn't been easy to build, but now that it was almost done, I had no misgivings or doubts that Holly and I would happily grow old within its walls, on its deck, and within the forest that enveloped it.

"You ready to get all that stuff off the trailer?" Walter said.

"In a minute. Why don't you start loosening everything up? I'll be right over."

The air was sharp and slightly disagreeable as I stood on the deck and gazed across the ravine. While I could taste the smoke, I couldn't see it, because the pines blocked my view.

With a five-minute walk through the forest, I'd be at the north side of the Long Trail house. While Holly and I no longer owned it, there would never come a time when we would stop thinking about our life there and how the fourteen years we shared under its roof had irreversibly changed our daughters and us. No matter how long we lived in this new house, it would never affect us like the colonial-style red-brick house hidden on sixteen acres of loblolly pines.

A tiny voice said to me: It's not over yet. If it was, why did you practically give yourself a hernia loading up all that furniture? You could still lose that house and this one too.

If I had to sacrifice one of them, which would it be? The one we were about to leave, where most of our possessions still were—or the one where we would live out our remaining years but which held no emotional power for us yet? I had no control over what was about to happen or not, so why even concoct such a choice? But how could I not?

"You OK?" said Walter.

"As much as I'll ever be," I said. "And just think: we get to undo all of this in a day or two."

With a weak smile, he nodded his agreement. I couldn't even summon up a weak smile.

March 1, 2009, 4 p.m. The fire chief of the Heart of the Pines Volunteer Fire Department lived directly across Long Trail from our property in a spec house that Walter and I had built in 2005. Roland had been a firefighter in the Milwaukee area, an hour south of my hometown, and he and his wife, Marsha, decided to give up Wisconsin winters when he retired from the fire department where he worked for many years.

They bought a house from us with many of the environmentally conscious features that Walter incorporated into our new one: native limestone exterior, energy-saving windows, cellulose insulation crammed into the walls like a thick blanket, and wood heat from a technologically advanced and highly efficient woodstove. Like each of the Walter-designed houses, Roland and Marsha's had a special touch: a burnished, curved handrail leading to the second floor fashioned out of a rough piece of metal that my building partner found in a salvage yard.

The fact that the fire chief lived across the street from us bolstered my confidence that the fire wouldn't hurt us. While I didn't expect Roland to lead his team of volunteer firefighters in a selfish way, it seemed reasonable that he would make sure his neighborhood was protected. Before Holly and I started carrying things back into the house, I gave him a call.

"Do you think it's safe to sleep at our place tonight after we put our things back?" I said.

"No guarantees, you understand."

"I know that. So give it to me straight."

"Unless something dramatic changes, those of us on Long Trail will be OK."

"What about Walter?"

"I'm less sure about that. But if you made me guess, I think he's going to be fine as well."

I gave Holly the thumbs-up and we got to work, with Miranda pitching in.

Halfway through the job, I had to say what I couldn't stop thinking: "What a waste of time and effort all of this was."

We argued a bit, and Holly got me to admit that it would have been fool-hardy to sleep in our house in defiance of the county's evacuation efforts. But I was pretty sure I knew what I'd do if sometime in the distant future we faced another evacuation order. I'd fight the urge to pack up, except for perhaps a handful of small pots I could put in a box or a large bag, including one that I received from a woman I admired as much as anyone I'd ever met.

THE GRADUATION GIFT

Elspeth Rostow was the female half of a Washington power couple from the 1960s. She was the longtime wife of Walt Rostow, President Johnson's national security advisor during the Vietnam War. She was sixty-eight years old when I took my first class with her at the LBJ School.

A native New Yorker transplanted to Texas as part of President Johnson's retirement retinue, she was impossibly elegant and well spoken, someone who clearly had been a beauty when she was young. Her grammar was faultless and her thoughts unfailingly coherent. It often seemed like she was reading from a carefully prepared script rather than speaking off the cuff. She was demanding but kind, with a sense of humor that was so subtle as to be almost undetectable.

Early in the second semester of my first year, I began developing a relationship with her that I could not name or define. During the times I visited her in the darkly lit and oversized corner office where she met with her students, our conversations would inevitably veer between the professional and the personal. Over time, she learned about my pottery career, my first-born daughter, my moonlighting as a church organist, and the house I was building.

I couldn't figure out how to address her. Calling her Elspeth would have been grounds for dismissal. But Professor Rostow seemed too formal and distant. I settled for three pronouns into which I could pour my feelings without being caught: "you" when I was speaking to her directly, and "her" or "she" when I referred to her in class.

One early afternoon during my last semester, I mentioned that our new house was next door to someone almost exactly my age who I expected would become a friend and sports buddy. When I said his name, she looked at me with a very straight face and said: "You must know that he was conceived in our bed. When Walt and I were out of town, of course."

The straight face became a little mischievous as she went on. "His parents were our neighbors and they sometimes stayed in our house when we were away. On one of those times, your future friend came into being."

If I had doubted it before, now I had proof. She was more than my teacher, even if not quite my friend.

Shortly before my final semester ended, she summoned me to her office. With a warm smile, she gave me a small box tied with a ribbon.

"It's your graduation present," she said. "It's not much, but I think you'll like it."

It was a small stoneware cup made by Bernard Leach, one of Lucie Rie's contemporaries and a giant in the twentieth-century pottery world.

"It's right that you should have it," she said. "You will undoubtedly appreciate it even more than we do."

For the next twenty-five years, I prominently displayed the pot in each of the three houses we occupied. I rarely touched it for fear of damaging or dropping it. It was more than a valuable object. It was a reminder of the person who gave it to me and whom I revered.

When we moved into our new house, I put it on a built-in maple wood shelf behind our bed next to my other favorite small pots. It was at its final resting spot.

March 12, 2009, noon. The county issued the "all clear" notice several days after my chat with Roland, and life returned to normal except for the several dozen individuals and families who got burned out. One of them was a silver-haired man with a long ponytail who lived above a large garage where he worked on classic cars.

Because of nothing more than very bad luck, his live-in garage was reduced to a total ruin while less than fifty feet away another house still stood and the pine trees remained green and vital. The randomness and totality of it was cruel and unexplainable.

About a week after the fire was fully contained, I turned west from Cottle-town Road just past this man's burned-out property, parked my car a hundred yards in, and walked along a narrow gravel path to a six-acre tract we had bought in 1991 soon after Miranda was born. The path dead-ended at a flat area at the top of a high ridge that I had cleared that year in anticipation of building a house more suitable for our growing family.

Shortly after I was sworn in as county judge, my mother-in-law, Betty, decided she wanted to live closer to us. Since Holly and I loved our "best small house in America," we didn't want to say good-bye to it. But if Betty bought it, it would remain in the family and we could use the proceeds to build a larger house on more secluded land, ideally with a view.

The plan was sealed when we found a heavily wooded property with spectacular views to the south and west. I hoped to again enlist Walter to lead the construction crew. On a cool and bright afternoon, we stood on the spot where the future house would sit, and he gave me an opinion I didn't ask for and certainly didn't want.

"It's pretty amazing, isn't it?" I said. "Nobody will know we're here and yet we'll be able to see for oodles of miles in two different directions."

"And what if there's a fire?"

"Why am I not surprised you'd bring that up?"

"Your house will sit on the highest point around here, with one, very narrow escape route."

"We own the land. It's kind of too late to be thinking about paranoid scenarios like that."

He was as exasperated by our inability to anticipate the property's most obvious risk as I was by the insouciant way he found fault with a done deal.

"If a fire was heading in our direction, we'd evacuate, just like you would," I said. "You only have one way out, too."

For a few minutes we tried to keep our emotions under control as he explained the science of a wildfire on a ridge. No matter how bad the fire was, it would be at its worst on our property because of its exposed position relative to the land surrounding it.

"So the upshot of all this is that by the time we hear about a fire, it could be too late?"

He nodded.

"You knew we were thinking about buying this place," I pointed out. "Why say all of this now?"

"But this is the first time I've actually seen it."

I couldn't deny that Walter was right, as he almost always was whenever we disagreed about the details of a project. But the fears he had stirred up quickly faded because Betty changed her mind soon after the site was leveled and the debris hauled off. We held on to the property in anticipation of outgrowing our house, as the children got older. But then the Long Trail house became available, and we sold it.

Now, as I walked up the ridge, I saw that Walter had probably understated the foolhardiness of our original decision to buy the property. Every tree was dead, and many were nothing more than charred stalks, their branches vaporized.

When I saw the fire shoot across the highline, I thought about the houses, businesses, and vehicles in its path. I didn't think of the catastrophic loss of trees and wildlife. But now I saw what a wildfire could do to an ecosystem, and it was unspeakable.

From the top of the ridge, I looked down the three adjacent hillsides as they plunged more than a hundred feet to level ground. Everything was black except for the soil, which was an off-white color, a mixture of ash and loam. The trunks of the largest pines looked like boiling tar had been poured over them.

If the Long Trail house hadn't sidelined our plans, we would have lost everything, including our lives if the fire had broken out in the middle of the night instead of early afternoon. For a moment, I couldn't stifle the scene: the five of us trapped in a dark house with the electricity cut off, unaware of what was about to happen. It was an image as toxic as a radiation overdose.

For several weeks, as I passed the unlucky man on Cottletown Road, I couldn't help glancing across his ruined land to the what-could-have-been ridge. Then, as we settled into our new house, with the next chapter of our lives just beginning, my imaginary apocalypse vanished.

LIVING AMONG THE PINES

The drought that bred the wildfire didn't let up during the first summer in our new house. Then Holly and I rejoiced when October ushered in many months of beneficial, soaking rain. A wet and chilly winter gave way to a green and heavenly spring.

More than our other three properties, the one where we now lived showed us what the Lost Pines could be when the soil was moist and the temperatures hospitable. This was because the prior owner had selectively culled non-native species and water-hogging cedars in a way that opened up the forest by creating space between the largest trees.

Shortly after we bought the property, we hired a small crew to finish what the prior owner had started. They cut down and shredded dead trees, stubby scrub oaks, and yaupon holly. Unlike our previous forest cocoons, the result was a private arboretum of loblolly pines and sinuous oaks. They were far enough apart that each mature pine could be enjoyed and appreciated on its own, yet close enough to maintain the forest's essential character of density and overflowing life.

Like most postadolescent trees in the Lost Pines, mine had shed their lower branches, leaving the bottoms unadorned while the upper sections branched out in individualistic patterns, some relatively straight and others like thick pieces of flexible tubing with the bends locked into place.

A pine tree that naturally grows upward takes a temporary detour to the side if it is trying to find a pathway to sunlight that is blocked by one or more of its neighbors. As a loblolly grows, the tree's point, made up of soft and supple tissue, adapts its direction to where the light is. Then, as the bark grows out, the tree widens and the center solidifies and the curve begins to harden in place. The eventual result is an organism whose flexibility is utterly incongruous with its strength, mass, and apparent hardness.

For most pines in search of light, this means a curve in the trunk. Several of those that stood as sentries along our driveway, however, had split in the middle, with two opposite curves growing upward, parallel to one another like a narrow horseshoe.

The tree I loved the most was a living monument to the ability of loblollies to toy with gravity. Even with the biological science firmly in mind, it was hard to grasp how this tree was able to support its enormous weight while growing out of the ravine's creek-bed at an angle, then reversing itself halfway up, then taking another sideways detour before straightening up at the top.

Many trees in the Bastrop County area had been planted by the Civilian Conservation Corps to replace pines that had been clear-cut in the 1920s, but this one almost certainly was a natural-born citizen, a descendant of the original Lost Pines, a creature that was well on its way by the time the Depression-era arborists came around. My enthusiasm for this tree bordered on the obsessive. No one who visited our home could avoid the short walk from our deck to the tree's base or the nature talk that went with it.

I began most of my days with a fifteen- or twenty-minute tour of my largest pines, neck craned upward, and grateful for a moment of mindfulness no matter what else was going on in my life. I would grow old with these forest senior citizens, most of them older than my father and some older than my grandfather.

November 3, 2009, 2:30 p.m. On a faultless, crystalline day with a pleasant but persistent breeze, I took the long way to Bastrop by driving Park Road 1C. A few minutes after I crossed the boundary of Bastrop State Park, I began to smell smoke. I didn't have time to panic because I quickly saw its source. A serious-faced middle-aged park ranger dressed in a brown uniform was overseeing a controlled burn. The fire was crawling along the forest floor, making steady progress but in no danger of turning into a conflagration even though it hadn't rained for many weeks. I parked on the opposite side of the road and got out.

"Howdy," I said. "You been at it for a while?"

"For a couple of days now. Some of the locals have been kind of freaking out, what with the memory of that big fire still fresh in their minds."

"Well, you're talking to a local who had a close call with that one. And I'm not freaking out because I know this sort of thing has to be done."

"I'm glad we're doing this," the ranger said. "But I'm not under any illusions about the big picture."

"Which is?"

"There's decades of fuel built up in the forest surrounding all those subdivisions up Highway 21."

"Same thing south and east of here. What's the worst-case scenario?"

"Depends on how dry and windy it is."

"Let's say another nasty drought like 2009 and the kind of wind we always get with a cold front."

"It would be hard to contain for a long time. There wouldn't be much anyone could do except wait for the wind to die down and the humidity to go up. As for how much damage it would cause, the best I can say is use your imagination."

"I look forward to it not coming true," I said as I shook his hand.

"You and me both."

As I reached the fork in the road just east of the main camping areas, I decided to pay a short visit to the park's highest point, where the Civilian Conservation Corps had built a small pavilion during the 1930s. Like the cabins and refectory, this structure was constructed of native red sandstone dug up from the sandy soil into which the park's loblollies had sunk their taproots. I sat on a bench that faced out across a good portion of the park.

From this place, all I could see was the forest ceiling, a tufted and impenetrable canopy of dark green. This is why Holly and I still lived in the Lost Pines after suffering through suffocating summers and periodic dry spells that pulled my spirits down as much as the blizzards and subzero temperatures of my youth. It was also why an invasion of tree-lovers followed our example, eventually tripling the county's population since our arrival.

The park ranger was a practical man, so our brief discussion of what could happen was limited to facts about fuel loads and population density. But looking out over the forest put his fears in more poignant terms. Some day, given the right conditions, Bastrop State Park's beauty could be its undoing. Those who moved to the Lost Pines because the trees had seduced and captivated them would be implicated in their destruction.

That park ranger wasn't the first person who had warned me about how a forest's natural fire cycles could be short-circuited by adoring and oblivious humans.

Early in my term as county judge, the Bastrop County real estate community became agitated about the possibility that the endangered Houston toad could slow down, or stop, local property development. I put together and chaired a working group to study the issue. The long-term goal was creating and shepherding a federally approved plan to balance environmental needs with economic ones. The working group included a biologist from the state parks department who was an expert on the toad's breeding habits based on his field research in Bastrop State Park.

He invited me to go with him on one of his nocturnal visits to an ephemeral breeding pond on the park's eastern boundary. One warm and humid early spring evening, Holly and I accompanied him and his assistant to a pond a half mile into the park. We left our cars at the edge of Park Road 1C and walked by flashlight along a narrow path. It was muddy and squishy from a recent rain.

As we walked, we heard a chorus of male toads letting loose with their high-pitched trills. He said that the wet conditions almost guaranteed a full pond and lots of activity.

When we got to the pond, Holly and I sat at the edge as the biologist and his helper geared up. They strapped on hats with a single out-facing light—like a coal miner—put on tall, rubber boots and grabbed a net.

The din came and went in short bursts. It was like being in a toad singles bar, with the hustlers trying to outmaneuver one another in pursuit of the females and then taking an agreed-upon time-out to catch their breath and dream up their next set of pickup lines. Each time the males started up, the lights would be trained on the nearest sounds. The brownish toads, which were two to three inches long, sat on the edge of the pond or on dirt or rock outcroppings. When they trilled, the loose flap of skin under their mouths puffed up into a red ball.

The biologist had a work ritual that demanded concentration and timing, so Holly and I left him alone. As we walked back, I barraged him with the questions that had been piling up in my mind. Was the toad population healthy and growing? How many did he think were living in the park? How many toad ponds did he monitor? What was the endangered amphibians' long-term prognosis? Did he love his job? Could I do this with him again?

All of his answers were positive. The park's toad population was thriving and its future was bright, assuming benevolent weather patterns and sensible park management. Most of it made sense on its face. Then he said something counterintuitive.

"Rain keeps the ponds full," he said. "But the toad also needs periodic fire."

"Say what?"

"The needles and brush have to burn off every so often. If that never happens, it just keeps piling up. There's going to be fire eventually. The only question is whether it will be beneficial or catastrophic to the toad."

With Amelia in tow, I accompanied him another evening to the park's largest ephemeral pond, deep in the forest and accessible on a path that began across the road from the stone pavilion. In the coming years, my two youngest daughters and I would regularly visit this place on humid late winter or early spring evenings when the temperature was in the 70s or warmer. Amelia finally tired of it, but Miranda didn't. Besides the biologist, I doubt there was anyone in Bastrop County who was on closer terms with the county's most famous critter than Miranda and me.

Bastrop County's two most famous species couldn't have been more differ-ent. One spent most of the year burrowed beneath sandy loam and clay, while the other spent every day reaching ever higher for the sun. One was reclusive and rarely seen; the other was impossible not to see. One was lucky to live for several years; the other lived for a century or longer.

Yet in one fundamental way they were the same. Their survival was at risk from the area's increasingly unreliable rain and the growing number of humans who lived among them.

As I got up from the bench, I paused a moment at the base of one of the largest pines within immediate walking distance. Fifteen years before, Holly's parents and siblings joined our family here to say a final good-bye to her broth-er Kevin, who had died suddenly and unexpectedly.

Kevin loved the Lost Pines when he lived with us during the time he helped build our second house. Nobody in Holly's family could think of a more suitable place for his ashes than a pine forest that would always be there. In death, he would coexist in the earth with the remains of pine trees from the ages and be shaded by the ones whose life was a blessing to all who visited and loved Bastrop State Park.

We knew that spreading Kevin's ashes at the tree's base might not be legal. But that didn't mean it wasn't right and proper and necessary.

CHAPTER 3

Summer 2011. At the end of August 2011, Tropical Storm Lee abruptly and unexpectedly came to life in the Gulf near the Texas coast. Weather forecasts trumpeted the best chances for meaningful rain in months. Everything was lining up for a landfall on the Texas coast, with Central Texas on the storm's wet side. If the right conditions came together, the soil on our land would be transformed from the consistency of pulverized concrete to a dense and dripping sponge.

Along with everyone else in Central Texas, I hoped Lee heralded the beginning of a historic drought's end.

After thirty years of living among them, the Lost Pines had taken root in our souls. That is why we felt like a member of our family was slowly dying when it stopped raining late in 2010, almost exactly a year after the first lovely rains that ended the prior drought. A dome of desert-dry heat settled over Bastrop County, a killer that stalked the Lost Pines as remorselessly and ruinously as a viral pandemic. On my daily visits to the trees on our property, my feelings changed from admiration and reverence to anxiety and fear. As a dry and hot spring turned into something far worse, our hearts cracked along with the soil as pines and oaks on our land turned from green to brown, succumbing in their weakened state to disease or insects. Some were immense.

Many large trees on Park Road 1C surrendered to the drought's lethal effects. As I rode my bike through the forest, I could barely force myself to look up or to the side because of the multitude of trees that had devolved from living objects of grace and strength to inert roadside hazards.

Central Texas is an oven every summer. But in 2011, the thermostat broke. One record after another fell. The high pressure that held the heat in place sustained the drought, repelling storm systems and stiff-arming the rain from neighboring states and the Gulf of Mexico.

Each time a sliver of hope crept into the forecast, I watched the weather radar on my computer with the compulsiveness of a gold miner scouring his pan for any glint of yellow. My investment in time and emotional energy was never rewarded.

In August, Texas recorded the all-time hottest average temperature for any state in America since scientists started keeping records late in the nineteenth century. During that month, Holly and I began and ended each day with a ballet of soaker hoses and an increasingly malignant sense of helplessness. We would coil our hoses around a cluster of mature pine trees that were barely alive and check several times a day to make sure the water was going into the ground rather than running off the powdery soil. Eight or ten hours later, with the sun feeling like a mortal enemy, we'd gather them up and spread them someplace else.

In the same way a child can't resist picking at a scab, I made myself miserable on a daily basis by scanning the tops of my trees with my hand as a make-shift visor, looking for evidence of creeping death. If I saw discoloration in a tree's needles, I would debate with myself whether it was stressed, condemned, or already dead. I began a mental inventory of those I would have to cut down during the winter and tried to imagine what my property would look like without some of my daily companions.

For several days after Tropical Storm Lee formed, I obsessively updated my browser with the latest tracking maps and forecasts from the National Weather Service. But after this merciless tease, the storm showed its true intentions. Rather than unloading inches of rain on plants, creatures, and people that desperately yearned for it, the storm set its sights on Louisiana, Tennessee, Virginia, and the Eastern Seaboard.

September 4, 2011, 8:30 a.m. As its parting gift, Lee coughed up a dry heave of blistering wind that spread west until it reached Central Texas. This is what Holly and I felt the morning before Miranda's twenty-first birthday.

With the tops of our trees swaying in the wind, Holly watered her flower gardens and I checked on the irises we had optimistically, and perhaps foolish-ly, planted the prior week.

"I think we're feeling the first hint of fall," Holly said.

"I doubt that very much. This wind feels like a fan pointing out from an oven. If you ask me, it's evil. Nothing good is going to come of it."

Holly's exasperated frown didn't change my mind, but as I sniffed several ripening cantaloupes and noticed a newly formed baby watermelon, my mood lightened a bit. The tomato plants were still green and would start flower-ing again soon. The lavender-colored morning glories and flowering hyacinth beans had taken over two sides of the garden wall and, like the tomatoes, would have a growth spurt as the days shortened and the nighttime temperatures moderated.

When we first moved to Central Texas, we grew our own food partly out of economic necessity. But money had nothing to do with our new vegetable and flower gardens. Now, as we approached our third autumn in what we could no longer consider our "new" house, our plans were clearly working out, drought or no drought.

As we sat down for our traditional Sunday breakfast of pancakes, fresh fruit, and whipped cream under the kitchen skylight, Holly said, "Our gardens are finally to the point we imagined them when we first bought this land. Despite everything that's happened this year, our work has paid off. It's all beautiful and what we hoped it would be."

"You're right. I feel very good about how it's all turned out. I'll feel even better if it starts raining again.

"When, not if," she said.

After we cleared the dishes, I told Holly, "You know what I'd like to do? Play 'Clair de lune' for you. I started working on it around Memorial Day, remember? Seems like a good way to mark the turning of a seasonal page."

After three months of practicing, the warm, shimmering pool of notes that Claude Debussy gave the world was sufficiently in my fingers and memory that I had moved from wrestling with its difficulties to reveling in its loveliness and changes of mood.

This was thanks to Anton Nel, the man who awoke in me the artistic impulses that slept for the two decades after I fired my kiln for the last time.

THE VIRTUOSO'S NEW STUDENT

Anton came into my life through a chance meeting I had with Van Cliburn at his namesake piano competition at the Bass Performance Hall in Fort Worth. Bass Hall was designed in the tradition of a European opera house, with a high domed ceiling and two fifty-foot angels carved from Texas limestone standing over the entrance.

In 2009, as I had for the two prior quadrennial competitions, I took my seat near the front for the preliminary round and marveled at what I heard and saw with a bit of envy mixed in. During a break one evening, following a recital by a blind pianist from Japan that brought the audience thundering to its feet for three curtain calls, I went outside for some fresh air and was startled to see Van Cliburn standing near the edge of the sidewalk by himself, smoking a cigarette. He was taller and thinner than I would have expected, but his large hands were no surprise. We faced each other for a few seconds, and then he broke the ice.

"That was stunning, don't you think?"

"No kidding."

"His ovation was richly deserved, and not just because he's blind. He played beautifully."

"This may seem like a stupid question, but do you have any idea how someone who can't see the notes can learn that music?"

"I'm told he memorizes it, measure by measure, by listening to recordings," he said.

"Well, however he does it, it borders on the miraculous."

"I agree. Do you play?"

"In a manner of speaking, but nothing like any of these people. I can read music and play slow movements, but anything complicated or fast is beyond me. Whenever I play at home, my family leaves the room." He chuckled. "I took piano lessons as a kid, but never learned any serious technique."

"It's never too late to start working on your scales."

"I don't know about that," I said. "I'm a middle-aged guy with lots of responsibilities."

"Still, you should think about it." He stomped out his cigarette and went back inside before I had a chance to shake his hand.

I acted on Van Cliburn's challenge several weeks later by impulsively sending an e-mail to the head of the University of Texas Piano Department, an internationally recognized virtuoso. I asked if he would give me piano lessons.

From his summer residence at the Aspen Music Festival, Anton responded almost immediately, and we agreed to get together at the start of the fall semester. The Thursday after Labor Day, I met him in his sun-dappled office in the UT music building. I shook his hand, and he motioned for me to sit down in a chair behind a pair of black Steinway grand pianos that sat next to each other like oversized, identical twins.

Anton was a trim forty-something man with very short hair, full eyebrows, and a penetrating, serious gaze that occasionally broke into a smile. His hands were smaller than I would have guessed, with lean, compact fingers. Both of us wore shorts and open-collared shirts, and our pale complexions had a rusty, late-summer look of too much sun.

"Tell me a little about yourself," he said.

I described my childhood lessons, my two decades as the organist at our church in Bastrop, and the Yamaha C3 grand piano I had acquired through my grandfather's legacy. Then he motioned to the piano bench of the Steinway nearest the door.

"What are you going to play for me?" he asked.

I was worried that if I didn't sound polished and professional, I would have no chance of becoming his student. So I opened my copy of *The Well-Tempered Clavier, Book 1* to the dog-eared page and started playing the Prelude in B-flat Minor tentatively, with a dry mouth and shivering knees. Things went downhill from there.

"I know that wasn't very good," I said when I stopped playing. "I've played the organ in church for hundreds of people, all without a trace of anxiety. But just now I was so nervous I could barely play."

Over the two decades that I played the organ, I had cultivated two pianistic musical sins that were as obvious to Anton as the sunburn on my face. The first was fingering based on guesswork rather than the collective wisdom of pianists over the ages. The second and greater one was my disinterest in musicality. What I lacked in phrasing and sensitivity I more than made up for with inadvertent accents and monochromatic dynamics.

"Are you willing to forget what you think you know and start from scratch with me?" he asked.

"I assume you don't mean I need to forget how to read music or where to put my fingers on the keys."

"In a way, I do mean that. Right now, all you see is notes that correspond to keys on the piano. That isn't music. You undoubtedly need technique, but only so you can learn to play beautifully."

I couldn't wait a second longer. "Does this mean you're willing to be my teacher?"

"That depends. I would start you with a C major scale, played very slowly. You will need to stop playing the pieces you like, even just for fun. And you must be patient. Are you willing to do all that?"

It was an all-or-nothing offer with no negotiation. So I agreed, and that was all it took for me to become Anton's least accomplished student.

I was almost out the door, then stopped and turned around. "You've left no doubt that my playing doesn't measure up. Why waste your time on someone like me?"

"It's an experiment," he said. "I need to see if I can teach someone at your level. Your lessons will be a test of my teaching as much as they will be of your learning."

I walked into Anton's office believing he could refine my skills, and I left wondering whether I had any skills to refine. Two decades of confidence were gone without a trace. In reaching out to Anton, I had either made a big mistake or been given a great opportunity.

"How did it go?" asked Holly.

"He's sending me back to kindergarten or maybe even preschool."

Rather than discouraging me, his diagnosis and prescription quickly became my blazing obsession. Over several months, I began to understand that careful fingering, combined with a slow and highly methodical approach to learning a new piece, would eventually put within my grasp many pieces that previously would have been unattainable.

The proximity of our ages, our shared love of piano music, a common genealogical history tracing back to the Netherlands, and a similar outlook on life meant that my relationship with Anton took on the added dimension of friendship in relatively short order. It wasn't long before my lessons started being less about technique and more about the point of technique.

A week before Christmas, and four months after that initial meeting in his studio, we hosted Anton and his partner, Bill, at our new home. I wanted him to see where and how we lived, and I needed my family to see and hear why I kept going on and on about my teacher's artistry and sensitivity.

As would become the ritual with each of his visits to our home in the pines, Anton played for us. He started his minirecital with a piece that brought Holly to tears—*Widmung* by Robert Schumann as arranged by Franz Liszt—and concluded it with Chopin's *Fantasy Impromptu in C-sharp Minor*, a piece that begins and ends with an angry torrent of notes wrapped around a lush and serene middle section.

When my parents came to visit late in 2010 to meet their great-grandson, Benjamin, for the first time, Anton and I put together a recital in honor of my mother, who introduced me to the piano and has played the organ in her church for decades.

On a brilliant fall morning, my daughters dutifully gathered in our living room, loyally humoring their old man despite their indifference to classical music. They were joined by Holly, my parents, and our dogs, who refused to be shooed outside. With our bulldog, Charlie, resting directly under the piano, I performed an entire program from memory and with a level of feeling that Anton said made him proud. My playing was no longer a broom that swept everyone out of the room.

With my mother beaming at me, I mouthed the words "Thank you" to Anton for everything he had done for me. He nodded and smiled. While neither he nor I knew it yet, he was just getting started.

September 4, 2011, 10:30 a.m. In the spring of 2011—eighteen months after my first lesson—Anton gave me a copy of "Clair de lune" and announced that I was now ready to learn this icon of the twentieth-century piano repertoire.

I started out by mapping the fingering for the right hand, then the left, and then slowly bringing them together. As the notes seeped into my fingers, I began work on the phrasing and dynamics. With each lesson, my understanding of the piece's structure and musical narrative grew. Within several months I was playing it at tempo, mainly from memory, with increasing confidence and growing ardor.

Now I would play "Clair de lune" as a gift to the long-suffering woman who had wordlessly endured the racket that came out of my piano for so many years. With a smile, Holly said, "Why don't you warm up a little, and I'll sit down when you're ready."

I played a few four-octave scales and said, "OK, I'm ready."

Four minutes later, the quiet arpeggios that end the piece rippled across the room. The look we exchanged with one another was enough. It was turning into a good day.

That feeling carried through the fajitas we ate and the beer we drank in the kitchen because it was too windy to eat lunch on the deck. With a full stomach, I barely lasted ten minutes when I sprawled on the brown leather couch to tackle the final chapters of a book I was reading.

When I awoke from my nap just before 3 p.m., the light in the family room was strangely off-color, a grayish hue that normally signified the imminent arrival of a thunderstorm. I practically leaped off the couch to check the weather radar. Maybe the forecasters had laid a giant egg, and we would get rain from Tropical Storm Lee after all.

"Hey, Holly," I said, "Check out my computer. Looks like there's rain northwest of here and it's moving in our direction." With her chin propped on my shoulder, we stared at the green blob over an area roughly the size of Bastrop State Park.

"Doesn't seem possible, but there it is," I said.

"That would also explain why it's gotten darker. Could be a big storm coming our way. Maybe that wasn't an evil wind after all."

I had barely conceded the point when the phone rang and Holly answered. Less than a minute later, with her back and shoulders rigid and face drained of color, she said: "That was Jeri Nell. There's a fire."

"Where?"

"She's not entirely sure, but it's somewhere near the park."

"So that explains what we're seeing on the radar," I said. "It's smoke."

"She says Walter thinks we should leave right away because of how the wind is blowing."

"But it's coming straight from the north. Hard to see how it could get this far to the east."

"She was pretty emphatic that we should go right now."

"We should be worried about your mom's place, not ours. If it's a big fire, it could cross the highway like in 2009."

"I'll call Amelia in case she's there. She needs to get out if she is."

The first of a half dozen calls was made: lots of rings and then Amelia's voice-mail message. "I'll keep trying to reach her on my cell phone," Holly said. "In the meantime, I don't think we should question Walter's judgment. There's no harm in leaving for a day or two."

"I suppose you're right, assuming we can find a place to stay."

"Should we grab anything?"

"We learned our lesson last time," I said. "All that work for nothing. If things change, we can always come back and get our stuff."

We shooed the dachshunds and Charlie into Holly's SUV. Rather than fighting with the dogs for space on the backseat, Miranda rode shotgun with me. As I packed up my computer, Holly tried Amelia's phone again. This time she got the manic busy signal that is symptomatic of a network veering toward overload.

"I can't reach her. It won't even ring."

"Keep trying. Although I'm sure she's OK."

I followed Holly out the driveway and onto Cottletown Road. None of us paused to look back or let our neighbors know what was happening. We didn't bother to grab a couple changes of underwear or our feather pillows that were a virtual necessity for a decent night's sleep. We left Miranda's birthday presents sitting on the dining room table.

AMELIA

In 2007, Walter and I built a house for my mother-in-law, Betty. We nestled it into a steep lot, inspiring her to name it Hill Haven. It was located in the middle of the Colovista subdivision, a sprawling development southeast of Bastrop that bordered the Colorado River on one side and the southern fringe of the Lost Pines on another, with a golf course tying it all together.

Less than a year after she moved in, she changed her mind and returned to Dallas for health reasons. The limestone-clad single-story house, with a garage that angled out from the house almost like an afterthought, stood empty for a while. Then Amelia decided she wanted to live there.

My middle daughter has my narrow-faced northern European look and her mother's accommodating and kind disposition. The silly and just-between-me-and-her nicknames that I gave her multiplied over the years to the point where I almost needed an app to keep track of them.

She was a lovely child, with thick blond hair and an impish smile. In her preschool days, she was a shameless show-off, darting about and jabbering away. Even during her gawkiest early-adolescent phase, the camera was kind to her. Now she was a young woman who was dazzling when dressed up and primped.

When she was in elementary school and shared a bedroom with her little sister, I would often take my place beside her while Holly labored to calm Miranda down on the bed across the room. After I read to her and the lights were out, Amelia would wiggle tight against me and quietly sing, note- and word-perfect, from her repertoire of Disney movie songs, sometimes mimicking a catchphrase from one of her favorite animated characters.

I tried to mold her personal interests after mine. When the sixth-grade Amelia said she was interested in marine biology, I gave her a mask, fins, and snorkel in the hope that she would be my future dive partner. She put on her gear a couple of times and then retired it. After one season of grade-school basketball, she emphatically refused to follow in her older sister's auspicious footsteps. After a couple of outings on the tennis court, we agreed there was no reason to buy her a racket or look into lessons.

She was definitively her mother's daughter—an elegant ballet dancer in high school, a patient teacher of preschool dance students, and hardwired not to pick a fight. Holly and I shared the credit for her voracious reading habit. But there was one thing I alone could take credit for: the pleasure she took in a glass of high-quality wine.

Amelia was inside Hill Haven, dusting and vacuuming, when the fires broke out and coalesced, barreling southward in her direction.

September 4, 2011, 3:15 p.m. As Miranda and I neared Highway 71, we came upon a jagged row of cars and pickups on the right shoulder with people taking pictures or looking through binoculars. As I reached the highest point of Cottletown Road, I saw what they saw and quickly pulled over.

"Miranda, I have to get out and get a better look at what's happening."

"Why? Mom is ahead. We need to stay with her and the dogs."

"We'll only be here a minute. Stay in the car."

I took my place in a crooked line of unkempt people who were dressed for a lazy holiday weekend. Hardly anything was said as we stared at the spectacle to the west. The smoke had congealed into an enormous black snake that had slithered across the highway. The oily and impenetrable serpent was at least five miles long and a half mile wide. Within it, a succession of sharp bursts of yellow light flared up, burned intensely bright, and then disappeared.

I knew what this meant. The wildfire was digesting houses and commercial buildings in succession, one after another, each immolation documented with a flare. It was strangely beautiful and undeniably sad.

As I compared what I saw to the most obvious physical landmarks—a water tower and the cow pastures southeast of the forest—I had the same thought as when Jeri Nell called: it's blowing south too fast to affect us. We'd be spared once again, even though many people we knew and cared about were probably already homeless or about to be.

While I had a general idea of the fire's location, I couldn't tell where it was in relation to Colovista or the small developments where some of our friends and acquaintances lived. The longer I stood on the crest of the hill and stared, the scarier Amelia's situation became.

My phone rang. "Where are you?" Holly practically shrieked.

"I pulled off the road to get a better look," I said. "I had to size things up so we know what our options are."

"There's no time for that. I'm at the highway, and we have to figure out how to reach our daughter. I keep getting that horrible busy signal."

"I'm getting into my car now. I'll be there in a second."

My few minutes had been well spent. Unlike Holly, I now knew the general situation and what our daughter had to do if she was at Hill Haven. She must leave immediately and go east toward Smithville on two perpendicular county roads that would take her to Highway 71 less than a mile from us. If she went the other way, working her way toward Bastrop on the county roads that paralleled the engulfed highway, she would likely run headlong into the firestorm as it blew south and west.

I was the only person in our family who understood this. If Holly was skeptical, I had to convince her. If Amelia resisted, I would hold my ground. I would not be talked out of what I knew.

Miranda and I pulled alongside Holly's SUV with our cars pointed toward Austin. It was impossible to see more than a few miles down the highway because smoke had swallowed all four lanes. Near the ground, all we could see was an enormous black smudge as impenetrable as ink. Around the smudge, gray and black smoke curdled up and out.

Highway 71 appeared to dead-end at hell's front door. Traffic was being rerouted back toward us.

"You still haven't talked to her?" I asked Holly.

"No. What if we can't reach her?"

"All we can do right now is head toward Smithville. You keep trying and I'll call Robb and see if we can stay with him until the danger passes. If you reach her, tell her she needs to join us."

"How? The highway is blocked."

"If she goes east on those back roads, she'll be on the safe side of the fire."

"How do you know this?"

"I could see it when I was standing on the top of the hill."

She nodded. "OK."

"If we can't stay with Robb, we'll need to get a room in town. If we wait much longer, there might not be any left."

I got back in my car and followed Holly.

Halfway to Smithville, Holly called. "I just heard from her. She's OK."

"Are you sure?"

"Yes. I'd still be talking to her except that we lost our connection. She was inside my mom's house when the power went out. She went outside to see if anyone knew what was going on and one of her neighbors told her about the fire and that she had to leave immediately."

"So where is she now?"

"In her car."

I called her and immediately got through.

"Where are you right now?" I asked.

"I'm creeping along in a line of cars," Amelia said. "The cops are directing traffic. They wouldn't let us on the highway. We're on a side road."

"You're going toward Smithville, right?"

"No."

"Why not? It's the only safe way out."

"I thought about that and almost did it. But I changed my mind."

"Why didn't you call me? I could have told you what's happening."

"I decided to follow other people out."

"But why not just me ask where to go?"

"I'm sorry. But how I was I supposed to know you knew more than anyone else?"

"So it's too late to turn around?"

"Totally. I'm almost to the highway on the other side of the fire. I've been in my car for the past half hour."

I didn't see any point in arguing with her.

"We tried calling you before we left the house. Why didn't you answer?"

"I turned my phone off because I was cleaning the house."

"Do you have any idea how worried we've been?"

"I didn't know anything was going on until the power went off and my vacuum stopped working. If that hadn't happened, I'd still be at my house."

I later found out that my conviction and certainty might have killed her if I had reached her before she left. What I thought was the opposite of what was happening.

My preferred route was about to be engulfed by the time her neighbor told her to leave. Going in the direction of Smithville would have put her between the main fire and one of its southeastern appendages with no safe way out.

Amelia evacuated as the fire was bearing down on the other escape routes. Those roads became a death trap soon after she traversed them. Nobody can say whether it was fifteen or thirty minutes or even a bit longer. But she could have been trapped, just like those who perished in the California fires, if she had been lazier about her reaction to the power outage or sought my advice before setting out.

My beloved daughter got out safely by following her instincts instead of turning to her all-too-confident father. Maybe a higher power was at work as well.

September 4, 2011, 3:30 p.m. By the time we reached Smithville, the fire had filled the western horizon. It was no longer inconceivable that it could jump the river, just as it did the four-lane state highway. Robb and Sherri's house no longer seemed like a good idea.

"We don't think we should head in your direction after all, buddy," I told Robb. "I can't believe I'm saying this, but maybe you should think about evacuating yourself."

"We've been having the same conversation."

We'd been friends with Robb as long as with Jeri Nell and Walter. For most of that time, we lived less than a mile from his hand-built place on Cottletown Road. For years, Robb and I assembled a group of our buddies on a weekly basis for pickup basketball games at his place and then mine. But several years earlier, he had remarried, sold his property, and moved to a rural area south of Smithville near the river.

"What are you going to do now?" Robb asked.

"We'll probably check into a motel and wait it out for a day or two. We really didn't pack enough stuff to go to Austin. Be safe, OK, dude?"

"You too."

There was only one plausible place in Smithville we could stay, and we went there immediately, thinking it would quickly fill up. It was a motel on the highway next to the hospital. It wasn't one of those la-di-da places where you practically need a forklift to clear the bed of all the extraneous pillows. It was just what we needed for a night or two because, standing in the parking lot, we'd have an unobstructed view of the fire's length from north to south.

"Do you have any rooms left?" I asked the owner.

"Yes, but it's lucky you got here when you did. There are only a few left."

There was a No Pets sign on the wall. "We have dogs. Will that be a problem?"

He frowned. "How many?"

"Three."

"How big?"

"Two little wiener dogs and an English bulldog. Don't worry, they're house-trained and they hardly ever bark." Given the situation, my lie seemed a forgivable offense.

He thought for a second. "Ordinarily, I wouldn't allow it. But with the fire, I guess it's OK."

It was the first of many small graces.

Since we hadn't packed anything, we had nothing to unload except the dogs. Without collars and leashes, we had to carry the dachshunds to the room and corral Charlie up a flight of stairs with our knees and hands, trying to keep him away from other evacuees who were also settling in. Except for the few times we had boarded them at the vet during a family vacation, this would literally be the first time they would have to act like normal dogs, with boundaries and limits on where they went and what they did. I had a hard time picturing it.

I went to my car to get my computer just as the trim carpenter who worked on each of the houses Walter and I had built drove up in his pickup, pulling a covered trailer. His teenage son was with him. They were sweaty and wearing T-shirts and shorts.

Like so many of our longtime friends, Steve had designed and built his own house and workshop, a project that he had never completely finished. Now firmly in his middle age, he lived with his family just north of the highway on a bumpy county road that was halfway between our neighborhood and Amelia's. He had the lean physique and wiry arms of someone who did meticulous, physical work.

I called out to him. "Hey, Steve, any idea where the fire is at?"

"I can't say for sure where it is. But I know where it's been. It was getting ready to tear into our place just as we were leaving."

I gave him a quizzical look.

"It's gone," he said. "As far as I know, nothing's left."

He delivered this news like he was giving the time and temperature.

"Are you sure? How do you know?"

"Trust me. I know. We got the stuff in this truck and trailer and that's about it."

"What about all of your tools?"

"Some of them are in the trailer. But most of them are gone. Jon got wiped out, too, including that classic car that's been sitting in his driveway since who-knows-when. He'll be here any minute."

His son wandered off, shuffling his feet, his eyes glued to the ground.

"I don't know what to say, Steve. This is awful."

"We'll get by. It's only stuff."

"It's a lot more than that. It's what you built. It's where you raised your kids. It's how you make a living."

The brief silence was unbearable. "Whatever you need, you can count on us," I said.

"That's OK."

"No, I'm serious Steve. You're going to need help, there's no way around it. I promise we'll be there for you. So will all your other friends."

I wanted to throw my arms around him, perhaps in the hope that it would shake loose the kind of reciprocal emotion I was expecting. Instead, we stood opposite one another, hands stuffed in our pockets.

"Thanks for saying that," he said. "Right now, I have to check in and unload some of this stuff in our room. Maybe I'll see you later."

Holly came outside a few minutes later, about the time Jon was driving up.

"I saw you talking to Steve," she said.

"Him and Beth are wiped out. I told him we'd help them in some way."

"You did?"

"Of course. How could I not?"

"A better question is, How could you? We might soon be in the same spot ourselves. And even if we're not, what can we do?"

"I had to say something. I don't see what's wrong with trying to be helpful."

"Put yourself in their shoes. What can we, or anyone, realistically do about their situation?"

"Put yourself in my shoes. What would you have said, given that we're OK and they aren't?"

"Let's not argue, OK? We just got here and I'm already exhausted from worrying about our daughter."

As we tried to keep our voices from spreading across the parking lot, Jon walked up, shook our hands, and flashed a warm smile. He was literally the first person I had met in Bastrop County, back in 1979. Over the years, the hair on his head had gone topsy-turvy, and now a full salt-and-pepper beard was splayed out beneath a shaved dome. He lived among the pines in a large ramshackle house filled to the rafters. Very little was ever thrown out.

"Steve's already told us," I said. "I feel terrible for you."

"We're safe and that's the main thing," said Jon. "We can replace most of what we need. And a lot of what we had, we can probably do without."

Jon's optimistic view of the world was normally a tonic. But I felt my neck tighten as I listened to him downplay what had just happened to him and his wife. I didn't doubt his sincerity. In fact, it would have been easier if I did. His response was so different from what I knew mine would be that I could process it only by trying to get away from it.

"We'll probably have lots of time to talk, Jon. Right now, we probably should get up to our room. Miranda is up there by herself."

"Of course. Don't let me hold you up."

A minute later, with the air-conditioning running so loud we practically had to shout to hear ourselves, I said to Holly, "It makes no sense. Jon loved the forest too. How can he be smiling?"

I avoided Jon's sunny disposition for the rest of the time we stayed in the motel, several doors from his room. Miranda enjoyed the brief snippets of conversation she shared with him on the steps or when each of our doors was open. But I wanted to reserve the right to fling myself into a pit of despair if things went badly for us without being shamed by others who had more effective coping mechanisms.

The hotel quickly filled up with a combination of people who already knew their fate, those who feared the worst, and those in a third group that included us. Being in that group created its own set of problems as Holly and I bounced between our room and the impromptu conversations breaking out in the parking lot and on the concrete stairs.

"It's hard to know what to say to some of these people since the fire hasn't gotten us yet, and I really don't think it will," I said. "Are we supposed to feel guilty compared to them?"

"I don't think guilt is the right word, but I get your point."

"It all feels so awkward and strange. Maybe we should just stay in our room."

"You can do that, but I'd rather spend as little time in there as possible. It's dark and claustrophobic, especially with the dogs."

"Are you worried?" I said. "About what might happen to us?"

"Not like you, I imagine. Whatever is going to happen, we can't do anything about it."

"I know. But how can you not care?"

"I can care without worrying."

"What's the difference?"

Silence.

"Well, whatever you call it, I want to know what's happening," I said. "Maybe I can find something on the Web. Surely the county has some useful information up there."

"Go ahead," said Holly. "I'm going to sit out here for a while with Miranda and the dogs."

Social media sites were burning up with rumors, secondhand information, mindless speculation, and pleas for information from those who didn't know what to think or where to turn. Taken as a whole, the information was contradictory, off-kilter, and boiling over with fear and frustration. I couldn't stop reading it, however, because the only thing worse than bad information in an unfolding catastrophe is no information.

I spent the most time on the county's emergency management Facebook site, trying to sort out the conflicting and over-the-top statements about who was saved and who wasn't, especially the growing chorus of know-it-alls who pronounced the Colovista subdivision doomed. While I didn't necessarily believe it, I knew there was a very good possibility that Hill Haven had burned along with everything Amelia owned except her car.

This was an awful situation, but still better than having to give up all that Holly and I had accumulated over three decades of marriage and our practically new home. It wasn't a real choice, but it felt like one, because how could the fire ask the Fritz family to sacrifice both?

"How much longer are you going to keep this up?" Holly said an hour before midnight.

"I guess I should stop. I can't believe the county isn't putting out any useful information."

"Maybe they don't know anything."

"Then they should at least say that. And explain why they don't know."

"You're just working yourself up. If you keep it up much longer, you'll never get to sleep."

I closed my laptop and tried to get comfortable with my head on a pillow that felt only slightly more comfortable than a sandbag.

As I stared at the ceiling, my anxiety rose. I believed we'd be OK in the end. But what if we weren't? How would all of us—but especially Miranda—cope with the loss of our home and keepsakes on the day she became a legal adult?

NAMESAKE

At this time of night, twenty-one years before to the day, I was driving Holly to Austin much faster than the speed limit. If a police officer pulled us over, I had a good excuse: "My wife is in labor, so we'll be on our way now, thank you very much." Hillary and Amelia had each been born around midday, so this would be our first night baby if she came into the world with the same alacrity as her sisters.

Miranda did indeed honor the waste-no-time family tradition, arriving soon after Holly was checked in. I fell asleep on the too-small couch in Holly's room after the wondrous sight of finger and toenails as perfect as they were tiny, and the slightly envious and left-out feeling of a father watching his newborn sleep on his wife's belly. When I woke up well after sunrise, it was to the sound of a quiet conversation between Holly and a nurse.

"She's our third daughter," said Holly.

I could see the nurse pointing to me through my squinty eyes. "How does he feel about that?"

"Probably disappointed, although he won't admit it. But at least she's his namesake."

"You gave her a boy's name?" asked the nurse.

"His name is Randy. Her name is Miranda."

"Nice."

"My sentiments exactly," I thought.

It was a lovely, quiet start to a momentous journey, like the dead-calm surface of a harbor at daybreak before venturing out past the breakwater into the adventurous waves and searing sun.

September 5, 2011, 7 a.m. While we slept, the fire slowed down as it moved eastward and came upon the riparian area along Alum Creek, reaching the place where the 2009 fire began. With relative humidity rising, temperatures moderating, and the winds diminishing, the fire took an overnight time-out, saving its worst for Labor Day.

The first thing I did when I woke up was go to the parking lot to stare at the towering plume of smoke that was now blanched white and fluffed up across my entire visual horizon. Learning nothing from this, I went inside and jumped back into the county's online cauldron of speculation and gossip. With the curtains drawn, our west-facing room was almost as dark as it had been when we went to bed.

"You're back at it already?" Holly whispered, with Miranda still asleep.

"There are a lot of people saying Colovista is gone. Hard to believe they're all wrong just like it's hard to believe the county is still clammed up. I think we have to tell Amelia to prepare for the worst."

"I suppose. But we should wake Miranda before we make the call. She deserves to be a part of all of this.

"I agree."

"Miranda, wake up," Holly said. "Happy birthday, dear."

"You're officially grown up now," I said.

"Thanks, Dad. Thanks, Mom. But it doesn't feel like a birthday. I'm worried about our house, and I don't even have any presents to open."

"If I can get them later today, I will," I said. "Otherwise, you can open them once we're back at the house, safe and sound. Right now we have to call your sister with some bad news."

"We think you got out just in time," I said after Amelia answered on the first ring.

"Are you trying to tell me I'm wiped out?"

"We don't know for sure yet. But, yes, we're pretty sure that's what happened."

"I don't have any clothes." She started to cry.

"You won't lack for anything you had," Holly said. "As soon as we can all get back into our house, we'll go out and get whatever you need."

After a makeshift and unsatisfying breakfast, I made the first of several trips to the overlook on Park Road 1C about halfway between Buescher State Park and Cottletown Road, eluding the law enforcement barricades and turn-back points.

This was the place on my bike rides where I would stop and rest before turning back. The overlook mainly faced the south. But if I stood at its eastern point, I could see the wedge of land that almost reached our place.

A group of cars and pickups were parked at cockeyed angles to avoid blocking the narrow road. They belonged to several of my neighbors and other people I didn't recognize. With the temperature rising and the wind picking up, we stood and conferred at the edge of the bluff with a fifteen-mile view to the southwest where the fire was adding to its list of victims. The combination of wind and fuel was pushing the fire in all directions, like an expanding balloon.

A sense of dread hung over our conversations. We were a sweaty and grimy band of pilgrims on a forced journey that we hoped wouldn't take us to an undiscovered country. One of my fellow pilgrims was a woman who lived less than a mile from us in the direction of the park road. Judy was nearing retirement age, lived alone, and worked in the real estate and title business.

"Unless the wind does something different, we'll be among the lucky ones," she said.

"Some of the people at the motel where we're staying already know they're burned out."

"How are they handling it?" Judy asked.

"Better than I probably would."

"Maybe after things are back to normal in a week or so, I'll see you and your daughter riding around on her golf cart."

"Now that's something I can definitely picture," I said. "Right now, I think I'll go and see if anyone at the fire department can tell me something worth knowing."

"Good idea. Let me know if you find anything out."

"Will do."

The Smithville Volunteer Fire Department was located on the town's main drag. With the trucks and firefighters in the field, the stone and metal firehouse that took up half a city block was strangely quiet and calm. The enormous and high-ceilinged room where the fire trucks were normally parked was empty. There was no sign of a calamity in progress.

I went into the room where the firemen had their monthly training meetings. Several women were standing near tables piled with food and coolers filled with drinks and bottled water. With his arms resting on his belly, the fire chief sat in a folding chair in the center of the room. He was dead-eyed from a night without sleep and not in a mood for questions. I asked them anyway.

"What do you know about what's happening around Cottletown Road?"

"We got men and trucks out there. We're making a stand. If we have anything to say about it, the fire's not getting there."

"I was just at the overlook and the fire seems totally out of control with the wind blowing again."

"What were you doing there?"

"What do you think? I had plenty of company."

"I'm sick of wasting my breath on people like you."

"It's not dangerous there."

"As if you'd know."

"Any idea how far east it's come?" I asked.

"It's going in every direction."

"Who's coordinating all of this?"

"Each department is doing its thing. There's no giant plan."

"Why isn't the county telling the public what's happening?"

He answered me with a stare.

"OK, OK. I get it," I said.

The congenial man who had installed our heating and air-conditioning system, and who lived near the house where Amelia and Miranda were born, stood behind the chief, saying nothing and barely blinking.

"How about you, Earl? Any idea what your situation is?"

"I've got a chimney left."

"How do you know?"

"I saw it."

"When? How?"

"A little while ago," he said. "I just got back."

This news felt like a punch to the face.

"What else did you see?"

"Like the chief said, they're making a stand."

We stood with our arms at our sides, our eyes locked, our voices flat. Feeling awful for him, I tried out a new line. "I'll probably be in the same situation as you pretty soon."

"Maybe."

"Well, I guess I better get out of your hair. I know you guys have things to do." They didn't roll their eyes at me, though they had every right to.

Five minutes later, I was back in our motel room, prepping for what I assumed would be a disagreement with Holly.

"I'm almost positive we're going to be OK, but it would really help to know for sure," I said.

"I hope you're not thinking about going back."

"Why not? Besides, all that time I wasted on my computer last night drained my battery and I've only got a little bit of power left on my cell phone. We can't go for days like that. We need to stay in touch with our daughters."

"Our room has a phone. You know, the kind that plugs into a wall."

"We also need clean clothes and underwear."

"Can you get my birthday presents, too?" said Miranda.

"Those will be the first things I take," I told her.

"We can get most of what we need in LaGrange," said Holly.

"Not my birthday presents," said Miranda.

"Why buy stuff that we already own?" I said.

"So you're going to risk your life for some stuff we can easily do without for a few days?"

"That's leaping to a pretty dramatic conclusion, wouldn't you say?"

She gave me a look that said about a dozen things all at once.

"Wouldn't you feel better if you knew our house was still there?" I asked her.

"That's the real reason you want to go back. At least you're coming clean."

"How about this? I'll check around to see if anyone knows for sure that it's safe to go back. If I can't find anyone to do that, I won't go."

I didn't have to ask around very long before I got the answer I was looking for. A stone-faced man with a receding hairline and thick eyebrows who was staying several doors down from our room told me he had just returned from seeing his burned-out place. He lived close to Earl, within a block or two of the house that Walter, Kevin, and I built.

"I came back on the park road, and it looked OK most of the way."

"So you passed Cottletown?" I asked.

"Sure did."

"Did you see any fire trucks?"

"Yup."

"Where?"

"At the intersection. If they're still there, they might make you turn around."

"I'm willing to take that chance."

"They gave me a nasty stare. Lucky for me I was driving away from the fire."

"Let me worry about that," I said. "The bottom line is, I'm good to go, right?"

"You'll be a lot safer than I was."

I got my answer. But there was one more thing I had to know.

"We used to live near your place, in a house set back from the road with a rather complicated metal roof and a tall arched window," I said.

"I know the place."

"Is it still there?"

"How could it be? Nothing else around there is."

Lucky for me, I had work to do. I didn't have time to let what he said sink in.

CHAPTER 4

September 5, 2011, 11 a.m. I didn't look back at Holly as I walked across the parking lot to my car. I'd be back in less than an hour with no harm done, no foul committed.

With the wind at full throttle, and the temperature skyrocketing, I began my evasions of law enforcement obstacles. The view toward Austin across the highway was a wall of smoke rising from the ground to at least fifteen thousand feet. A prop plane approaching the Smithville airport from the west would have been invisible.

I kept my focus by putting together a mental list of the other things I needed to get besides Miranda's birthday presents, my electric chargers, and several changes of clothes. It was mainly bathroom stuff—contact solution, toothpaste, toothbrushes, dental floss, and face soap—and our must-have feather pillows.

I passed the overlook—now almost completely overrun with vehicles and people—and took a detour. If the fire was going to block my way, I didn't want to encounter it on the park road: turning around quickly on such a narrow road would be difficult. So I took Old Antioch, a county road that exited the pines into meadows and pastureland. Going this way would take a little longer but would also be safer. After all, how could the fire spread without trees?

I was tempted to open my driver's-side window to monitor the smell of smoke, but it was too hot. After I passed the overlook, I didn't encounter a single person. All of the firefighting equipment was gone as well.

I was beginning to think I was completely alone when my phone dinged. It was a text from my next-door neighbor Gordon, the man who sold us our land in 2007. I stopped in the middle of the road and read it: "I'm out here now. All OK so far, anything I can do for you folks?"

This was classic Gordon, a very independent man and a good neighbor. Of course he was still hanging around, given his libertarian streak and love of his land. His text made me smile because now I not only had company—I was also vindicated.

Nothing was different as I turned into my driveway and parked next to the curved, herringbone brick walkway. "So everything's OK," I thought. "Not that I ever really doubted it." I tasted the slightly sour air as I walked to the mahogany front door.

Holly had left a yellow sticky pad on the kitchen island. The light from the tubular skylight was pure and intense, the haze removed like cloudy water passed clean through a membrane. I sat on one of the four wicker stools, took a cheap pen from a nearby drawer, and made my list.

As I glided from room to room, I stashed the first set of items—Miranda's birthday presents and our toiletries—in a paper grocery bag that I carried in my left hand. With my right arm, I cradled our feather pillows against my chest. As I put all of it in the backseat of my car, I wondered if the air had gotten smokier in the brief time I was in the house.

My second and third trips around the house were focused on wicker baskets of jeans, shorts, undies, socks, and the diving equipment I needed for a trip I was taking in three days to Cocos Island, off the southwestern coast of Costa Rica. As I piled all of it into the trunk, I no longer wondered about the smoke. It was definitely getting worse.

I crossed off all the things on my list. With one foot in my car and the other on the driveway, I stared at my house, leaning over the door with my elbows. I didn't believe our home and land were in any more danger than I did when I drove off twenty-one hours earlier. But what if I was wrong? How would I explain what I left behind when I had a chance to save it?

I went back inside and began gathering up the framed photos of our kids at various points in their lives and the old-school snapshots we had taken with actual film. They'd be easy to put back, so what was the harm in taking them?

Next on the no-brainer list: our passports and birth certificates, never mind the fact that I could replace them online in less than an hour. And I couldn't pass up a framed letter that Lady Bird Johnson had sent to me when I was county judge.

Now, as the light outside grew a little dusky, I faced the hardest choice: what to do with my pots and the art Holly and I had collected over three decades of shared aesthetics and personal taste.

Should I wrap up my favorite pots and the Bernard Leach cup, and carefully stack them on the front seat of the car and the floor, hoping that none of them would go flying from a sudden stop? I did that once before, with Holly's help. I didn't want to do it again.

Holly had hung one of her grandfather's large oil paintings over our fireplace. As an experiment, I tried removing it carefully. When that didn't work,

I ripped the hanger out of the wall, leaving behind a nasty little hole I was not looking forward to explaining later.

There were too many pastels, oil paintings, and limited-edition prints on the walls, and Holly had hung them in a way that made them difficult to remove, as I had just learned with the oil painting. It was best to leave them be.

I heedlessly walked around the house, wasting valuable time. If I had stopped to think clearly and honestly, I would have made different and far wiser choices.

On the Christmas morning following the fire, I received a gift from Amelia along with a brief letter, the kind that any parent would cherish until the end of time. As I read it with soggy eyes, it suddenly occurred to me: this was the latest in a procession of notes and letters and drawings from my kids that I had squirreled away in the middle drawer of the pine desk Walter made for me and that I regularly took out and reread. This was the newest installment in twenty years of daughter-to-dad artifacts that charted the growth of my relationship with my children, each item dripping with emotion and blissful remembrance.

But I never gave them a thought, nor did I even remember them, until I read my daughter's Christmas letter.

I was snapped out of my autopilot mode by the sight of Gordon standing in my driveway, his roundish face radiating a weird combination of geniality and dead-level seriousness and his thinning hair whipping about. He was wearing a T-shirt and shorts, and his car was parked behind mine on the circular driveway.

"You never answered my text," he said.

"Dude, I've been too busy gathering up my stuff. I was going to text you later."

"I didn't even know you were here till I saw your car."

"Well, here I am."

"Much as I hate to say it, I think it's time for us to get out of here."

If Gordon—the last man standing—was saying this, who was I to argue with him? "Maybe it's good you pulled up," I said. "Now I have a reason to leave."

"Just because I'm going doesn't mean you have to."

His statement was precisely backwards.

"Let me take one more walk through the house and I'll join you," I said.

I went back inside and was suddenly stricken by the vulnerability of everything I saw, like a parent watching an oblivious child wander toward the street.

The ash floor in the living room was where my grandson Ben and I had spent the prior Memorial Day weekend together while everyone else was out of town. On our knees and haunches, we played with blocks and built towers out of Legos. I read him books, picked up the messes he made as he crawled about, and marveled at what had come to me in my middle age.

The kitchen island under the incandescent skylight was the altar where we held our family rituals built around food. I piled the tomatoes, peppers, and melons I had grown over the past four months on the countertop to the left of the island. The plates we received as wedding presents more than three decades ago were stacked on the shelves above the dishwasher. Our wood-handled silverware—also from when we got married—sat in the top drawer near the sink.

The bookshelves Walter made were crammed with books Holly and I began accumulating in our college days at street fairs where several paperbacks could be had for less than a cup of coffee. Looking at the oldest and most threadbare books, I saw our college minds reflected back. Some were embarrassing (was I really a Marxist then?), some inexplicable (how could anyone read that turgid philosophical stuff?), but most were choices I would still make (Flannery O'Connor, Faulkner, Shakespeare, Thornton Wilder).

Not counting the books I'd bought most recently, most of them hadn't been touched in years, except for when we boxed them up and moved. But throwing any of them out was unthinkable. They were a literary map of our marriage and side-by-side intellectual evolution. We'd keep them for the rest of our lives.

On the farthest-to-the-right bookshelf were the frayed and barely-holding-together children's books that were passed down from daughter to daughter. I had read each of them to my daughters in the same way: lying in their beds, side by side on our backs, with the smell of their baths in their hair. Sometimes I would read part of a sentence and they would finish it. With *In the Night Kitchen* propped on my chest, we'd laugh at naked little Mickey standing next to a giant bottle of milk as they pointed at his wiener. They'd growl the *Wild Things* growl or come under the spell of Oscar Wilde's "The Selfish Giant," not making a sound except their breathing.

The books leaned against one another, stockpiled for overnight visits from Ben and his future siblings or cousins. We'd wait to replace them until they fell completely apart.

Across from the bookshelves was a small closet where we kept our games, sports equipment, and VHS videos we intended to convert into digital format. As I took a quick look at the labels on some of them—dance recitals, family vacations, and home videos of the girls when they were newborns, crawling, or barely walking—I chided myself for waiting this long to cash them in for DVDs. I promised myself that not another Christmas would go by before we started watching them again, as we used to do in the Long Trail House, splayed on the L-shaped leather sofa with the girls in their pj's and me in my sweats.

As I passed Miranda's bedroom, I thought of her harvest of Special Olympics medals for running, long jumping, and relay hanging in her closet. Some were from the regional meet held each spring just north of Austin and others from the annual state meet in Fort Worth the week before school let out for the summer. I had seen her win almost every one. They rattled against each other whenever she slammed her door. It was a happy sound.

Except for the hole in the wall where the oil painting had been, everything was the same as the last time I was in the family room, waking from my Sunday afternoon nap. But I could no longer deny that this might be a moment I would later recognize as the dividing line.

If my intuition was right, there was only one small thing I could do about it, with Gordon waiting for me in the hazy and tangy air. I reached for two dust-coated bottles of French wine at the bottom of my wine rack so that I could keep my promise to Amelia.

With a bottle in each hand, I kicked the front door shut. After locking it, I led Gordon out of my driveway, casting a final sideways glance at the house and wishing I had snapped a pic on my smartphone before setting off. As I began my drive back, I noticed that Gordon was no longer visible in my rearview mirror.

Five minutes into my ride, I was thunderstruck by what I had done. My car was filled with stuff that could be replaced in an afternoon while the items that could never be replaced were still there. I made a quick U-turn, determined to gather up my Lucie Rie–like bowls, Elspeth's gift, and my favorite wood-fired pots, starting with the ochre one. If that meant stacking them loosely on the backseat of the car, without protection, I was now willing to take that chance.

As I turned back into our driveway, with the acrid wind buffeting my car, I realized why I had lost sight of Gordon. He had stopped to lock our mutual gate, a red cast-iron bar that swung across our shared driveway. It was the first time either of us had done that since we lived there.

I could have unlocked the gate and done what I set out to do. But the voice inside my head urging me back was drowned out by another one: "Gordon is gone. Not only that, he locked the gate. He's not coming back. Are you seriously going to stay when he, of all people, has bailed out?"

I looked at what Gordon had done with a combination of regret and relief. My home, my trees, and my garden were now off-limits, a No Trespassing sign posted over my life as I knew it.

Many months later, as I again tried to make sense of the decisions I made during that last visit, my therapist said something that hadn't occurred to me until that moment: "Gordon probably saved your life."

I called him to ask why he had locked the gate. This was the first time we had spoken since a chance meeting a week after the fire.

"What were you thinking?" I said. "Why did you do that?"

"I knew the fire guys could always cut the lock if they had to get back there to protect our places, so I locked the gate to keep out people who shouldn't be there. Who knows who'd be roaming around and what they'd be doing?"

"I can't remember you ever locking the gate before."

"That's true."

"Why did you decide to evacuate?"

"The smoke."

"I knew it was getting worse, but it never occurred to me that it might be dangerous until you showed up."

"You were inside most of the time."

"Don't you see what all this means?" I asked, my voice gurgling.

He said nothing, perhaps wondering if I had posed a trick question.

"You probably saved my life. Do you realize that?"

It went on like this for several minutes. Simple, declarative sentences delivered by him in a steady voice and by me in a throaty, cracking sputter. While the concept of my death remained abstract, the unintended gift he gave me was as real as my nearly exploding heart.

For almost a week after the fire, I berated myself for what I saved that late morning compared to what I left behind. Holly and the girls countered that I should be glad I got out alive, an assertion I dismissed as unsubstantiated and overly dramatic. They said that if I was determined to castigate myself, I should focus on the idiocy of my decision to go back.

Each side felt obligated to dig in despite the pain being dished out. Finally, at their insistence, I sought out a neutral opinion. I called a pediatrician friend who lives in Miami.

"I can't stop thinking about what I should have taken but didn't," I said. "I know it was getting smoky, but I'm almost certain it was several hours before the fire came through. I could have saved everything."

"So why didn't you stay?"

"My neighbor sort of talked me out of it."

"Tell me what it was like as you went back and forth."

"Each time it got a little worse. I could also see the color of the light changing."

"Was it getting harder to breathe?"

"A little. I probably started coughing a bit."

"You realize, don't you know, that most people in fires die of smoke inhalation? They're already dead when the fire gets to them."

"I know that. But if I had started coughing hard, or found it really hard to breathe, I would have left. Give me some credit."

"You're talking about smoke asphyxiation. You're forgetting about carbon monoxide poisoning or reduced oxygen levels in the air. You could have been overcome so quickly, you'd have passed out. You would have been helpless to save yourself."

This assessment was confirmed six months later during an afternoon visit with two Texas Forest Service employees. As we talked, I mentioned that I had briefly gone back on Labor Day while the fire was raging. "Why would you do that?" the man said. "What on earth were you thinking?"

"I had to get my daughter's birthday presents and the chargers for my computer and phone, and somebody told me it was probably safe to go back."

"You realize how ridiculous that sounds?"

I nodded.

"You shouldn't have done that," said the woman.

"I know that now."

"When did you go back?"

"Late morning."

"When do you leave?"

"Around noon."

"If you had waited any longer, there would have been nothing left of you."

CHAPTER 5

September 5, 2011, noon. I turned back toward Smithville. As I neared the intersection with Old Antioch Road, I saw two old friends who lived near our first house. Joe and Jean were standing on the side of the road, staring at a low black cloud that could have passed for a gathering thunderstorm. It had a greasy, somewhat satanic look.

I got out and briefly joined them. "That looks sort of ominous," I said.

"We know," Jean said. "We've been watching it for a while now."

"Any idea which direction it's going?"

"It's hard to say."

"Well, so far, so good," I said.

They looked at me skeptically. I could hardly blame them.

"You went back and got some stuff?" Joe said.

I didn't want to explain what I had and hadn't taken, so I cut the conversation short. Less than an hour later, after another stop at the overlook, I was back at the motel, stockpiling our clothes and Miranda's presents in our room. I hid the bottles of wine on the floor behind the passenger seat because I wasn't ready to sort out for Holly or myself the mixed messages sent by my decision to save them.

I had made that promise to Amelia during a trip to Europe the previous summer.

BURGUNDY

We were in Europe because of a different promise I made to my youngest daughter.

Miranda's unique qualities endow her with serenity and an effortless ability to set aside the slights and minor insults that tend to take up residence in the minds of most people. While these are great gifts—the kind people of means often invest considerable sums to chase after—they come at a cost, one of which is being shortchanged on some of the experiences her siblings enjoyed.

That is why, after her sisters enjoyed a three-week romp through Europe thanks to the generosity of their maternal grandmother, I promised Miranda that I would take her there on her graduation from high school in 2010 to even the score. Because her graduation would coincide with Amelia's new baccalaureate from the University of Texas, I invited her to come along as her graduation present as well.

Early in August, we left for nearly two weeks in England, France, and Switzerland. While most of this time would be spent in London and Paris, I carved out an overnight trip to Burgundy because I couldn't bear the thought of traveling across the Atlantic without visiting one of the world's shrines to wine: the legendary Côte d'Or.

Accompanied by my sister-in-law Laura, we arrived in the heart of Burgundy without any idea of how to finagle tastings at the sort of wineries I was interested in: family-run operations that produce rarified juice in small amounts.

We pulled into Beaune around noon on a summer's day that seemed ordered up by the French Tourism Bureau. With temperatures in the 70s and a sunny sky, we parked our rental car on a cobblestone side street and meandered past houses and shops imported from a bygone era, with exposed timbers and plastered walls.

While the town's enchantment was undeniable, we had work to do. To get our bearings, we went to the Visitors' Center. Little clots of tourists were assembling for walk-throughs and tastings at the largest and most commercialized wineries in the area.

This wasn't what we came for.

Sensing my disenchantment, a young woman with blond hair pulled back and a welcoming smile took my arm, pulled us aside, and asked what sort of experience we were looking for. With Laura acting as translator, we got the skinny on how to savor the delights of Burgundy like a knowledgeable local.

"Monsieur, what sort of domains are you interested in?"

"I'd like to visit the ones that are too small to export their wines to America."

"That won't be any problem at all. Go to any village you choose and look for the small signs with the names of family-run domains. Knock on the door and see what happens."

"We hope to do tastings," I said.

"Of course, Monsieur. They rarely get visitors, and many of them love it when they do."

This was the opposite of what the Burgundy wine tour websites had said. It seemed too good to be true.

"What do we say?"

"Just tell them you are interested in learning about and tasting their wine. This is their passion. Why wouldn't they want to share it with you?"

With this advice buzzing in our heads, we went south in search of the kind of Chardonnay that can be bought in America only by those with a fistful of cash. After knocking on several doors in Meursault to no avail, we were greeted by a winemaker who was clearly glad to have visitors wanting to sample his artistry.

While two of us were hard-core wine lovers, Miranda had no experience with alcohol of any kind, and Laura was an indifferent drinker at best. But the sublime output of Meursault and Puligny-Montrachet beguiled and seduced everyone in our group. If we didn't impose discipline and restraint on ourselves, we would roll out of every winery happily incapacitated, free of any mortal care, and teed up for deadly disaster on the road.

So we took our time and ratcheted back the size and number of the pours as well as our domain visits.

We went north the next day to Gevrey-Chambertin in search of world-renowned Pinot Noir. At 10 a.m., we gathered around a small table in a dark cellar. With our eyes straining to get used to the dim light, we surveyed several racks of bottles as a young man pointed us to a semicircle of chairs.

"We are honored to have you sample our wine," he said. "We are very proud of it."

He looked younger than his twenty-something age and he had to bend his head as he reached for some bottles in the cellar's arched corner. Standing in front of a large grandfather's clock, wearing chic wire-rimmed glasses, a T-shirt, and jeans, he initiated a tasting I will never forget.

"We have several vintages of our premier cru that we are pouring and one of our grand cru. What would you like to start with?"

We worked our way through two wonderful pours. Then he opened the Grand Cru and filled three glasses—the kind with the generous, bulbous bottom—leaving less than half of the bottle. Amelia and I solemnly and attentively swirled, sniffed, peered, and took a glorious initial sip. As they had at the other wineries, Miranda and Laura would share a glass. But for whatever reason, Miranda took one look at the Grand Cru and belted it down like a giant shot, wiped her lips, and flashed a goofy grin.

As any serious oenophile knows, wine is as much about family and celebration and shared experience as it is about taste and color and smell. To memorialize this experience for my wine-loving daughter, I made a suggestion to Amelia.

"What would you think about me buying two bottles of the Premier Cru and saving them for your wedding, whenever that should be?" The look on her face was all the answer I needed.

On the day we returned to America, I packed the bottles as carefully as I could in one of our suitcases. Twelve hours later, I exhaled with relief when I saw that they had survived the trip. The bottles took their place at the bottom of my wine rack, with a film of dust settling on them over the next year. They went untouched until the minute before I led Gordon away from our house.

September 5, 2011, 5 p.m. Virtually everyone at our motel gathered on the west-facing side to snap photos and make cell phone calls about what we were seeing.

The fire's smoke plume had roiled up past the twenty-thousand-foot mark, roughly half the height of the mushroom clouds that climbed over Hiroshima and Nagasaki. Our entire visual horizon to the west was taken up with a fluffed and heaving cloud that was now backlit by the descending sun. What had been white was now saturated with a yellow hue that grew more striking and beautiful as the sun sunk lower.

An hour earlier, as the fire's march eastward became undeniable, Holly remarked, "That can't be good" and we exchanged prognostications with a group in the parking lot who shared our unease. Nobody said anything now.

It was a naked and unapologetic display of immense natural power, overwhelming and indifferent to any human need or desire. It was awful, because of what it had already done to dozens of our neighbors and friends. But it was also gorgeous and breathtaking and like nothing we were likely to ever see again.

"I probably need to take a picture of this," I said, reaching for my phone. "Otherwise, nobody will ever believe it when we try to describe it."

"You better not," said Holly.

"Why?"

"It would be like taking a picture of a bomb going off. You don't need to be reminded of this ten years from now. Please put your phone back in your pocket."

I did as I was told.

With my mind reeling from the spectacle, I staggered into our motel room. Out of habit more than anything, we turned on the local news. Governor Rick Perry, hot off the trail of his still-promising presidential campaign, was surrounded by a group of state and local politicians squeezed around a podium in the Bastrop County Emergency Operations Center, each apparently trying to outdo the others with their no-nonsense expressions.

The governor had on his "Have no fear, I'm in charge" face. After giving the fire the credit it was due, he went through a brief litany of vague promises and unpersuasive commitments. After about five minutes of this, we turned the TV off.

I felt a wave of nausea boil up. By now, I was convinced that meaningful human intervention was impossible until the fire wearied of its excesses or simply ran low on the fuel it was gluttonously devouring. What I did not need was the pious affect and solemn pronouncements of men who I knew were already calculating the odds of the political gains and losses that inevitably follow in the backwash of a disaster. Compared to what I saw from the window, the sight of these so-called powerful men rendered so small on the motel TV extinguished any hope I had left that things would improve anytime soon.

I made one last trip to the Smithville Volunteer Fire Department. I found it hard to keep my eyes on the street. The backlit and yellowing tower of smoke demanded my attention and respect.

"What's happening in the Cottletown area?" I asked the first firefighter I saw.

"Take a look at the map. Everything we know is on there."

I did as he suggested and didn't learn anything.

"Please help me understand this," I said.

"What don't you get?"

"OK, I'll just get to the point. I live about a mile from the park road. Is my place still there?"

"What does it look like?"

"My house is barely visible from the road. It's on the right side if you're coming from the highway."

"Does it have kind of an open field along the road?"

"It sure does."

"I think we were there earlier today. We parked our trucks briefly in the field."

"So it's fine, then?"

"It was OK then. I haven't been back since."

"What time were you there?"

"A little before noon."

"That's about the time I was there. But I never saw any trucks."

"You probably got there right after we left. Not very smart of you."

"Maybe. But I'm still alive, right?" He didn't take well to my attempt at a joke.

"You haven't been back since?" I asked him.

"No, none of us have. Too dangerous."

Back at the motel, the three of us went through the routine of a family trying to act normal.

"Miranda, do you want to open your presents?" Holly asked.

"It doesn't feel like a birthday at all. I don't want to open them now."

"Maybe opening them will make you feel better," I said. "Take your mind off things a little."

"I don't feel like it."

"Maybe we can celebrate your birthday by getting a hot dog at that trailer on Main Street," I said.

"Sure. OK," Miranda said. Holly declined the invitation.

The hot dogs tasted good even though my stomach felt gnarled and twisted.

"Do you think our house is OK?" Miranda said as the two of us ate our dinner.

"For most of today, it seemed like it, but now I just don't know."

"This is turning into a horrible birthday. When Hillary and Amelia turned twenty-one, think how much fun they had."

I was ashamed. A milestone birthday was about to end, and I had spent it fretting at the overlook and chasing after tidbits of truth that didn't exist.

We took our dogs to a park along the Colorado River and let them run around while we made and took phone calls from family members and friends. Our message was the same to all of them: "We are guardedly optimistic although the situation is undoubtedly grim. Many of our friends are homeless, as are Amelia and one of Miranda's friends. We will soon find out whether we are in their company."

Rather than chase squirrels or bother the other people at the park, our dogs nervously stayed close to us. We couldn't help wondering what they knew.

"I assume you've tried calling our answering machine?" said Holly.

"Of course," I said.

"And?"

"It just keeps ringing. Which doesn't necessarily mean anything."

When we returned to our motel room, I logged back on to the county's emergency operations Facebook site against my better judgment. Someone had sent a link to a website that supposedly mapped the progress of the fire with great precision based on infrared satellite imagery.

"Holly, take a look at this."

"What is it?"

"You see those little tongues of flame? They indicate where the fire is or has been. According to this, we're OK and so are Walter and Jeri Nell. Another narrow escape, just like 2009."

I kept updating the browser and the image never changed. I didn't believe or disbelieve it. But it gave me a way to channel my obsession.

Throughout the evening, we could hear people talking outside on the balcony and near the stairs. I guessed that about half the people in the motel were wiped out and the rest of us didn't know. I couldn't bear the thought of more conversation with any of them.

I couldn't figure out how to pass the time. Recreational reading was unthinkable. Miranda's birthday was unsalvageable. Everything on TV seemed idiotic or worse. Going to bed was pointless, given the racing and uncontrollable thoughts in my head. The only topic worth discussing with Holly had already been beaten to death.

Despite the hollowness of the time ticking away, it was impossible not to sense its gravity as well. We could be down to the last few hours of what we considered to be a normal life and I was squandering it by doing nothing except wishing it would pass more quickly.

Around midnight, I went to bed certain of nothing except that I would go out at first light to find out the truth for myself and nothing was going to stop me. For six hours, I hovered in that dreadful state between being barely awake and not quite asleep, obsessively checking my watch. I finally reached the point where the entire idea of sleep seemed foreign; I wasn't sure what it was or how I would recognize it if it came upon me.

As my mind wandered into dead ends and through menacing alleyways, I tried to imagine what I would see in several hours. Would it really be possible for a house as solid as ours, with a stone exterior and a metal roof, to burn down? And what if it had? Where would we go? How could we live? What would a typical day be like in the months ahead?

At 6 a.m., feeling bone-tired and sore, I got up and put on a fresh T-shirt, shorts, and socks.

"What are you doing?" Holly murmured.

"I'm going to find out what happened."

"It's still dark outside. You won't be able to see."

"I will by the time I get there. I can't sleep and there's no point in me laying in bed."

"Don't you think it's too dangerous?"

"Obviously not."

"What if you can't get through?"

"At this point, I'm a pro at getting to where I'm not supposed to be."

There was a rumor of daylight toward the east as I set off. Law enforcement had gotten more emphatic about their roadblocks and barricades, so it took purposeful misdirection to shake off the officers. I drove part of the way with my lights turned off.

I reached the overlook just as it was becoming light enough to see across the valley. It was warm but not uncomfortable.

For a few minutes, I stood alone at the edge, entranced and sad and guardedly optimistic. I was torn between staying where I was—with my hope still intact—and making good on my commitment to see what the fire had or hadn't done.

A person I had never seen before appeared on Park Road 1C from the direction of Cottletown Road. I was curious why he was walking alone at that time of the morning, but not enough to ask.

"Morning," he said.

"Howdy," I said. "Where are you coming from?"

"Down the park road a bit."

"I was just getting ready to go that way myself. Any reason I shouldn't?"

"Not really."

"So it's safe?"

"You're looking at me, aren't you?"

I described where I lived. "You know where I'm talking about?"

He nodded.

"Well, how does it look?"

"Like it always does."

"The fire never got there?"

"Apparently not."

"I figured that, but it's good to know for sure."

"Glad to be of help," he said.

With this good news, I had no reason to linger at the overlook. For most of the drive up Old Antioch Road, nothing was different. But when I reached Cottletown Road, it all changed. The area where I had lived twenty-three of the past thirty-one years was transformed into a tree mortuary rendered gray by a slightly hazy dawn, a film of white ash covering the ground, and no living thing visible in any direction.

How could I square what I saw with what the man at the overlook told me? Who was he and how did he get there? Was it really possible he walked three miles from my neighborhood in the dark? Even though I had seen him less than fifteen minutes ago, I couldn't recall the details of his face or even what he was wearing. Maybe I was in the middle of a dream where I gave a ghostlike stranger the job of telling me what I most wanted to hear.

But I knew this wasn't a dream. In a dream, reality is jumbled up, illogical, with no apparent beginning or end. Everything I saw made perfect, if dreadful, sense and flowed from Jeri Nell's phone call less than two days before.

Where there had been dense forest, I now had an unobstructed view that went for a mile or more with tendrils of smoke slithering up from the ground. Several enormous loblollies that stood like iconic sculptures in a large field were seared from top to bottom, many decades of growth undone in an instant.

It was like the landscape had been flayed, the skin of life surgically peeled off.

I opened both car windows and drove slowly. With only a mild breeze and most of the smoke out of the air, the menace of the prior day was replaced by silence and the calm of finality. Everything I saw was familiar and strange, real and unreal, close and distant. I was witness to a rupture in time, the past ripped away from the present, as if the two had never been joined.

I crossed the intersection with Park Road 1C and things got worse. The home of Judy, my acquaintance from the overlook, was gone as was Robb's old place. I passed Hudson Road, which led to Jeri Nell and Walter's property, and I knew their thirty-five-year-old home—with the elevator for Jess and the artifacts of a long life together—was gone.

Our gate remained locked, so I parked the car and walked from the high point of my land to the turn where the house site came into view. My pine trees were blackened, their tops singed and bottoms blistered. There was no sign of several large oaks except for the smoking holes in the ground where their roots had been. They looked like dinosaur tracks.

There was no evidence that the trailer house of our next-door neighbor ever existed. All that remained of a decrepit car was a scorched frame.

I made the turn on the driveway and saw how my former friend and artistic partner had betrayed me. I later learned that this ruthless act began with spot fires breaking out from flaming hailstones launched from the main inferno as it closed in on our pines, oaks, and home.

The hail of baseball-sized embers—the catapulted remains of other trees that were already in the throes of a fiery death—announced the death sentences of the trees Holly and I kept alive with our soaker hoses and unformed prayers. A minute or two later, the executioner arrived.

Did my loblollies smell the smoke and sense the air's heat as they inhaled carbon dioxide and swayed in the wind? Did they feel anything as the hail of fire went from a trickle to a downpour? Does a living creature surrender its life to a fire without pain and in silence?

Everything Holly and I did that summer to wage war against the drought was instantaneously undone as a literal wall of fire passed over our ten acres. Within seconds, virtually everything was on fire, including the creatures that lived there: snakes, insects, deer and birds that hadn't gotten away, and the feral cat who slept in the drainage pipe underneath the driveway.

Our trees were torpedoes of flame, the ground was a carpet of flame, and our house looked like someone had put a giant blowtorch to it. The thermometer in the house topped out at 2,500 degrees, like my old wood kiln, hot enough to warp even the quarter-inch steel plates that braced my carport, and revitrify any pot that survived.

The wall of fire passed quickly, the thermal imprint of the horizontal tornadoes embedded in the landscape, but the flames stayed around until there was nothing left for them to eat. Stumps in the ground, some as wide as three or four feet, kept burning until there was literally nothing left but their footprint in the dirt. The combustible materials of our house burned and then smoldered, eventually turning into fine ash.

Like a terminally ill patient who has yet to get the diagnosis, I realized we had already lost everything as we watched the conflagration the previous afternoon magnify to a pinnacle of horrifying and spectacular beauty.

My roof was a crinkled mass of metal that looked like someone had driven over it repeatedly and then stomped it in the middle for good measure. Like a perverse grace note, a tiny flame still burned near the front of the house. I realized immediately that it was the last gasp of the propane still in the tank, expiring at the point where the hot water heater had been. It reminded me of an eternal flame in a cemetery.

I was there for less than a minute. My mission was complete, and I didn't need to inspect the corpse or do an autopsy. As I walked back up the hill, I marveled at how the forest's ineffable beauty had been traded in for ugliness and an awful smell oozing from the doomed trees. I wondered what I would do if I didn't have a family to go back to.

I felt nothing as I drove back to the motel. I didn't rehearse a speech or imagine what I would say to Holly and Miranda or even contemplate the mystery of my dry eyes. I drove slowly because I knew I was eating up the last morsel of time before I plunged into a new life, clueless about where to go and what to do.

When something intelligible finally did pop into my head as I passed the abandoned overlook for the final time, it was the words and music of Pink Floyd, a symphonic blast of guitars from my youth. My mind had summoned up the chorus of "Comfortably Numb."

As I neared the motel, with the rising sun attacking my eyes, I saw Holly standing in the parking lot. Her face seemed to say "I already know," and it woke me from the dream of the past half hour. We shared a sobbing embrace as I croaked, "It's all gone. Nothing's left."

Barely able to get the words out, I went into our room and delivered the news to Miranda. She reached into our chests and pulled out our hearts with her response: "Losing our house is the worst birthday present I could ever have."

September 6, 2011, 7:30 a.m. Hillary and Amelia were awake when they got our call.

"I just got back from our place," I said. "We're wiped out."

Amelia gasped. "So both of our houses are probably gone. Everything we own."

"It appears so, although we won't know for sure until somebody can get back into Colovista in a few days."

"Luke is going to try this morning," Amelia said. Luke was her longtime boyfriend.

"That seems like a really bad idea," Holly said.

"Probably, but I doubt I can talk him out of it."

"Jared's parents are out of the country for the next two weeks," said Hillary. "He's going to check with them about whether you can stay at their house until they return."

"That would be a lovely gesture," Holly said. "We're going to gather up the few things we had in the motel and probably head in your direction in an hour or so after we find something to eat."

I called my parents next.

"Dad, can you get Mom on the phone as well?"

"She's out for a short walk. Do you want to call back in a few minutes?"

"I will, but not before I tell you why I'm calling. The fire came through our neighborhood yesterday, and our house was lost. I saw it with my own eyes this morning just after daybreak."

"I don't know what to say." His words barely found their way out of his watery windpipe. I knew it would be easier for both of us if I let him cry in peace.

"I'll call back in a few minutes."

The only task I could think of, besides checking out of the motel, was to notify the post office that, for the first time my adult life, I was homeless with no forwarding address. Before going inside, I called my parents again. My father answered.

"Did you tell her?" I asked.

"Yes, she wants to talk with you, but she's still crying. She needs a second."

"Dad told me the terrible news," she said in a wheezy voice. "What are you going to do now?"

"We're probably going to stay at Hillary's in-laws' for a week or two. After that, I have no idea."

"What about Amelia? Is her house OK?"

"Probably not."

The next wave of sobs was unleashed. Although I didn't cry, a wave of nausea welled up so strong I barely fought it off.

I tried to picture my parents thirteen hundred miles away, unable to help us or show us their pain. How would I feel if I were in their place, with my daughters in anguish and me unable to do a thing about it? In some respects, I thought, they're going to be in worse shape than us for at least a day or two.

As I walked up to the large wooden door of the post office—a 1950s building with metal grates over the customer service windows and a glassed-in notice board framed with dark wood—I tried to imagine how the conversation would go. I recognized the man behind the window, although his name didn't come to mind. He was clad in a uniform and sat on a stool.

I didn't want him to feel sorry for me, but I also didn't want him to be indifferent. A smile would be better than a frown, but only if it was barely noticeable.

"I suppose you can guess why I'm here," I said.

"Why don't you tell me, just in case."

"We're burned out. What happens to our mail now?"

He looked me straight in the eye. "First off, I'm very sorry for your loss."

"Thank you."

"We'll hold it for at least the next few weeks. We can't do that indefinitely, but we understand that it might take a little while for you to find a place to live."

"Do I have to fill out some paperwork?"

"You will eventually. But for now, just letting us know is enough. Your mail carrier was already aware of your situation and those of your neighbors."

"So just telling you is good enough."

"Yes. In the meantime, if you authorize it, someone can pick up your mail on your behalf so it doesn't pile up too much."

Wanda, an artist friend of ours who lived in town with a couple of wiener dogs, seemed like a good possibility. For many years, one of her landscape paintings of the Lost Pines had hung alongside my piano bench.

"Have you had very many people come by for the same reason as me?"

"Not as many as you'd think in Smithville. The Bastrop Post Office is very busy, though. A few of the firefighters are among those who lost their homes."

"Like who?"

"I know you'll understand that we can't mention names."

Without apparently even thinking about it, this civil servant had performed a high-wire act of professionalism and empathy. I shook his hand to show my gratitude.

Dealing with our mail was an understandable and attainable task with a beginning and an end. Given the black hole of my future, I wanted to drag it out a little longer, so I paid a quick visit to Wanda, a trim and attractive woman almost the same age as Holly and me with a full head of graying hair and a bountiful, deep-throated laugh. As I walked up to the front door of her single-story, rambling house, I could see the drought had exacted its price on her garden, a wondrous and overflowing patch of life in better years. The yipping of her dogs announced my arrival.

"I'm sorry I don't have time to visit, Wanda. Holly and Miranda are back at the motel, and we're getting ready to leave for Austin."

She looked confused.

"The fire got us. Probably Jeri Nell and Walter as well."

I welcomed Wanda's embrace.

"I'm here to ask a favor. Would you mind picking up our mail every couple of days?"

"Of course, I'd be happy to do that. What about your dogs?"

"What about them?"

"If you need a place for them to go, I wouldn't mind if they stayed with me, at least until you get settled in somewhere. I know dogs can complicate things."

When I returned to the motel, Holly and Miranda were in the parking lot with Charlie and the dachshunds. They were still without leashes, but they were minding their manners, perhaps because of the cloud that had descended over their human companions.

On my way from the post office, I had decided that focusing on practical tasks would be the best way to keep my mind away from dangerous territory.

"I was just over at Wanda's. She's agreed to pick up our mail for us. Even better, she offered to keep the dogs."

"Absolutely not," Holly said. "They're going with us."

"I'm not saying we have to do it. But wouldn't you feel better, knowing we have that option?"

"There is no way I'm going anywhere without our dogs."

"It'd be one less thing for us to worry about, at least in the short run."

"I need them for emotional support and they need us for the same reason. Please don't bring that idea up again."

Perhaps the topic could be revisited later, at a less tender time. I soldiered on to my next idea.

"What would you think about me calling Steve and Linda? Maybe we could move back into our old house."

"How do you even know it's still there?" Holly asked.

"You really think that enormous brick house could be destroyed? That place was like a fortress."

"If you're right that it's still there—and I don't know how you can be so sure of yourself—I'm against that idea too," Holly said.

"But why? What's wrong with it?"

"It's bizarre. That part of our life is over. Can't you see that?"

I really couldn't.

"Why can't I at least give them a ring to see if it's even possible?"

"You can move back there if you want and they let you. But Miranda and I won't be joining you."

It was another discussion for later. I had one last task.

"Can you at least wait for me to call the insurance company? I don't even remember how much we were insured for. I need to find that out and get the paperwork going."

"No. All of that can wait. Let's get something to eat and then get out of here."

After we returned from an indigestible breakfast of fast-food sandwiches, during which I kept my head down in the hope that nobody would ask what our situation was, I was startled to hear someone calling my name from across the motel parking lot.

"Hey, Randy, it's me, Bob. You still remember me, right?"

Of course I remembered him. He bought the first house Holly and I built, a structure that would never have survived our construction ignorance without my grandfather's intervention.

"YOUR WALLS WILL LOOK LIKE A SNAKE!"

My maternal grandfather was an unassuming, bespectacled man nicknamed "Casey." He had a kind smile and gentle disposition. For most of his working life, beginning with his escape from the public school system around the time he entered adolescence, he designed and built small and immaculately efficient brick homes. These homes, many of which were built during the Great

Depression and in the decade following World War II, still stand to this day in much the same shape he built them.

Like many adults in the Wisconsin blue-collar community where I grew up, he clocked out at the end of the day able to see exactly what he had accomplished. He rarely spoke about his work, but he didn't need to. Its craftsmanship and integrity were self-evident. One of my earliest memories is of accompanying him to a construction site, carrying a tiny lunch bucket.

With my grandfather as inspiration and role model, I convinced Holly soon after we stumbled on the Lost Pines that we could build our house and my pottery studio ourselves, even though all I knew about construction was how to hammer a nail. I had no doubt we could figure it all out by reading a couple of books and occasionally picking my grandfather's brain.

When I told him what I had in mind, he said, "Do you have any plans?"

"I don't really need detailed plans. And we can't afford them anyway."

Silence.

"What are you going to build?" he asked.

"The studio and house will both be simple rectangles on a pier-and-beam foundation. I'm thinking of using telephone poles to support the sills. I read that they are long-lasting and cheap."

"I don't like the sound of that. You're just going to stick them in the ground?"

"That's not the way I would have described it. But, yes, I suppose that's what I'll do."

"Who is helping you with all of this?"

"Nobody," I said. "But I was sort of hoping you'd give me a few tips as I need them."

"How are you going to figure it all out?"

"With some books I got from the Austin library."

I chose to ignore the message his questions and pauses were sending. So the plan was set, and on the first day of the new decade Holly and I broke ground on the place where I would make pottery for almost six years. When we finished after three months, I had a studio that was functional and definitely not pretty.

"How's it all looking?" he asked several weeks into the project.

"Pretty good," I said. "Our subfloor is going to be the final floor, since it's a pottery studio and will be messy all the time. The walls are up and we'll start framing up the rafters any day now."

"What about the ceiling?

"There won't be a ceiling. I'm going to have exposed rafters. That's what I'll see when I look up."

"And your ceiling joists?"

"Why would I need those if there's no ceiling?"

"If you don't have them, your walls will look like a snake," he almost shrieked into the phone.

I got it. Ceiling joists tie the walls to one another. It was the first of several occasions when he stepped in to save us from ourselves.

If the pottery studio was version 1.0 of our building efforts, the place where the mistakes we made would have the least long-term visual or structural offense, the house was version 1.5, an improvement but still rough enough to affirm our inexperience and rudimentary skills. With plywood shelves and a curtain where a bathroom door should have been, it was nothing like the ones that followed.

For over six years, Holly and I lived in this house without air-conditioning or health insurance, grew much of our own food, and earned a subsistence living off our artistic endeavors and the occasional sale of our excess garden produce.

The lack of privacy in our little home was fine for a baby but no good for a three-year-old girl. After replacing the rickety front door with one that was attractive, secure, and set off with a window that Jeri Nell etched with the outline of a pinecone, we placed a classified ad in the Austin paper that perhaps promised more than we could deliver. Nevertheless, several weeks later we received a call from a man who said, "I would like to respectfully make an offer on your lovely property."

September 6, 2011, 9 a.m. Now I was looking at the man who made the offer. Bob looked different, but I immediately recognized him.

"You still own the place we sold you?"

"Absolutely. Long time no see."

"It has been a long time."

Bob had remarried, so the necessary introductions were made.

"I wish we were saying howdy to each other under better circumstances, though," I said. "I'm sorry to have to tell you this, but I'm sure your place is gone, just like mine. I was on Cottletown Road a couple of hours ago, and it's bad."

"Actually, our house is still there," Bob said.

"I'm telling you, I've seen what the fire did."

"We have too. We just got back from there. Our house made it."

Apparently my former friend fire had made a colossal and boneheaded mistake. How could that wooden structure on pier and beams—clad in cedar that aged into a silver hue, with lofts instead of bedrooms and a living area only slightly larger than a monk's cell—still be standing while our stone and metal home wasn't? An injustice had been committed. Where could I go, and to whom must I appeal, to straighten things out?

"So you're telling me your house, the one I built ages ago, is like a little island in a sea of devastation?"

"Yes I am."

I wondered if Bob and his wife would be happy or sad or both as the months wore on and they looked out on what used to be the forest surrounding their house and my old pottery studio, which they had converted to other, more practical uses.

With questionable sincerity, I said, "I'm glad for you, Bob."

He smiled and nodded.

Because my car was piled up with the artifacts of my last visit, Miranda rode alongside Holly with the dogs crammed into the backseat, Charlie wheezing and unable to get comfortable while the wieners paced and pawed at one another.

With the section of Highway 71 between Bastrop and Smithville shut down, we had to chart our trip to Austin through a combination of back roads that would take us south of Bastrop until we could cross the Colorado River and get back on the main highway.

I had two choices as I drove: start compiling a mental list of what had to be done or distract myself with podcasts or music. Holly's summary dismissal of the three tasks that seemed most at hand closed out the first option, so I defaulted to the second. I started out with a *Writer's Almanac* podcast I had downloaded the morning of the fire. This is what I heard Garrison Keillor say:

The Great Fire of London started on this date in 1666. The fire broke out near London Bridge, at the house of Thomas Farynor, the king's baker. One of his workers awoke at two in the morning to the smell of smoke, and the family fled over the rooftops. The blaze spread rapidly, helped by strong winds and drought conditions.

I listened in a stupefied state as Keillor briefly described one of the major fire events in Western history. The similarities between the causes of the London conflagration and the one that continued to rage out of control in Bastrop County were hard to believe. The podcast was an almost absurd coincidence.

It was only at the end of this brief tale that the podcast came to life for me in the form of a double dare:

There was one positive outcome from the fire, though: It may have halted the progress of the plague, which had been ravaging the city for the past few years. The rats and their disease-carrying fleas perished in large numbers.

Within days of the fire, architects Christopher Wren and Robert Hooke, and diarist John Evelyn, had all submitted plans for the rebuilding of the city; all of them called for making the streets more regular. In the end, almost all the original layout of the city was preserved, although the streets were widened. Wren was given the task of rebuilding fifty of the churches, including St. Paul's Cathedral, which remains one of his masterpieces.

The first dare was: can you find something positive in the destruction of the Lost Pines and the property you loved so much? The second was: can you rebuild a house, and perhaps a life, that is better than what you had?

PART II

COLLATERAL DAMAGE, COLLATERAL GRACE

CHAPTER 6

September 6, 2011, 9:30 a.m. When a person's life is unexpectedly blown off course, the unmapped journey begins with mundane questions that sometimes turn into profound ones.

With the fire in my rearview mirror, the questions came quickly. Where would we find temporary housing for the months to come and how would we furnish it? What would we need just to be presentable in public or eat a meal? How does an insurance claim get started for an immense loss?

Do we rebuild or start from scratch somewhere else? Is this a one-time chance to leave a drought-stricken state and start fresh someplace else with a bucket of insurance money? Could we live anywhere away from our grown children?

What does it mean now for our life to be normal? Is there such a thing as normal?

As I neared Austin, the weight of these questions came together in a simpler one: Why can't I just lie down and sleep for the next few months?

We met Hillary, Jared, and our grandson Ben at a strip mall in far south Austin. The look on the face of our eldest daughter was a combination of sympathy and determination. She began with some practical details of how we would temporarily settle into her in-laws' house.

With Hillary and Jared leading the way, we arrived at the last house on a short cul-de-sac in a neighborhood of cul-de-sacs. The Jensons lived in a large, sprawling two-story house with a full dining room and five bedrooms, two of which were oversized, with king beds. Except for the bathrooms and kitchen, most of it was carpeted. Several doors led to an expansive and lush backyard. The house was comfortable, tidy, and well kept.

Because of Jenson family allergies to animal hair, we decided to make the two-car garage the temporary home of our dogs, even though the concrete floor was a heater without an off switch and the air was as still as a tomb.

We piled all of our things in the living room, scoped out the Internet connection, and made a quick inventory of what we would immediately need, mainly toiletries and food. There was also the matter of collars and leashes for our dogs, an unprecedented intrusion on their lifetime habits of roaming at will, doing their business where they wanted, and barking at whatever interested or annoyed them.

I volunteered to stay behind and send out the necessary emails while Holly and Miranda went shopping.

I called up my e-mail and saw that Anton had already sent a message: "You do not need to respond to this, since heaven knows, there is a lot to do and to think about. I realized after I spoke to you that you don't have a place to play the piano, or practice or do your music—this breaks my heart. Can I please extend an open invitation to you to come to my house to play or listen to music anytime? I have lots and lots of music you can use, as you know."

One problem solved: I would have access to a piano and music.

To my friends and professional colleagues, I sent this note: "My beautiful place is ashes. We lost everything but the important thing is nobody in my family was hurt. My daughter lives in another house that I built and we don't know the status of it. More later as I regroup."

Almost immediately, the replies starting coming in: short and heartfelt condolences and offers of help. While I expected nothing less, reading and re-reading them felt good. For a moment, as I went into the living room to take a short break, it occurred to me that things were going to be easier than I would have thought. Except for the brief outburst in the parking lot with Holly, I hadn't even cried, and surely that must say something about my inner strength.

I was taking it like a man. Even if Holly and Miranda melted down, nobody would have to worry about me.

That thought had barely registered before it hit me. For at least fifteen minutes, I cried more intensely and deeply than I could remember since the days when Miranda's cognitive abilities were vaporizing before our horrified eyes.

For someone who hardly ever cried, the tears were more unnerving than cathartic. Nobody had died, my marriage wasn't crumbling, my health was intact, and we still had our friends and extended family. Had the fire outed me as a closeted emotional weakling?

In a daze, I wandered around the spacious Jenson house before taking a seat on a couch in the living room to stare at the totality of our possessions. That's where I was when Holly and Miranda returned.

"What are you doing?" Holly asked.

"Looking at what's not here: my pottery, the Bernard Leach pot, your grandfather's pastels, the oil painting in the hall."

"Don't forget the Chagall."

"Nice of you to remind me, although I hadn't forgotten that."

"You should be thankful you saved anything," Holly said. "If you had stayed much longer, you might be dead now."

"I don't believe that for a second. I was there, I had time, and I wasted it."

"You can beat yourself up over this if you want. But we're all alive and safe."

Although I knew I wasn't going to win this argument with Holly or anyone else in the family, I had already won it with myself. I would accept no forgiveness or absolution.

With dusk looming, we introduced the dogs to their leashes and took them on their maiden walk in the direction of a narrow greenbelt two blocks away. The dogs had been roasting in the garage since we arrived, and only Izzy was bouncy and ready for fun.

Our goal was to get them to the greenbelt as quickly as possible, but things didn't go as planned. Messes were quickly made in some of the neighboring yards just as people were returning home from work or taking an evening stroll. We didn't have the necessary equipment to pick up after them, but we had a good excuse.

While nobody was unsympathetic, it was obvious that our explanation had landed with a thud. We cut the walk short.

"Judging from how a couple of them reacted, you'd think we'd just committed a crime," I said.

"You act like they owe us something," Holly responded.

Nobody in the Jenson house expected to sleep well that night, and nobody did.

September 7, 2011, 10 a.m. On Wednesday morning, I called my insurance agent and learned that a representative of the company that wrote our homeowner's policy would be on site to answer questions and start the paperwork. Before I left for Bastrop, Amelia called.

"Guess what? My house didn't burn after all," she said. "I can't believe it."

"How do you know? How can you be so sure?"

"Luke saw it for himself. All of the houses around us are OK as well."

"Are you serious? How did he get back there? All the roads are shut off."

"He snuck back with his cousin. He said he was dodging little fires on the side of the road."

"Do realize how insane that sounds?"

"No more insane than what you did. I feel awful about what's happened to you and Mom, but I'm so happy I have a house to go back to."

I found the insurance company rep in a white trailer parked a mile west of

Bastrop. He was in his early thirties and wore short sleeves and a tie. He had the faintly sympathetic smile of a funeral director. It was clear he was used to being around people whose world was flying apart. We sat on folding chairs, facing one another, next to an aging laptop and a pile of paperwork.

"Please accept my sympathy for what's happened," he said. "I know we can't replace what you've lost, but we can at least do our part to help you move forward."

For a moment, I felt sorry for the young guy. For the next several days, he'd be a confessor, a therapist, a clergyman, a financial counselor, and a vessel into which the underinsured would pour their frustration and denial. The only way someone could do a job like that is to turn people into objects, situations into words on forms. I'd try to cut him some slack.

"I'm familiar with your coverage amounts," he said. "If your house is a total loss, as we expect, you'll receive the full-insured amount. For your possessions, you'll need to make a detailed list of everything you owned and its replacement value. You'll also be entitled to a monthly allowance while you're living in temporary housing."

This opened up a range of temporary living possibilities I hadn't expected.

"Why do we have to make a list? Trust me, you could write me a check right now for the full amount and we'd be far from even on what we've lost or how I feel."

"It's a requirement," he said. "I wish it wasn't."

He wrote me a check as an advance on our immediate expenses. I shook his hand and started to leave. But a conversation in one of the trailer's other rooms stopped me. A man who looked to be in his sixties was wringing his wrinkled and sun-speckled hands. His cap was resting on his lap, and a ring of sweat had glued what was left of his hair to his head.

A mild disagreement about whether some equipment was insured seemed about to flare into something more serious. The man's voice, which had been carefully courteous, was starting to rise, and the pace of his words was picking up. "I'm not asking for help. This is business and I've been a good customer." I couldn't bear to hear how the man's plea turned out.

I guessed it would be a week before I returned, so I decided to take a quick drive through Bastrop. Smoke still gathered and hovered in the east, and Highway 71 remained closed. National network satellite trucks, heavy equipment, and dozens of insurance company trailers and tents squatted wherever flat, vacant space could be found. Helicopters flitted over and near the smoke.

Before I left Austin, I scanned several major newspapers online and watched some of the morning news shows. Bastrop County was national and international news. Apparently no one had died, but the property damage was approaching unprecedented levels. A national news reporter interviewed one of our friends and her daughter. They were wiped out but would be fine. Others whom I didn't know said the same.

So it was apparently possible to lose everything and tell the world not to worry. And do it without a frown or a tear and maybe even something masquerading as a smile.

Emergency operations were being coordinated from the town's stucco-clad convention center, and the parking lot was jammed. I drove by slowly and found a place to stop. A crowd gathered near the front door. People pointed at and touched a large map. Some were hugging. Children clung to adults. There were no smiles here.

What would be worse if we kept living around here: being around people like this or the cheery folks on TV?

While a battalion of government officials were on hand, I knew who was ultimately in charge and responsible. By Texas law, that was the county judge, and he was in a far more precarious and exposed position than I was in 1991, when the inverse of a wildfire happened.

In 1991, just before Christmas, the clouds ruptured over the reservoir lakes formed by the dams built with Lyndon Johnson's pestering and Franklin Roosevelt's acquiescence. With the floodgates open, the Colorado River below Austin rose to its highest level in a generation, inundating homes, wrecking roads, and cutting off people in low-lying areas. The state lent me a helicopter, and I took to the air several times a day to assess the damage while the waters kept rising.

Two days after the flooding began, Governor Ann Richards arrived by air to personally give me the news that the president had declared Bastrop County a federal disaster area.

For the first and only time in my term, I had the power and authority to wrestle a major public problem into submission. I met those whose properties along the river were damaged and gave them access to the financial resources that come with a disaster declaration. I escorted federal officials around the county, showing what needed to be fixed and coming up with a plan to get the work done fast and visibly, so those in the affected areas wouldn't lose hope. I felt useful and invigorated and optimistic.

While the flood was a major event, it didn't ruin lives or lay waste to Bastrop County's defining feature. I knew the wildfire would be far different. The burned-out families would find little comfort from solicitous and well-meaning county officials. Bastrop State Park had suffered a lethal blow. Those in charge of fighting the fire were days, if not weeks, from conquering it. In the meantime, other houses would burn and trees die as the fire retraced some of its steps and ventured into new territory.

I pictured the meetings that were undoubtedly happening in the convention center. The room would be jammed and stuffy, with uniformed officials holding up the walls, their arms crossed and faces grim and expressionless. Administrative employees would be shuttling in and out, rushed for time and consumed by their new duties.

I'd seen enough and turned back toward Austin. Sucked into an eddy of ambivalent and conflicting emotions, I was slowly coming to the belief that I must abandon the community I formerly led, assuming I could convince Holly and Miranda to join me. I couldn't imagine living among the scorched and acrid leftovers of the Lost Pines. Bumping into acquaintances unsure of how to respond to our situation, or repeatedly reliving my experience through other fire victims, were intolerable possibilities.

Not even two days had passed, and I was thinking about life-changing choices.

REALPOLITIK

These thoughts would have been unimaginable on New Year's night, 1991, when I took the oath of office before an overflow crowd of over three hundred people in the county courthouse's largest room. On the first row of the middle section were Hillary, then a grade-schooler; Amelia, a toddler with a burn mark on her forehead from a wayward New Year's Eve sparkler; Miranda, a baby sleeping in Holly's arms; my parents; and Holly's mother and siblings. At my instigation, a group of folk musicians played the national anthem, and a woman from a local church sang a gospel version of "God Bless America." I delivered some remarks to the crowd about my plans to modernize county government. Instead of frowns or frosty stares, I got a standing ovation.

If someone had asked me at my swearing-in what a county judge is, I would have said the county's chairman and CEO. My model was based on truisms for any medium-sized organization with a seven-figure budget. The man in charge has subordinates. There are penalties for failure to perform. Change can come partly from persuasion, but orders are sometimes necessary as well. Someone has to have the last word.

This was the theoretical model. It was nothing like the actual one. My first year in office was a seminar on the realpolitik of Texas county government.

While I held the county's top office, there were almost twenty other elected officials who viewed themselves as being on roughly equal footing with me, especially the other four members of the county's governing body. To their way of thinking, we all worked for the same absentee boss: the voters.

By the time the flood happened, with my chairman/CEO concept in the ditch, I was living by a new set of rules. Anyone with an election certificate on the wall owes me no duty or sense of allegiance. Change is as hard as the status quo is easy. A good argument is worthless when I'm outnumbered. Only the voters can punish nonperformance, and they're usually not paying attention.

I saw no need to map out the personal relationships and animosities among the various elected officials and longtime county employees. I didn't care who was on the outs with whom, who gossiped or broke bread or drank together, and who owed a job to an accommodating politician.

By refusing to pick sides in courthouse squabbles, I alienated both sides. By not slinging back beers when others were, I couldn't draw from a wellspring of affection when I really needed something. In my own eyes, and those of my supporters, I was above-board, even-handed, professional, and data-driven. In the eyes of others, I was an aloof, isolated, and self-centered know-it-all.

I was indifferent to the spoils of elective office that many others savored—a fancy title, prominence in the community, and a blizzard of invitations. What revved my engines was fixing things and dreaming up unexpected solutions to social or financial problems. I came into office with lots of ideas and voluntarily left, after one term, with most of them still in their seed packets.

September 7, 2011, 11:30 a.m. I had barely thought about any of this in more than a decade. But my emotions were boiling, and I needed a place where I could pour them without scalding my family. It was easy to seize on the lamentable memory of people and experiences that I would be glad to leave behind as I said good-bye to Bastrop County for now and perhaps permanently. I just needed my wife and youngest daughter to agree with me.

I found Holly and Miranda in the garage, where it was 20 degrees hotter than the house and not a molecule of air moving. They were sitting in folding chairs. Holly had Dottie in her lap and was rubbing Charlie's head. Miranda's arms were wrapped around Izzy.

"What are you doing in here?"

"We're with the dogs," said Holly. "They're comforting us."

"How long have you been in here? Your faces are beet red."

"I don't know. Probably a long time."

"Don't you think you should take a break? It's awful in here."

"We'll come inside when we feel like it."

"When you do, we need to talk about something," I said. "It's important."

Holly nodded, her faced locked on Charlie.

"Miranda, don't you want to come inside now?" I asked.

"Mm-mm."

I checked my e-mail and there was a note from the couple who bought our Long Trail house.

> *Well, unfortunately, our place didn't make it. The fire chief had to climb over fallen trees on the driveway to approach the area, but only two fireplaces were left standing. In fact, he's dispatching a unit to put out some areas that are still burning right now. Thank god he was able to check for us. He told me that there were two waves of fire that went through our neighborhood and probably it was the one last night that did it.*

The idea of moving back into the house where we raised our children into adulthood was officially dead.

September 8, 2011, 6:30 a.m. On Thursday morning, I stumbled from the bathroom into the kitchen, my head throbbing from lack of sleep and every joint stiff and uncooperative. I was annoyed at how much time I had wasted during the night in a wakeful and fidgety state. I could have put those wee hours to far better use working on the inventory list.

I logged on to the Austin newspaper's website. As part of its wildfire coverage, the paper had published a map of the burn zone. While the edges were jagged, and the overall shape was asymmetrical, the thirty-four thousand acres looked like a giant's teardrop. Our devastated property was an invisible speck in the right-hand side of the teardrop's bulge.

Taken in the context of all the families that were wiped out, we weren't even a rounding error. By the time the county published its final inventory of destroyed homes several months later, the number reached almost seventeen hundred families. Our home and property would be a single line in a very long list for a wildfire that was a quantifiable record-breaker.

Besides showing what happened, the map also showed what could have happened but didn't.

Shrink the teardrop by less than 10 percent and the entire Cottletown area is spared. Fatten it and hundreds more homes burn. Fatten it even more, and all of Bastrop burns on the west side and the world-renowned M. D. Anderson Cancer Research Center goes up in smoke on the east. Tug at its bottom, and the fire jumps the river and ends up God-knows-where.

I looked more carefully at what the thirty-four thousand acres included:

almost all of Bastrop State Park; the neighborhood where our kids caught the school bus when they were little; an array of small subdivisions north and west of the park, with a random distribution of small houses, modular homes, and trailers; McAllister Road, the well-groomed main artery into Colovista; and portions of the Pine Forest and Tahitian Village subdivisions, a hilly and forested area of medium and large houses and Property Owner Association rules.

In taking more homes than any other wildfire in Texas history, the teardrop showed no socioeconomic favoritism or discrimination. By incinerating a much-beloved park that borders two heavily traveled state highways, the fire left a calling card with a grim message: "You will remember me for decades."

The Austin newspaper's fire coverage included an article that made me feel like I had just run into a glass door face-first.

"Holly, you've got to see this," I said. "It's about the two people who died in the fire."

The sharp edge in my voice made her frown.

"One of them lived on Walter's road. Not just that, he went back around the same time I did on Monday. Don't you see? He was there at almost the same time as me, just up the road. And he died."

"Now do you believe what I've been saying about how crazy it was for you to go back?"

"According to this, he was just a few years younger than me."

The newspaper gave no details about what happened to this man I occasionally waved at but never knew. I tried to imagine the two of us, separated by a quarter mile, going about our business as the light turned gray and the air soured.

I immediately understood the consequences of admitting what might have been. I'd have an almost unbearable set of new obligations: visualizing and feeling my death; beginning every new day with a greeting card cliché about the glories of being alive; bursting with gratitude every second of every day, regardless of what is actually happening in my life; and letting go of self-recriminations for making bad decisions while the fire raged. In addition to all of that, there would be the unavoidable speculation about my soul's relocation as my body's ashes blew away in the wind.

So instead of going there, I turned my attention to something less cosmic: where we would live for the foreseeable future. With little debate or consideration of other alternatives, we had decided to relocate to Austin. With Holly looking over my shoulder, I quickly realized I had neither the patience nor clear-headedness to page through screen after screen of rental possibilities on the Web.

"I have no idea how to make sense of any of this," I said.

"Maybe you should call Luke's uncle Kenny. He's a real estate agent in Travis Heights."

I reached him after a few rings.

"Luke told me what happened," Kenny said. "I'm very sorry for you and your family. Why don't you come by this morning? We can discuss what you need and then check out the best possibilities."

We piled into Holly's SUV and headed toward Travis Heights, the one place in Austin where I always imagined I could live if I was forced to adopt an urban lifestyle. Just south of the river, the neighborhood was the opposite of cookie-cutter, with a mix of architectural styles and streets that curved, angled, and dead-ended at greenbelts and parks.

With an oversupply of mature trees, including enormous live oaks with branches that stretched across entire lots or into the airspace of creek beds, Travis Heights was a felicitous blend of the old and the new, the modern and the classic. It was the sort of place where the well-heeled young and hip coexisted with those who were graying and living on the abundance of a successful, now-completed career.

The house Kenny shared with his partner was set back from the street. Next to a small in-ground swimming pool, it was a rambling two-story design, jammed with furniture, artwork, and several wine racks. Some of the wine bottles had pieces of paper stuck to them.

"What's up with these?" I asked.

"Funny you should ask," Kenny said. "Those are little hand-written warnings to Amelia and Luke not to think about trying out a sample. Their taste in wine is ridiculously high-brow for two people as young as them."

"I'm probably to blame for that."

"That's what I understand. When I was their age, I was happy to drink cheap, knock-off rosé from a bottle with yarn wrapped around it."

"Ditto."

Kenny was an easy guy to like. He had a full head of brownish hair and a wry, easy smile accented by hip, squared-off glasses. He wore khaki shorts and a collared short-sleeve shirt. His laptop sat on a glass coffee table, and he hunched over it with his legs splayed. I took note of the attention he paid to Miranda.

"So tell me what you're looking for."

Holly and I exchanged mystified looks.

"Do you have any ideas, Miranda?" asked Kenny.

"I need a bedroom."

He laughed. "I think I can find something with a couple of those."

As he clicked and scrolled with the speed of a pro, Holly and I silently stared at him.

"OK, let's start with the basics. Furnished or unfurnished? What area of town? How big? What's your budget?"

We answered with blank stares.

"How about this? Let me make a few calls and we'll take it from there. I'm setting aside the whole day. It's the least I can do."

After Kenny put together a list and printed it out, we hit the road in his SUV. After making a stop at a vacant brick house just down the street, we took longer looks at two pleasant, unfurnished two-story houses in a clean and quiet neighborhood ten minutes northwest of downtown. Trying to imagine our daily life in them was disorienting, and the thought of going on a buying rampage to furnish them was instantly unappealing. The immaculate lawns and sidewalks seemed ill suited to the habits of our dogs.

"Let's keep looking," I said.

"This next place is on Lake Austin and it's completely furnished," said Kenny. "The people who own it are living elsewhere for the foreseeable future."

Our spirits were momentarily lifted, but that didn't last long. The house was enormous and excessive. The carpeting was thick enough to asphyxiate a small animal, the walls were filled with self-congratulatory personal memorabilia, some of the colors were inexplicable, and the Western art was strictly paint-by-numbers. We were flabbergasted and downhearted.

It was time for a break.

As we drove to a popular hamburger joint at a very busy intersection, I struggled to understand why I felt so beat down. We had solid insurance coverage, which gave us more choices than many burned-out families would have. While the house we just left was an assault on our sensibilities, it would meet all of our basic needs, and why should we expect more than that when hundreds, if not thousands, of other people from our community would find themselves in far worse conditions in the coming weeks? With a jolt of shame, I reread an e-mail on my phone I had received the previous evening from Lynn, a good friend who worked for an international relief organization.

The thought comes to me that you have so much in common with the millions of people around the world that we work with . . . everything taken away in an instant because of natural disaster or war. I think of Somalia, which combines the disastrous effects of both. The shock must be overwhelming.

Yes, the shock was overwhelming. But that's where the comparison with Somalia, or the Japanese coast buried by the tsunami, or disaster victims anywhere else in the world ended. In the historical pantheon of disaster victims, the Fritz family didn't qualify. We were alive, we were uninjured, and our needs would be taken care of. What right did I have to complain or feel sorry for myself?

During the afternoon, Kenny kept excusing himself to make brief phone calls as we trudged through several more places, all unfurnished.

"I keep trying to imagine how we'd go about getting all the stuff we need," said Holly as we walked through an empty living room and kitchen. "There are the obvious things, like beds and a desk and chair for you and a kitchen table and maybe a TV. But there's so much else we'd need as well. Think of what we'd have to get just for the kitchen. Plates, silverware, glasses, cooking stuff."

"Makes my head hurt just thinking about it."

"And whatever we buy, we're stuck with it. It's what we'll be eating off of, and sleeping in, maybe for the rest of our lives."

"Making permanent decisions under pressure when we can't think straight. I can't wait."

We were nearing the end of the day, no closer to a decision than when we started, when Kenny finished another phone call and announced: "Finally. I've been working on this all day and I just got the green light to show you one more place. When you see it, I think you'll agree I saved the best for last."

Five minutes later, we arrived at a limestone-clad Spanish-style two-story house with a red tile roof. It was located several blocks from Kenny's place, in the heart of Travis Heights, on a steeply sloped lot that seemed impossibly large for central Austin. Built in 1934, the house was surrounded by many large, sculptural oaks that were as old as they were magnificent.

We raced from one furnished room to the next, our excitement growing. Finally, we gathered on the orange-tiled rooftop terrace with a stupendous view of downtown Austin to the north and the purplish fringe of the Hill Country to the west.

"Careful," I said to Miranda as we looked around, gape-mouthed. "Don't get too close to the edge."

"I feel like my breath is being taken away," said Miranda.

"So you like it?"

"Can we live here?"

"I don't know. But I hope so."

The beds were comfortable, we could easily see ourselves lounging in the evening on the sofas and chairs, and the kitchen was serviceable. There were several small decks on the first floor and a narrow sunroom just off the kitchen with tall stools surrounding an even taller, square table. It would be a delightful place to eat breakfast or play Scrabble.

The bathrooms were relics from the past, with small and stodgy sinks and slightly cockeyed doors that objected to being closed. One had a poorly lit shower where no one would linger. But these defects were immaterial compared to the house's virtues.

While the house was impressive, we could hardly believe the walk from one side of the two-acre property to the other. It included a long set of stone steps surrounded by trees and dense undergrowth that dropped at least fifty feet from the house's southern side to one of the three streets that bordered the property. Even though we were five minutes from downtown, it felt like we were in a forest. With no pines, it didn't look like Bastrop County. But it was green and quiet and like nothing we had any right to expect.

"This is really available?" I said. "We can have it if we want it?"

"Probably," said Kenny. "But there are still some loose ends I have to tie up. I'll know for sure in a few days at the most."

It seemed literally too good to be true: a fully furnished house in my favorite Austin neighborhood on enough undeveloped land to qualify as a small bird sanctuary. Not only that, we were two blocks from a large and winding city park with a swimming pool at the southern end and a wet-weather creek in the middle. If we had to be burned-out and homeless, we couldn't possibly hope to find anything to top it.

Hillary and Jared had invited us for dinner. On the way over, I said to Holly: "I've been thinking we should check with Walter or Jeri Nell to see if they know for sure what happened to their place. Maybe they dodged a bullet after all."

I first tried Walter's number, but it went immediately to voice mail. Then I called Jeri Nell.

"We're wiped out, just like you," she said.

"How do you know? Are you absolutely sure?"

"Positive. Walter went out Tuesday morning and checked on the whole neighborhood. We can e-mail some pictures he took of your place if you're interested."

"No thanks. I know what it looks like. Can you salvage anything from the house or Walter's workshop?"

"Walter may pick through it, but I doubt he'll find anything."

"What about your trees?" I asked, referring to the forty wooded acres surrounding the house and Walter's workshop.

"Most of them are dead. Maybe a few of them will make it, if we're lucky."

We talked for a few more minutes in monotones. There was no need to go into detail or crank up the emotion.

I hung up and turned to Holly. "Can you imagine? All of those special tools he designed and rigged up over the years? And the wood he salvaged and stored in those outside bins? And the stuff he was working on. It would be like if I lost my computer with no backup."

"Think of how long they lived in that house," said Holly. "The entire time we've known them."

"And the elevator they built for Jess. How are they going to get by without that?"

Our thoughts returned to the beautiful rental property we had found, though, so we were buzzing and upbeat as we took our places around Hillary and Jared's dining room table. The food was delicious; one-year-old Ben was chirpy and huggable. We couldn't stop talking about how our day had taken a dramatic turn for the better.

But then—like a runner who unexpectedly gets a debilitating cramp, or a musician whose memory goes blank in the middle of a performance—the sizzling emotions suddenly took hold. My three daughters looked at me, with a combination of dismay and amazement, as I began to bawl. Eating and conversation stopped.

My outburst was brief but dramatic. As I settled down, my oldest daughter said, "I may be wrong, but I think that was the first time I ever saw you cry, at least like that."

"Considering that you're almost thirty years old and that we've had some very difficult moments as a family, that seems a bit ridiculous to say," I responded.

"If it's happened before, I can't remember it. I'm serious."

"Just because you're serious doesn't mean you're right."

"You're like Granny," said Hillary. "You don't cry. That doesn't mean you're insensitive or hard-hearted. It's just that you have other ways of showing your feelings."

"I saw him cry when I was eleven years old," said Amelia. "When Grandpa died."

"You sure?" asked Hillary.

"Definitely. It made an impression on me."

Miranda joined in: "I don't think I've seen Dad cry either."

I didn't enjoy being analyzed in the third person. After a brief, awkward silence, Hillary posed the obvious question: "Why did you do that? Especially after you seemed so happy when you got here."

I had no answer.

"Give your dad a break," Holly said. "We've been through a lot. I don't think it's such a strange thing. In fact, it's probably healthy."

"I don't know about that," said Hillary, "but it's definitely unusual."

The evening's emotional fizz had gone flat.

We settled down to the main point of our visit: watching the first regular game of the new NFL season. It was seven months since my exultant soul had practically left my body as the final seconds of the 2011 Super Bowl ticked away to a Packers victory. As a lifelong fan, I have no choice but to suffer when they lose and exhale with relief when they win. For any ardent Packers fan— and there really is no other kind—watching a close game is a nerve-wracking affair that is more endured than enjoyed.

So it was an odd sensation to be indifferent to the ebb and flow of a wild and thrilling struggle with the New Orleans Saints. The game ended with the Packers defense stuffing the Saints running back at the 1-yard line to seal a one-touchdown victory. Instead of having sweaty palms and an amped-up pulse, I sat on Hillary and Jared's sofa like a piece of sculpture, barely breathing.

"You're in bad shape," said Hillary. "With a game like that, we should have been on you for the last hour to keep quiet so Ben doesn't wake up. But you've hardly uttered so much as a grunt."

We gathered up our things to leave.

After pulling me aside, Hillary said quietly: "I got an e-mail today from the priest of your church in Bastrop."

"Why? You haven't gone there in years."

"They never took me off the distribution list. Anyway, it's about some mental health services the church is helping to arrange. Do you want me to forward it to you?"

"You think I'm going nuts? Is that your point?"

"I thought you might be interested. I won't send it if you don't want it."

After a brief silence, I said, "Go ahead. It can't hurt, I guess."

As we drove back to Hillary's in-laws, I fantasized about the sleep I was certain awaited me. A body can take only so much, I told myself, and the reward for several nights of sleeplessness surely must be six or seven unbroken hours of oblivion. My anticipation was as palpable and physical as a man about to break a fast who smells bread baking.

Before going to bed, I read the e-mail from Mother Lisa:

As the reality of the loss and devastation of these fires settle in, we can expect that many in the Bastrop community will need mental health care. I am working with a group of mental health providers in Austin with spiritual training who will provide counseling over a sixth-month period in space that we will provide. It will be a privilege as a congregation to contribute in this way to the recovery of our community.

I was glad our church was doing something beneficial. But I didn't see what it had to do with me.

September 9, 2011, 7:30 a.m. The next morning, I sat down to a breakfast of cold cereal and take-out coffee with Holly and Miranda. We had just completed the morning's version of the twice-daily ritual of pulling the dogs past wary neighbors, shooing them across a busy street, and walking them along a skinny greenbelt down on its luck from the heat and drought. The wieners practically choked themselves on their leashes whenever another dog came close. Whoever was holding Charlie's leash risked a dislocated shoulder.

Nobody was smiling as we shut the garage door, replenished the water in the dog dishes, and then took our seats around a corner of the large Jenson dining table.

"It may seem like a very small thing, but I miss our fresh-brewed coffee," said Holly.

"I miss opening the door in the morning for the dogs to go where they please and do as they want," I said.

"I miss my room and my Wii," said Miranda.

After a few minutes of eating in silence, I said to Holly: "We need to get going on the insurance list. I was thinking that we could do this as a team. I can take a quick cut at the obvious stuff and then you can add to it, room by room. As you finish each one, I'll do the online research to estimate replacement value."

As I sat down at my computer, my phone rang. The caller ID displayed the name of a good friend and former work colleague. The reason for the call was obvious, and I debated whether to answer.

"Hi, Becky. I think I know why you're calling."

"Is your place OK? Is everyone fine?"

"No to the first question, yes to the second."

"So your place didn't make it?"

My voice choked up.

"I don't think I can talk about this right now," I told her.

"Can I call you back in a day or two? I know how much you loved your place in Smithville."

"You're right, I did. Which is why I can't talk about it now, and I have no idea when I will be able to."

Silence.

"I appreciate you calling, I really do," I said. "Maybe I'll holler back at you sometime. I've gotta go now."

So this is what it would be like as people reached out to me in person: compassion and empathy reluctantly accepted; emotions barely held in check; a dull, throbbing pain in my head; and a gnawing uncertainty about how to react and what to say.

I wasn't shutting myself off from those who cared about us. I gratefully read and reread heartfelt e-mails and text messages. But the sound of a human voice flipped open a trapdoor under my brain, sending it hurtling.

As Holly suggested, I started with the clothes in my closet. Most of it had come from a well-known and high-quality online retailer. While I regularly wore all of it in my last executive-level state job, my consulting work was mostly stay-at-home, which meant I had only sporadically worn the dressiest items over the past four years.

Nevertheless, I decided to replace all of it. I would do the same for my other stuff.

The beauty of my plan seemed undeniable. I would make two parallel lists: one for the insurance money and the other to begin rebuilding my life exactly as it was. Within several days, I would be well on my way to having everything in my closet that I had lost. Once that job was done, I could begin plotting with Holly how to replace the big items, like our super-thick and oh-so-comfortable bed, the brown leather couch that the three of us sank into while watching TV and where I had helped Miranda learn to read, and the black leather chair from our living room where I did most of my recreational reading. I would welcome discussion of how to find and buy the silverware and dishes we originally got when we were married in 1977. I wasn't sure when I would bring up the replacement of my grand piano, but surely the time for that treacherous topic would come soon as well.

Trees and paintings and pottery couldn't be ordered up. But lots of other things could be, and surely must. If the main effect of a fire is losing things, then what could be more therapeutic than replacing them with their identical or fraternal twins?

Several hours after I slapped back Becky's outstretched hand, I was smiling with satisfaction over what I had just ordered and would buy in the days to come. I spent a considerable sum on dress clothes that would arrive in less than a week. While they weren't exactly what I had before, they were close enough.

Tennis shorts, rackets, and armbands were also on the way. The NFL Store was sending me two Packers Super Bowl T-shirts that were exactly like the ones I had practically worn out over the summer. Later in the day, I replaced my tennis shoes, bandannas, and casual shorts by driving to a nearby big-box store and handing over my credit card.

Because I had an important business meeting in several days, I needed a set of formal clothes. Holly and Miranda needed some clothes as well, so the next day we decided to go to a nearby mall after I bought my dress shoes.

Even though I got to the shoe store shortly after they opened, they were already busy, and I had to wait. As I sat there, I overheard a salesman mention a "special discount for fire victims" to the family he was helping.

I wasn't sure what to think of that label. The fire had been unmerciful to the Fritz family, but did that make us "victims"? The word had an undertone of pitifulness that I found unappealing and maybe even a bit insulting.

But if we weren't victims, what were we? And why did I care how people referred to us if they did so in a spirit of benevolence and helpfulness?

A pleasant-looking middle-aged man called my number.

"I need a pair of brown dress shoes and some orthotics to go with them," I said. "In fact, now that I think of it, I might as well buy some black ones as well to go with the suits I just ordered."

"Sounds like you're stocking up."

"No, I'm replacing what we lost in the fire."

The expression on his face changed. "I'm so sorry to hear that," he said. "I can't imagine what you're going through. While I know it's not much, we're offering a discount for any families who lost their homes."

"That's kind of you."

"It's the least we can do." I remembered that Kenny had said the same thing two days earlier.

"Well, let's see what you have," I said. "I'd like to get something as close as possible to what burned up."

I described what I was looking for, and we scanned several dozen shoes. None of them came close to being twins with what I'd been wearing for years.

There wasn't an iota of impatience in his demeanor. But I soon felt foolish about what I was asking of him.

Fifteen minutes later, I was at the cash register, resigned to the two pairs of shoes I selected out of exhaustion as much as anything. Word of my situation had circulated among the salesmen, and a few of them gathered around to offer their sympathies and wish me well. I was grateful for these small gestures of concern but also embarrassed by how they looked at me.

As I drove to pick up Holly and Miranda, I tried to make sense of what had just happened. If I was now part of an increasingly famous tribe formed out of shared adversity, what was its name and distinguishing features? How did I want people to respond to my tribe? And what did we owe them in return for their solicitude?

"Did you get some comfortable shoes?" Holly asked as she and Miranda climbed into the car.

"I won't know until I wear them. I got a discount, though, and lots of hangdog looks."

"They're trying to be nice. What's wrong with that?"

"Nothing in principle. But you'll see what I mean when we get to the mall."

My prediction proved to be an understatement. While the men at the shoe store kept their emotions in check, the women who were put in charge of a tiny portion of my wardrobe let their feelings be known. We were part celebrities and part refugees from dire circumstances. We were objects of pity and props in a feel-good project.

A group hug was not out of the question. Perhaps someone would ask us for our autographs.

With my mind cramping up, I let Holly make the final decisions, and I walked out with a set of clothes nothing like what I would have chosen if it had been entirely up to me. While Holly and Miranda did their shopping, I excused myself to a couch in the mall's atrium. When they returned, they weren't carrying anything.

"Where's your stuff?" I asked.

"I changed my mind," said Holly. "It's too soon to be spending a bunch of money on things we may not need."

"You hardly have any decent clothes."

"We don't need them right now. I want to take our time before we make any hasty decisions we might regret."

"But they're offering us a discount. It won't last forever."

"That's hardly a reason to grab the first thing we see."

The lopsidedness of our situations forced a confession.

"You might not like it, but I've already spent a bunch of money on clothes and some other stuff."

"What are you talking about?"

"When I was working on the insurance list yesterday, I decided to replenish my wardrobe. I ordered it online. When it all arrives in a few days, it'll be like I never lost any of it."

"You bought suits and a bunch of dress shirts?"

"Yup."

"But you never wear suits anymore. In fact, you hardly ever dress up. All you need is what we just bought."

I wanted to defend myself. But I felt like a fool.

"I can understand why you did it," said Holly.

"That's all you're going to say?"

"We have to try to be kind to each other."

On the way back to the Jenson house, I called the company's customer service line. It was too late to cancel the order. When the boxes arrived the following week, I picked through what was there. I returned all of it except for a few shirts, three pairs of pants, and a gray suit.

Over the course of five moves in twelve months, I shuttled the clothes I kept from one closet rod to the next, where they hung, inert and largely forgotten. Seventeen months after I bought them, I put on the gray suit and the black shoes for the first time.

September 10, 2011, 6:30 p.m. Except for Hillary's branch of the family, the Fritz clan gathered Saturday evening at Anton's two-story condo in southwest Austin for dinner, music, and spiritual balm. His building was in a wooded neighborhood bordering a greenbelt and spring-fed creek. It was dominated by a black Steinway concert grand that ate up two-thirds of his high-ceilinged living room. It had a nickname: "the Black Beast."

Anton and his partner Bill went all out for us: a multicourse meal and two wonderful bottles of Pinot Noir from the same area in Burgundy where I acquired the wine for Amelia's wedding. The furniture was rearranged to fit the glass dining room table into the living room next to the piano, and there were six immaculate place settings.

As we sat down for dinner, my mother-in-law's name popped up on my caller ID. Betty got right to the point.

"I've been thinking about what I could do to help all of you. And it suddenly dawned on me today that you should have my piano."

I was too stunned to reply.

"Before you agree to take it, I was hoping Anton could check it out and make sure it's suitable for you. I only want you to have it if he thinks it's right for you. Can you contact him and see if he would be willing to do that?"

"You're not going to believe this," I said, "but I'm looking at him right now. We're at his place, getting ready to have dinner. And what's even more amazing is that he will be in Dallas week after next for a concert."

She let out a squeal of delight. "That's almost a miracle. Before he comes, I want to have it tuned and checked out by a technician up here. He can tell you whether it's in good shape mechanically and Anton can evaluate its musical potential. Once all that's done, I will arrange to ship it down there as soon as you're ready to have it."

"That could be as soon as three or four weeks," I said. "We have a good chance of renting a large house in central Austin."

Anton and Betty compared schedules and confirmed mutual availability. Within a few minutes, things were set in motion for me to receive a gift of incalculable personal and spiritual value, a joint legacy of my mother-in-law and fire, my friend-turned-enemy.

"Tell me a little about this piano I'll be checking out," said Anton.

"It's a Bechstein grand with a mahogany case. Pretty old, as I remember. She inherited it from her deceased aunt. I only played it a few times when Betty lived in Bastrop County, never seriously. I don't remember anything about how it sounds or plays."

"Bechsteins are mainly found in Europe, although my teacher in South Africa had one. You don't run across them very often over here. They have a unique sound, definitely different from the one you lost."

"Does different mean better?"

"Not always, but probably in this case."

After dinner, Anton pulled me aside briefly.

"If your mother-in-law's piano doesn't work out, there will be other options," he said. "Music is too important for you to be without. I've already made some preliminary inquiries. No matter what happens, you will have a piano that is right for you, and sooner rather than later. Until that happens, you are welcome to play mine anytime you need to make music."

After dinner, Anton played for us, starting with the Schumann piece he performed the first time he visited our Cottletown Road house. As the short recital progressed, thoughts of the fire briefly bled away. When he finished, we knew he had given us a great gift: beautiful music, passionately and faithfully performed; time suspended; grace for our bruised and tender souls.

Even though every member of the Fritz family wept during the Schumann, I was singled out. "Dad's been crying a lot," Miranda said. "We're starting to get used to it."

"Hillary seemed almost shocked by the sight of it the other night," I said. "I guess she momentarily forgot about the events of Miranda's birthday."

"Actually, we talked about that later," said Amelia. "I reminded her how much Dad's garden and trees and house meant to him. And she reminded me how he would badger us into checking out his vegetables and beloved toad pond every time we visited." She looked at me and said, "I understand why you're doing it. It's kind of touching, actually."

Hugs were exchanged, and we left Anton's condo in an emotional state that, if we could have captured and preserved it, would have made the coming days and weeks much easier to get through. But while the evening was ephemeral, like the music that formed its centerpiece, Anton's availability and support would not be.

The hours I spent with his concert grand in the days we lived at the Jenson's—in the company of Debussy and Chopin and Bach—were the only ones where the fire temporarily excused itself from my clamorous mind.

Anton's review of Betty's piano came in two weeks later, and it was a rave. "Her piano suits you," he said less than an hour after he checked it out. "Most importantly, it has a soul. That piano definitely has a soul."

"So no doubts?"

"None. It needs a little work. But once it has a tune-up, you will have a truly unique and wonderful instrument. I couldn't have found you anything better."

I immediately called Betty to accept her piano with my deepest thanks and arrange for its delivery the week after our move to Travis Heights. My Bechstein was born a continent away exactly one hundred years earlier, in the brief and tranquil moment before Europe became engulfed in one of history's greatest man-made horrors. It was brought to life by men with the national lineage of Beethoven and Bach. After a number of long voyages, it was about to be united with its most grateful owner.

September 10, 2011, 11 a.m. We returned to Bastrop the next day to attend a church service I expected to be difficult but necessary. We felt obligated to join other grieving families in the presence of many others who yearned to support us. And because the priest of our Episcopal parish was newly homeless, along with her husband and two dozen other church families, she might have a sensitive and appropriate message to console us.

Calvary Episcopal was a small church in the Gothic Revival style when we first became parishioners in 1980, with very old limestone brick, a rectangular bell tower, towering stained glass windows, and a ceiling supported by arched pine trusses. At the most, 125 people could crowd into it.

Now it was three times that size. During the year it was being rebuilt and expanded, the church briefly went through a deconstruction period in which the hulk of the old building looked like a French World War II ruin. The church was now a modern building with architectural allusions to its past, most notably the high ceiling and the stained glass windows behind the altar.

Holly, Miranda, and I took our seats in a pew near the front of the church. Martha, my right-hand helper when I was county judge, sat down next to me, whispered something kind in my ear, and softly patted my right hand with her left.

When it came time for the sermon, Mother Lisa climbed to the lectern with a purposeful look, her long and thick gray hair pouring from her head like a waterfall. I was relieved that our priest was not a man. With my eyes brimming, this is some of what I heard her say:

> *We don't understand why one house burns and the one next to it remains in a charred landscape. We don't understand why we didn't take what we most needed from our homes instead of taking, as one commenter on Facebook said, the bowling ball from the hall closet simply because the bag had a handle on it.*
>
> *We don't understand how we could have thought until now that life was fair, that we deserved either the good or the bad things that have happened to us—that our faith in God was some kind of insurance policy against disaster. We don't understand why it hasn't rained when in the gospels Jesus says that our heavenly Father knows what we need and will provide it. Those of us who lost our houses don't understand why the people who did not feel guilty. Those of you whose houses remain don't understand why we who lost our houses and possessions in the fire feel guilty taking your love-offerings of money and shelter and necessities, especially if we have insurance and know that we are not really destitute.*
>
> *We are trying to make sense of something that doesn't. So I hope that we'll be gentle with ourselves and with each other. We have to move beyond our guilt to be present fully to one another in the coming weeks and months and even years. As the smoke clears, the needs of our community will become clearer and the ways in which we can help each other will also become clearer. We have a very long process of recovery ahead once the danger of fire has passed.*

During the offertory, Mother Lisa reminded us that mental health services would be forthcoming through her efforts and those of others. She then invited all who had lost their homes to join her at the altar for a blessing. Each family was a knot of arms, hands, and wet cheeks.

As I knelt during the Eucharistic prayers, I noticed that a number of people who had known me for the better part of three decades were stealing looks at me. They reminded me of my daughters the night of the Packers game.

I was not ashamed by my emotional display. But I was also uninterested in prolonging it by lingering with others as they gave us their sympathy and prayers. After the service ended, I broke free of my wife and daughter, exited through a side door, and bolted for the car with my head down. While I wanted to thank Mother Lisa for her words and gestures, I wanted even more to avoid the inevitable questions about how we were doing and where we were living.

Two weeks later, we again attended Sunday services at Calvary Episcopal Church. With my body crusted over with fatigue and sleeplessness, I took in the sights of the church through the lens of my daughters' baptisms, the funeral of Amelia's godmother, Hillary's wedding, and several Sundays when my organ playing joined with the choir in musical offerings that left me dazed with happiness. My recollections were not nostalgic. Rather, like the memory of the forest we loved, they were cherished artifacts of a life that was growing dimmer by the day.

My emotions sloshed around during Mother Lisa's sermon, as the peace was exchanged, and while the choir sang. Like a sentry on patrol, Miranda kept her eye on me and made periodic gestures or whispers to her mom about her dad's condition.

As the service wound down and the final hymn began, I came to a regretful conclusion. Calvary was no longer a place of spiritual safety and nourishment. Instead, it was a place where I couldn't stop myself from wallowing in the past, my emotions unhinged and laced with self-pity. I felt like Pavlov's dog.

Several days later, I arranged to briefly meet Mother Lisa in her office after she had reached out to me with a sensitive and touching offer.

In 1983, I created a porcelain urn for Ash Wednesday services. Like many of my porcelain pieces, the covered vessel had a dull metallic glaze set off by several white stripes where the porcelain was exposed. It deeply gratified me to receive ashes each year from this pot.

After hearing about the loss of my pottery, she offered to return it to me. Handing me a cardboard box, she said: "Packing this up made me very nervous. I can't imagine what I would have done if I damaged it."

"Thank you for giving it back, although I have mixed feelings about accepting it."

"It's the least I can do," she said. There was that expression again.

There was a discomfiting silence. In addition to coping with her loss, Mother Lisa's pastoral duties had no doubt exploded. How could anyone do what was now being asked of her? How could she minister to those in pain and attend to her own grief as well? How could she help burned-out families when she faced a long list of practical problems, starting with where to live?

It seemed so overwhelming and unfair that I was unable to say anything to her. Everything that came to mind seemed pitiful and small.

Finally, I broke the silence by practically blurting out: "Well, this is probably the last time you'll be seeing any of us for a while. We're moving to Austin on October 1 and no telling when we'll be back."

"We surely want you back with us when the time is right."

She looked pained, and I could hardly believe what I had just said. Still, my words kept coming. "Hard to say when that day will come, if ever. We've got a lot of hard decisions to make, I'm afraid. Since you're sort of in the same position as us, I think you can understand what I mean."

"I certainly do."

"I assume you're not going anywhere, even though you probably wish you could."

"I expect that if you and Holly return, you'll find me right here."

"Even if we do move back, I'm not sure we'll keep going to Calvary. I don't like how the place affects me now."

"It's your decision. You don't have to explain yourself."

"OK, then. I guess I'll see you when I see you."

With my arms wrapped around the box, and my face pointed at the floor, I walked out of her office, mortified by what I had done and said but unable to turn around and make things right. As I got into my car, I felt like Pavlov's dog again, now gone rabid.

September 14, 2011, 10 a.m. A day after we moved into the Jensons' house, the county blocked all of the roads into the burn zone. State and local law enforcement officers in no mood to negotiate turned away property owners desperate to find out what had happened.

But as firefighters gradually contained the blaze, property owners were let back in, one area at a time, providing they had the proper county-supplied credentials.

I made appointments for the morning our neighborhood opened with our insurance adjuster and a local trash disposal service. My first stop was a big-box store where the county paperwork was being distributed. Several large shade tents were set up in the store's enormous parking lot. Volunteers from an Austin charitable organization, all wearing the same kind of shirt, handled the processing.

As I waited my turn, I was relieved that I didn't know any of the other families. After providing identification, I received the necessary form for our vehicles. A fortyish woman with sunglasses and dark hair pulled through a sun visor asked me: "Do you need any assistance at this time?"

"In what way?"

"Temporary housing?"

"No, we have a place to live in Austin."

"What about other kinds of help? We have debit cards you can use for food or to buy something you need right away."

"I'm OK. We had insurance."

"But that sometimes takes time."

"It's nice of you to ask. But I'm fine."

"We're checking with everyone, and it's good we are because most people don't feel comfortable asking for help."

"That I believe," I said.

"Even though they obviously need it."

"Yup."

"Just so you know, they're giving away shovels and sieves over there. And dust masks too, I think."

I knew she meant well. But I couldn't bear another second of it.

As I entered the burn zone, the first thing I saw was the border of Bastrop State Park where it ends at Highway 71. What had been impenetrable forest was now a landscape of scorched trees and clear views. It reminded me of the winter forest vistas I knew so well from my childhood in Wisconsin. Each year, green and lush summertime landscapes would melt into panoramas of naked deciduous trees, the aftermath of autumn's gorgeous purge.

That didn't happen in the Lost Pines because loblollies far outnumbered oaks. Where I lived, the forest was green and thick year round.

But now it wasn't. The state park was an impostor: it was masquerading as winter, but the white and gray on the ground were the opposite of snow and cold.

The gate to our property was open, which meant Gordon was back. Our insurance adjuster, Kenneth, stood at the bend in our driveway, taking notes. He wore a collared shirt with the name of his company stitched on it. His handshake was firm and warm, his tone of voice even-keeled without being cold. After exchanging introductions, he got down to business.

"I'm sorry for what's happened to you and your family. It's a total loss, so of course you'll receive the full insured value of the house."

"Should we do an inspection?"

"It's not necessary, but I don't mind taking the time if you think that would help."

We started at the front entrance. The curved brick walkway was largely intact up to the spot where the front door would have been. My favorite wood-fired pot—the ochre-colored urn that I proudly displayed in the entryway—was wedged underneath a panel of metal roofing.

The pot was intact. It had a fresh coating of melted ash, the unmistakable residue of a 2,500-degree fire, the same peak temperature as my old wood kiln. I wondered which of our possessions, or what tiny piece of our house, had fused with the urn's side and hardened as the ruin began to cool. Stepping over nails and broken glass, I picked it up with both hands, held it from the bottom with my left hand, and gave it a snap with my right forefinger and thumb.

It sounded as hollow and lifeless as a cracked bell.

"You can't imagine how finding this pot makes me feel," I said. "It's very fragile and compromised, but it survived."

He said nothing.

"I made this many years ago for myself, when I was about to switch careers from being a potter. Surely if this one made it, there must be others in there as well. I just have to find and dig them out."

We gingerly worked our way around razor-edged standing-seam roof panels where the carport had been. I knew exactly where to look for the remains of Miranda's golf cart.

The Christmas before her eighteenth birthday, Holly and I gave our youngest daughter a monogrammed chain with the key to a battery-powered vehicle I would teach her to drive, first on the dirt path that connected our Long Trail property to the one we had just purchased, and then on Cottletown Road at times of the day when traffic was light.

Teaching Miranda to drive that winter was like teaching her to read. I deconstructed each primary task—accelerating, braking, turning, yielding to other vehicles, stopping, and parking—into smaller tasks, like the phonetics of a written word.

At first we got on each other's nerves. I desperately wanted her to learn a skill that almost anyone else her age could do instinctively. Her near misses with trees and ditches made me jumpy and impatient, as did her tendency to accelerate with her right foot while braking with her left. She responded in kind when I insisted that she do the same thing repeatedly until she got it right.

And then, just like her reading, her focus and commitment were suddenly rewarded. She became fluid and confident, driving her golf cart like a miniature car, pulling over when other vehicles approached, braking for stop signs, pacing herself on downhill stretches, and pulling into her parking spot with no help from me.

Miranda's golf cart was a symbol of independence and accomplishment. But absolutely nothing of it remained—no melted frame and no warped struts.

On the main slab, hundreds of exposed nails and screws were scattered about and sticking up, and glass shards were everywhere. We left prints in the ash as we tiptoed along the edge of the space that had been the family room.

"At least the woodstove still looks like its same old self," I said. He nodded without a smile.

I jumped off the slab and made my way around the side of the house facing the ravine and garden.

"This is where the deck was attached," I said, pointing to the horizontal bolts sticking out of the concrete. "It was held up by three enormous aromatic cedar posts that a local sawmill custom-made for us. They had to find some very tall and straight trees to cut and mill those posts. I bet they practically exploded in the fire."

He gave me another nod and blank look. I pointed toward the slab's highest point.

"That's what's left of a curved limestone wall. The guy who built it really knew what he was doing. Right before he finished it, he said to me, 'I know how to bend a stone.' My deceased grandfather was a master brick mason. It would have amazed him."

Finally, he said something: "What was on that little slab over there? Where you were looking under the roof panels."

"That was a carport. The ornamental steel plates on the ground held the corners rigid. They were my partner's idea, part beauty and part function. Quarter-inch steel and now they're bent."

"Your policy will pay out on the carport based on its size and design. I'll be sending you some questions to come up with a valuation."

"I don't suppose I'll get anything for my trees or garden, will I?" It was a serious question.

"No. While I can only imagine what your trees meant to you, they don't have any insurance value. I'm sorry."

"I had to ask. Look at all of them. The brown needles and blackened trunks probably mean they're doomed. But it'll be a while before we know for sure."

He closed his folder and zipped up the side.

"Is that it, then?" I asked.

"I think so. I'll start the paperwork on the main claim. You'll be working with someone else on your contents. You've started your list, I assume?"

"Yes."

We worked out the reimbursement details for the Travis Heights rental house, and then he left. Without realizing it, I had just finished my first therapy session: I talked and someone listened.

I had a little time before the next appointment, so I looked for more pots. In my tennis shoes, shorts, and T-shirt, I wasn't dressed for the part.

I found several Indian pots we inherited from Holly's father and one of my pots in such a blistered and maimed state that I immediately decided to throw it away. But the dangerous conditions made it slow going, and I quickly lost my heart and nerve. By the time the disposal company reps appeared, I had decided to leave the cleanup to the professionals.

"So what can you do for me and how soon?" I said.

"We can remove all of this and give it a clean sweep. By the time we're finished, it'll be a bare slab with nothing on it."

"Please be careful. There may be some things in there worth saving."

"No problem. You're not the only person who's said that."

"I need to discuss it with my wife. But I'm guessing we want to be rid of all this as soon as possible. It breaks my heart to see it, so the sooner it's gone, the better."

With both tasks completed, I took a quick look at the gardens. Holly's flowerbeds bordering the curved walkway were a tangle of brown vegetation. But there were tiny pinpricks of green at the bottom of many stems. My morning glories and blooming hyacinth vines were shriveled and falling away from the garden fence. The melons had exploded and the remnants were well on their way to being devoured by ants. The tomatoes and peppers were a lost cause. In the midst of all this, however, several potato sprouts broke the dried surface of the bed that formerly held the spring potato crop.

I called Holly.

"You're not going to believe this, but there's a tiny amount of life in my garden. And your flowerbeds might come back. There are little green shoots where your perennials were."

"What about the trees?"

"Couldn't be worse."

"I have to believe that some of them will make it."

"We can't let Miranda see any of this," I said. "Not now and not ever."

"I agree. What are you going to do now?"

"Get our mail from Wanda's and then head back."

As I walked up the driveway, Gordon met me halfway. He wore a work shirt, jeans, and heavy-duty shoes.

I first met Gordon and his wife after we sold our Long Trail house but before we had moved out. They were initially wary of our overture to buy some of their land. But after we showed them pictures of the green houses that Walter and I had built, and after we enthusiastically embraced Gordon's vision for their land—strategic removal of water-hogging cedar trees, thinning of invasive plants, ephemeral ponds at the low point of natural drainage areas, and a live-and-let-live attitude toward the wildlife—they decided to sell us ten acres that bordered Cottletown Road on the western side. After walking the prospective tract with him, Gordon agreed to slightly modify its shape to include a wet-weather pond with a thirty-foot radius that he dug out for Houston toad habitat.

Gordon and his family lived in Austin, but he spent almost all his free time on his large property, planting fruit and pecan trees, tending to his garden, and never wearying of the endless job of selective clearing and thinning.

He sometimes paid us an unplanned visit. He was unemotional without being cool or aloof. But as our plans came to fruition, his satisfied smiles confirmed that we had become the good stewards that he hoped we would be. We were good neighbors to one another.

"How did you know I was here?" I said.

"Those trash guys told me. They're working up a bid for me as well."

"Looks a little different from the last time you were here."

"I think I know how you're feeling."

"Maybe. But you're smiling and I'm not."

"We'll get through it," Gordon said. "We can help each other."

"That'll be hard to do once I say good-bye to this place. Which I hope will be soon."

"It's a little early to be talking like that, don't you think?"

"Not really. Look around you."

"It's terrible, I know. But the forest will come back."

"On its own? Just like that?"

"With some help from us."

"And in the meantime, I'm supposed to be OK with all this? Can't do it."

"Well, I've put too much of myself into this land to give up."

"It has nothing to do with giving up. I loved the land you sold us because of the trees. Now I don't love it anymore for the same reason."

"You've really made up your mind?" he asked. "Only a week after the fire?"

"I made up my mind the day after the fire."

Gordon wasn't smiling anymore.

"You're an optimistic guy," I said. "I used to be one, too. Maybe I still am about other things. Just not this."

I shook his hand. "I admire how you're handling all of this, Gordon, I really do. But I'm too weak or discouraged to follow your example. And I don't even wish I could."

Wanda was gone, so I let myself in with the key she had left hidden for me outside. A week's worth of mail was piled up on her dining room table. I picked it up with every intention of leaving. But the many paintings, drawings, and sketches on Wanda's walls stopped me. I looked at them as a famished man might look at a freshly cooked meal. How lucky Wanda was to own all of this. And how strange it felt to be in a house with a roof, and four walls covered with art.

As I locked her house with the mail under my arm, it struck me that I was growing jealous of those whose life was marked by the ho-hum and the routine and who were surrounded by stuff so familiar to them that they probably didn't notice it.

CHAPTER 7

September 19, 2011, 9 a.m. We wondered what the dogs were thinking as we herded them into Holly's SUV the morning we relocated to Amelia's house in Colovista. We were moving because the Jensons were coming back from their trip abroad and our daughter had cleaned out the decaying and stinky mess in her refrigerator, the aftereffects of ten days without electricity.

For the next two weeks, we would live with her in a role reversal that no parent would want. We'd sleep on a twin bed in a spare room, eat her food, and lean on her for strength and whatever optimism remained in our family. Our twenty-three-year-old daughter would be the rock in our turbulent sea.

We divided everything we owned between our vehicles. Somebody with bad eyesight could have mistaken us for college students on summer break, schlepping our meager possessions from one makeshift living arrangement to another, except vagabonds wouldn't have a brood of yapping dogs as an escort.

Charlie jammed himself into the space in front of the passenger's seat, panting and slobbering. He looked as comfortable as a size 12 foot in a size 10 shoe. Miranda sat in back. Despite her best efforts, the nervous and agitated dachshunds roamed at will between the front and back, distracting Holly as they jumped on and off her lap. I drove alone, with every inch in my car taken up with what was left of our things.

As we turned onto McAllister Road, I thought of what I had seen from the high point of Cottletown Road an hour after the fire began. The bright yellow flares popping out of the smoke were now heaps of rubble much like our own.

As we neared Amelia's house, I suddenly and impulsively turned right onto the curved private road that once belonged to the man who developed Colovista and who had died several years before. As I drove up, I recalled a glorious spring afternoon almost two decades before when the land surrounding the driveway was so dense with trees and undergrowth that it was impossible to see his sprawling mansion teetering on the edge of a high bluff.

LES'S CHOICE

My friend Les had made a fortune in the Houston real estate market. On the surface, he was a jovial man, although I knew he had been a shark in the business world. As ruddy-faced as me, with two shocks of white hair parted almost in the middle and a slightly open-mouthed smile, he was large but not fat. He kept his emotions tightly under control. When he wanted to be friendly, he was a charming country gentleman. When he had a chip on his shoulder, it was best to steer clear of him. He lavished his philanthropic impulses on his alma mater, Texas A&M University. One of the student dormitories is named after him.

During the time I was county judge, we spent lots of time together, mainly playing golf. Les occasionally invited me to his house for dinner parties with people he wanted to impress or—as was more often the case—who wanted to impress him. It was one of the largest and most opulent in Bastrop County, with a twenty-mile view across the river to the south.

"You're pretty lucky to see this day in and day out," I told him at one of his evening get-togethers when we were the only two on the cantilevered deck as a brilliantly orange circle inched its way under the horizon.

He smiled. "No sunset is ever the same."

One sunny and mild April afternoon, Les asked me to come over and bring one of my daughters. Four-year-old and cute-as-all-get-out Amelia volunteered.

"So what's on the agenda?" I said as he met me on the driveway in shorts, a collared short-sleeved shirt with the A&M insignia, and cap.

"I'm going to show you something that I've been thinking about for a long time." He pointed to his lumbering and oversized black SUV that could have passed for a Secret Service detail. "And who do we have here?"

"This is my daughter Amelia." She grinned at him and wiggled into a comfortable spot between us.

Les drove us across the breadth of a subdivision and golf course he was about to develop. He called it Colovista, a word he made up that alluded to the property's most prominent features: the river and the views that surrounded it.

After an hour of driving across undulating fields among mature and beautiful pines, oaks, and cedar elms, he pointed south and said, "I have to show you something I'm calling Alleluia Corner." He had the audacious idea that the most picturesque hole of his course, and the two that bracketed it, would eventually be worthy of homage to the legendary trio of holes at Augusta National. We trudged up a steep hill and found ourselves gasping, at first from the exertion and then from what we saw. Amelia stopped yacking.

"This will be number 15, the signature hole," he said. "People will play the course just to experience this."

From where we stood, the Colorado River bent in two directions 150 feet below. The trees that bordered the river were tall, leafy, and magical, and not like what we were used to in the Lost Pines. They weren't better, just different. My friend bent down, dug through some dirt, and pulled out a flinty arrowhead, the evidence of human settlement on this ground from hundreds or even thousands of years ago. Then he found several more.

"Would you like a couple of these, little girl?" he asked Amelia.

"Sure," she chirped. "They're nice."

"Be careful, though," he said. "You can see how sharp they are."

We stood on the plateau, the western sun starting to sink and a warm breeze blowing. No wonder Les was so proud and full of expectation.

The subdivision and golf course came to pass largely in the way he described it to Amelia and me that Saturday afternoon. Les had the financial wherewithal to live anywhere in the world, and he chose the southern extremity of the Lost Pines for his retirement. Because I liked and respected him, I was glad he never had to see how the fire punished his choice.

September 19, 2011, 9:45 a.m. The blackened slab where his home used to be was strewn with twisted metal and bricks. The metal struts that supported the cantilevered deck hung over the cliff like bones with the meat picked off them. Judging from the lack of footprints in the ash, it appeared I was the first person to see any of it.

Les built his home on the highest point in Colovista, which meant it was one of the most exposed sites in Bastrop County. Like our doomed six-acre ridgetop property that was incinerated in 2009, his homestead took the absolute worst the fire had to give. The forty acres of trees that protected his privacy couldn't have looked worse if the air force had firebombed them.

"From the most spectacular place in the county to the ugliest," I thought.

"Where did you go?" asked Holly as I pulled into Amelia's driveway.

I tried to explain myself.

"You didn't think we might need some help carrying in our things?"

"I'm here now."

"We need your help and you're somewhere else, getting upset all over again I'm sure."

"It didn't make me feel good, if that's any consolation."

I was reeling from what I had just seen, but I clearly wasn't going to get any sympathy. It felt like an injustice.

With the air around us charged with testiness, we lugged some of our things into one of Amelia's spare bedrooms and the rest into the other.

"Where will I sleep?" Miranda asked.

"How about the sofa?" her sister said. "When you're ready to go to bed each night, we can spread out a blanket. It already has pillows."

Like she had done since the fire ruined her birthday, Miranda accepted the situation without complaint.

After things cooled down between us, Holly and I tried out the spare bed. It was barely big enough for two children, much less a pair of middle-aged adults. To be comfortable, we'd have to lie on our sides and face the same way. We'd have to turn over in tandem. It wasn't much different from our sleeping arrangements when we began our married days in a dingy and rickety second-floor suburban Chicago apartment with a smallish mattress on the floor.

Absent the facts, the situation would have been comical. But chuckling was the last thing I felt like doing as I wedged my body into one of my daughter's stuffed chairs and replayed the events that had led us to this point. Two weeks earlier, we were prepared for Amelia to live with us in the Cottletown house—the one now lying in ashes—for the indefinite future. We wondered how much help she'd need to replace her things. We tried to imagine how we'd balance our parental instincts and compulsions with our daughter's natural capabilities as an adult.

Now I wondered if it was possible to cross a line as an able-bodied adult dependent on a grown child.

The daily cycle of sleep envy and sleep deprivation that began at the Jenson house took complete control at Amelia's. I would climb out of bed in the morning, foggy-minded and headachy, sore from the cramped accommodations, and out of sorts that another night had turned out so differently from what I needed and deserved. During the day, I clung to the belief that I had reached the point where sleep would be physically unavoidable that night. After going to bed with a combination of anticipation and fear, a brief interlude of light sleep would turn into hours of wakefulness—my legitimate wages unjustly denied.

To make things worse, my insomnia unleashed a nightly stream of second-guessing and recriminations about a multitude of decisions that had brought us to this point.

A month before the fire, I read Jennifer Egan's novel *A Visit from the Goon Squad*. The fact that it had won the Pulitzer Prize was enough to get me past an off-putting title that hinted at mob violence and trash talk. I admired and devoured Egan's tales of interwoven lives, and how the passage of time can rough anyone up, not just those who make stupid decisions that unwind in unfortunate ways.

I got her point about time being a creature with no empathy or remorse. But as I read the book, I found little to regret in my life as I reflected on who I had chosen to marry, how my relationships with my children had turned out, my professional accomplishments, and the comfortable life I had created for myself in Central Texas. I decided that if Egan's goon squad paid me a visit, all it'd get would be a derisive laugh and the sight of my middle finger.

I was wrong about that. At 1 or 2 a.m. each night in Amelia's spare bedroom, it had its way with me, administering a beating with the punches of what-ifs and the knees-to-the-groin of might-have-beens.

Why did we move to a hot and dry state when we could have ended up in a place like Oregon or Northern California? Land in Sonoma County that was cheap in 1979 now cost a fortune. With better planning, and a lot more luck, we might have ended up with a vineyard and millions in equity instead of a heap-on-a-slab and land we'd be lucky to give away.

My fantasies about Northern California morphed into grandiose visions of forgone Silicon Valley fame and riches. Steve Jobs and Bill Gates were both born within months of me in 1955, and who's to say what could have happened if we had moved to the West Coast in 1979, precisely the moment before personal technology started changing the world?

But what if Holly and I actually had chosen somewhere else and built far different lives? There would be no marriage of Hillary and Jared and therefore no Benjamin. In fact, a different set of personal and professional circumstances could have meant fewer daughters or no children at all. Divorce couldn't be ruled out either. And just as riches could have poured over us, so too could have spectacular failure and the ruinous temptations that go with it. I could be an addict or homeless or both.

No home in Central Texas meant no trip to Colorado in 2003 and, therefore, a far different Miranda. Would I want a different Miranda? Should a question like that even be posed?

My dead-of-night mind was pernicious. Instead of channeling my insomnia in sensible and productive ways—giving thanks that Amelia and I didn't perish, planning for what had to be done in the coming weeks—I involuntarily rewound the tape on incidents in my life that felt like punishments for who I was and how I did things. At the top of the list: my up-and-down relationship with Barbara Jordan and my ersatz job interview with a future president.

THE PRICE OF BEING MYSELF

Barbara Jordan was the most visible icon at the LBJ School and a professor sought out by almost every student. On the first day of the 1984 fall semester, I joined nineteen other lucky students around a long conference table with Professor Jordan in her wheelchair at the head seat with a fierce gaze and elbows perched. Her voice and elocution were as impressive and intimidating as I expected they would be. The class was Policy Development, which meant it was a vessel for her many tales of coming into power and making use of it.

"I could not have been elected without the Voting Rights Act and the 'one man, one vote' Supreme Court decision," she explained to her adoring students one memorable day with the autumnal light from the nearby parking lot saturating the room.

To my eyes, as well as her own, Professor Jordan embodied what the civil rights and voting rights laws had done to transform American society for the better. For several months, during private talks in her office, she stoked the idea that I should join the brotherhood and sisterhood of elective office. With her encouragement, I began to see myself as someone who could be trusted to do the right thing if I was given the power to improve people's lives. I could hardly believe how lucky I was to have a personal bond with her.

Then one day in early November, to the shock and embarrassment of my classmates, we had a brief and rancid falling out. The class was discussing the various ways in which political campaigns are funded, and I mentioned that I found the British method of pure public financing to be particularly attractive.

"What is it about this model you like so much?" she asked, her eyes narrowing behind her largish glasses.

"I think it does away with the corrupting influence of money."

"So you think people who take political contributions are automatically corrupt?"

Given her storied history in Texas politics, and the inevitability of her having accepted a lot of contributions over the years, I could see where this was going. "You're asking me to make a blanket statement, which I'm not sure I want to do," I said. My mouth was dry and my legs shook a little.

"Why not?" she said in a voice so deep it practically made the floor vibrate. "You said something, and I'm asking you to be more specific about what you meant."

"Look, I'm only saying I like the British way a lot better than how we do it here."

She lowered her gaze and asked, "If you like it so much, why don't you just move over there?"

I felt blood rising to my face. Perhaps I had unintentionally insulted her, but that was no reason for her to overtly insult me.

Nobody said anything as Professor Jordan and I stared at one another. Finally, with the air's frigidity seeping into every corner of the room, I said, "I think you owe me an apology."

Except for the two of us, every head in the room faced the floor.

"I beg your pardon," she said.

My voice was surprisingly steady. "I said I think you owe me an apology."

"And why is that?"

"Well, on the first day of class, you set out some ground rules, one of which was mutual respect. And just now I don't think you did to me what you expect of us."

After what seemed like a year, through teeth so clenched it was a wonder her face didn't lock up, she said, "I'm sorry for what I said to you."

For the remaining weeks of the semester, she and I debated topics that I knew had been devoid of controversy since she began teaching. I couldn't help picking a fight, and she couldn't resist returning fire. We took no pleasure in it, but we also couldn't seem to stop ourselves.

How could I have let my nearly pathological need to speak my mind squander the opportunities that might have come to me if I had remained on the short list of Barbara Jordan's favorite students? Where might I have ended up if I hadn't shamed her into that apology?

With my wife quietly snoring, time's goon squad kneecapped me with the memory of my one-on-one encounter with George W. Bush.

In 1997, I became acquainted with a prosperous businessman who was an informal adviser to the Texas governor. One day he and I discussed career options in his Houston office, full of family photos and mementos of his business and civic accomplishments. He was a genteel southern gentleman of the old school, soft-spoken and seemingly impossible to ruffle.

After discussing a range of possibilities, he agreed to arrange a meeting with Governor Bush in which I would pitch him a few of my many ideas for turning the machinery of state government into something less lumbering and creaky. With any luck, Bush would see me as I saw myself: a self-confident dynamo who could crank out bright-eyed concepts for him in the morning and figure out how to turn them into reality in the afternoon.

And so it was that I found myself one bright and hot July morning in the high-ceilinged anteroom of the governor's office, waiting to be ushered in. After the inevitable wait that always seems engineered to remind the supplicant of who's in charge, I was led into the governor's office, a wood-paneled, oversized room. Governor Bush rose from his desk to shake my hand. His chief of staff stood to the side.

"Sit down and make yourself comfortable," said Bush. He leaned forward in his chair, put his elbows on his desk, and gestured with his head to the other man.

"This is Joe, my right-hand man. He probably seems scary, but he's really just a lovable teddy bear who's only here to make sure I don't get too far off script."

While Bush was trim, of medium build, and apparently as friendly and approachable as his supporters and handlers assured the country he was, his aide had the look of a drill sergeant and the demeanor of an IRS agent who has just caught a tax cheat in the act.

"So what are we here to talk about?" asked Bush.

His question startled me. I assumed he knew I was there to talk myself into a job in his office. "You're asking me why I'm here?"

He laughed. "All I know is that a mutual friend of ours suggested we get together for a little visit. So here we are."

I quickly realized I had the solution in my hand. I handed Bush a list of the ideas I originally intended to present as evidence of my worth. "And this is what?" he asked.

"Some of my ideas for reforming state government that I've been thinking about for a while," I said. "Unfortunately, I didn't bring a copy for Joe."

"That's OK. I'll give him mine after we finish up. So walk me through your list."

Fifteen minutes later, with Bush's feet now up on his desk, and his fingers knitted together behind his tilted-back head, we were laughing and enjoying one another's company, and I concluded that I really wanted to work for this amiable man.

"So what's the bottom line here?" said Bush. "You've got all these good ideas. Now what?"

"I want to work for you and make them happen."

"Really?"

"I know it's sort of unconventional, what I'm proposing. But I'd like to be something like a special projects director, if that's the right term."

Turning to his chief of staff, he said: "Can you set up some interviews with him and the usual suspects? See what might be possible?"

"Of course, Governor." They were his first words since we both sat down.

For five more minutes, Bush and I chatted and yukked it up. By the time I left his office, it seemed certain that I would soon be in his orbit, with many more genial encounters in store and his reflected glow giving me the necessary authority to turn my ideas into actual achievements.

"Got a minute?" asked Joe as soon as we were free of Bush's gatekeepers. He pointed to his office and marched me in.

He didn't waste time or words. "I don't know how you got past our usual screening procedures and ended up in there. But I can assure you that this is not how we do things here. You managed to get the governor interested, and he asked me to show you around, so that's what will have to happen. But there's a big difference between you having a few sit-downs with his senior staff and your dream coming true."

By the time he showed me out, I was deflated, my bubbly encounter with Bush now completely flat. After the senior staff visits he arranged, my communication with the governor's office went radio-silent. Then, purely by chance, I ran into Joe one day at the Capitol and he agreed to wrap things up within a week, one way or the other. He turned down my offer to immediately put me out of my misery.

True to his word, he called me several days later and offered me a job in Bush's budget office. "We posted it several weeks ago. It isn't as sexy as what you probably think you deserve. But it's yours if you want it." He gave me the quick-and-dirty on the job's duties and salary.

"What are the odds of face time with the governor?" I asked.

"Slim to none."

I didn't want to be rude, so I asked a few more benign questions and then said, "Thanks, but I think I'll pass." Three years later, almost to the day, Bush delivered his acceptance speech to the Republican National Convention.

Who knows what would have happened if I hadn't brushed away Joe's outstretched hand? When Bush moved into the Oval Office, he set up an administration top-heavy with Texans, some of who had started with him in state jobs with similar duties to the one I was offered. I would have had three years—an eternity in the world of politics and government—to prove my ability and trustworthiness in an office with lots of turnover as his senior staff cashed in their chips to work on the presidential campaign.

Were these incidents emblematic of some deep failing in me that unleashed a chain reaction culminating in our present, pitiful situation? How much different would things have turned out if I merely followed the example of almost everyone else I knew: know your place, keep quiet, salute authority, and find no fault with the status quo?

September 23, 2011, 9:30 a.m. As the days at Amelia's progressed, my sleeplessness became more than a guarantee of bodily debilitation and cascading self-doubt. It began to manifest itself like termites in the building materials of my brain.

One morning, I drove back to the Smithville post office. The same good-hearted man who helped me the morning after the fire was at the window.

"Good to see you again. How can I help you?"

"We're moving to a rental house in Austin on October 1 and we need to forward our mail beginning that day."

"It will take a little time for the changes to hit the system, so it's good you're doing this now," he said. "Fill out this form and I can take care of the rest."

He gave me a pen and form, and I began by accidentally reversing my old and new addresses.

"May I please have another form? I made a mistake on this one."

"No problem."

Another form immediately led to another mistake.

"Can I have another one, please?"

It happened again.

"Once more, from the top," I said.

This time he had a solution. "Why don't you let me fill this out for you? I can take what you've already written and ask you the remaining questions."

"It can't be this difficult. I don't understand."

"You've got other things to think about. I'm glad to do it for you."

Feeling humiliated, I took an armful of mail to a semiprivate spot in the post office and weeded out the junk. Seeing our old address on each piece made my stomach hurt.

Several days later, during a break between racquetball games, our foreheads glistening and our T-shirts pockmarked with perspiration, I described this experience to one of my brainy buddies, a cancer researcher with a doctorate who lost his home on McAllister Road.

"To be honest, given what we've been through, I don't think that's strange at all," he said.

"But it was such a simple form. A fourth-grader could have filled it out."

"I'd trust a fourth-grader more than myself on lots of things these days."

"You finding it almost impossible to concentrate?"

"Are you kidding? I make simple, stupid mistakes all the time," he said.

"And sleep?"

"What do you think?"

"And nothing to be done about any of it, I suppose," I said.

With his lips slightly upturned, he shrugged.

At least it was a comfort to know that his formerly topnotch mind was becoming as mushy as mine.

I compared notes on the situation with Walter. We both agreed it seemed to take twice as long to accomplish half as much, assuming we even had the energy and focus to do that.

"I know some people over the years have taken exception to how I do things," I told Holly one night, as we got ready to brush our teeth in Amelia's second bathroom. "But nobody, and I mean nobody, has ever accused me of being inept or out to lunch."

"The way things are now, the horrible way we feel, it isn't going to last," Holly said.

"So you say. All I know is I've gone from helping a half-million kids to wondering some mornings if I still know how to tie my shoelaces."

MY GREAT CAUSE

Although it seems impossible to believe today, there was a time not long ago when Congress and the president linked arms and did something meaningful and wonderful to help struggling families. The new program's spiritual grandfather was my role model Wilbur Cohen.

The Children's Health Insurance Program (CHIP), which came into being during the Clinton administration, gave states the flexibility to create subsidized health insurance programs bred from their cultural, demographic, and political DNA.

In 1998, my boss at the Texas Department of Health asked me to join forces with a man in a sister agency to start working on the Texas version. My new partner, Julian, and I had personalities and work habits that were mirror images of one another. We built a powerful partnership by combining our relative strengths and looking past our respective shortcomings.

Julian and I had been around government long enough to understand the opportunity and obligation that we had been given. If we did our jobs well, hundreds of thousands of Texas parents would gain peace of mind and their kids would get the medical and dental care they needed. For a results-obsessed guy like me, it was a miracle.

In the hurly-burly world of Texas state government, Julian's cautious temperament and Quaker upbringing made me think of a monk patiently and carefully picking his way through a street teeming with people and activity, all of it noisy and some of it disreputable.

The slow pace and dead ends of policy-making in a large bureaucracy didn't rile him up. In his dealings with legislators and the governor's office, he draped himself in a cloak of deference that never took on the color of obsequiousness. He was always aware that all the good we intended to accomplish together could be undone by an unfortunate remark uttered in the wrong setting.

I worked fast and efficiently, sometimes cut corners, loved to kick the tires on untested ideas, and harbored a rebel's attitude. When it came to the uninsured children of Texas, it wasn't easy for me to safely harness my zealotry.

He was a perfect counterweight to me. I was the flaming ball to his pool of deep water.

We put together two side-by-side teams, working in separate buildings. He took care of the legal and policy-making side. I was in charge of operations.

In 1999, the legislature authorized the Texas version based on a conceptual design the two of us developed. Governor Bush's budding "compassionate conservative" national identity meant we had to build and launch a juggernaut that showed Texas state government cared about its children.

The first sign that our work had national implications came almost immediately. Shortly after we got our marching orders, the deadline got moved up by five months. The second sign appeared on a day trip to the district of a powerful legislator who was firmly in the Bush-for-president camp.

We were dispatched to his West Texas hometown in a state-owned plane. We had barely arrived before he got right to the point. With a smile—the kind that inspires terror rather than affection—he wrote "428,000" and "September 1, 2001" in big numbers on a flipchart. Translation: Julian and I must enroll 428,000 children within seventeen months. Succeed or else.

On the trip back, we compared notes and did the math.

"It's a ridiculous goal," I said. "It can't be done."

"We'll find a way."

"You know what this is all about, right?"

"The children."

"Whatever, dude. Just because you're not willing to say it doesn't mean it's not true."

I delivered the news to my team the next day.

"Julian is being his usual stoic self," I said. "But I'm not going to lie to you. We're being set up to fail, and all because a certain person wants to be president. The best we can hope for is to help as many children as we can before we all get the boot."

My cohesive and supremely competent team and I moved forward at a breakneck pace. Working out of a standard-issue office building in northwest Austin, I cultivated an environment that was as raucous and fun as it was productive.

Everything about CHIP was why I got into government in the first place. I had one big strategic goal—bring health insurance to a ton of Texas children—that devolved into a series of tricky tactical problems. My biological need to get things done was continuously gratified.

The fact that our marching orders boiled down to a single number yielded one unexpected but wonderful dividend: we were left to our own devices so long as progress was clearly being made. Any state bureaucrat quickly learns that external overseers and internal second-guessers almost always suffocate a new idea before it can leave its crib and start crawling around on its own. But we had free rein to do what we thought necessary if the numbers kept rocketing up, which they did.

Besides Wilbur Cohen, my other professional role model was my grandfather, Casey Buteyn. At the end of each day, he knew what he and his staff had done. With each new monthly enrollment report, we knew how many more children had affordable health care, many for the first time.

Julian's optimism—whether sincere or feigned—proved to be right. By the time Texas CHIP was two years old, more than a half-million Texas children had the medical and dental care they needed and their parents could sleep easier.

Julian and I, with our tiny staffs, had embarked on a great cause and left our mark. No matter what followed in our careers, nothing would surpass it. I had proven to myself that my self-confidence was legitimate and a creative and sometimes contrary attitude could reap rewards in a bureaucratic environment engineered to suppress it.

Now, with my chronic sleeplessness and increasingly porous mental faculties, the strategic thinking and management skills of my CHIP days seemed like a hallucination. Not only was it hard to believe I would ever regain them, it seemed hard to believe I ever had them in the first place.

September 29, 2011, 10 a.m. "I'm going to run a few errands in town," I told Holly on a bright and hot Thursday morning.

"What for?"

"I just need to get some odds and ends. I won't be gone long."

The need for my lie was self-evident. If Holly knew I was going to inspect what the fire had done to the ecosystem of our daughters' childhoods and most of our marriage, she would have tried to talk me out of it, and we'd waste more time channeling our grief and exhaustion into another argument.

With my stomach in knots, I turned north on Alum Creek Road into the neighborhood where Amelia and Miranda were born. I passed what used to be the homes of several former friends and one of Hillary's childhood buddies. Nothing left.

Then I pulled into the property where Walter, my deceased brother-in-law Kevin, and I teamed up to build the cedar-clad house in 1986.

I stood on the scorched concrete slab where the house had been, my forehead drenched with sweat and my heart like a stone in my chest. Some of the nails I had hammered twenty-five years earlier poked up from the ash. I walked around the slab's perimeter, imagining each room and the wonderful things that had happened there.

This was the place where I would return if, like Emily in *Our Town*, I was given the opportunity to relive a day of priceless normality.

I would pick a cool, clear day in November 1991, with the smell of pancakes and fresh fruit filling the kitchen, and crystalline autumn sunlight pouring into the skylights. I would delight in baby Miranda scuttling across the pine floor Kevin and I laid, sanded, and sealed. Toddler Amelia would be bouncing on her parents' bed and chattering away. Grade-schooler Hillary, pretty with her ponytail, would be reading a book or practicing a dance step on the deck or playing with the dachshund. Holly and I would smile at each other, awash in what we had and what we assumed was to come. At the end of the day, we would read to our daughters, lying flat on our backs, side by side in their beds, with me next to the tulip-themed wallpaper Hillary had chosen for her bedroom. Before going to bed, Holly and I would stand on the wooden wraparound deck and gaze at the clear night sky through pine tops animated by a cool breeze.

A wildfire axiom hit me for the first time. Many icons of grief are tangible representations of a lost loved one, like a letter or an old picture. But now I knew that a wildfire's heirlooms are the absence of things, a void where something of great value and personal meaning once existed.

That house was an enormous heirloom of my life with my children when they were very young. It predictably and gratifyingly brought forth memories of some of my life's happiest moments. Now the heirloom was inverted into something-not-there.

It didn't matter that I hadn't set foot in the house since the day we moved out. Just driving by it, as I regularly did, was enough to warm my insides. Its absence felt like someone had found eight of the most important years of my life on a DVD, including the formative years of my children, and wiped it clean with no backup.

I continued down Alum Creek Road to Park Road 1C. I had correctly guessed that the link between Bastrop and Buescher State Parks had been hit hard, given its density of fuel. But nothing could have prepared me for what I saw.

A firestorm had ravaged this dense, verdant section of the Lost Pines. A horrific conflagration had passed through, and the trees that remained were utterly scorched. Some of them held a few lonely limbs, while others were little more than a stalk. The remaining pine bark had boiled and blistered. The forest's understory—a tangle of vegetation where armadillos and raccoons foraged, insects hid, birds nested and fed, and toads burrowed—had been converted into a dark and ugly powder, ash mixed with sterilized topsoil. Holes where trees had been were everywhere.

The devastation was absolute, and the voice inside my head reacted to it by spouting platitudinous questions and clichés.

How could this happen?

Could it look any worse?

I literally can't believe it.

Nobody would believe this unless they saw it with their own eyes.

I'll never forget this as long as I live.

As I neared the road where we had lived for almost a quarter century, I noticed a small group of young black men gathered near the intersection with Cottletown Road, digging through rubble and dumping trash on a flatbed trailer. This was the destroyed home of Reverend Williams, an African American minister I first met in his church twenty-two years earlier as I campaigned for county judge. This warm-hearted man with a deep laugh and salty hair was entering the same spiritual netherworld as me. I needed to speak with him.

He was silently sitting in a blackened metal chair, leaning back, wiping his forehead and impassively watching the junk slowly get piled on the trailer. Greetings and how-do-you-dos seemed beside the point, given the circumstances.

"I just came down the park road," I told him. "I don't know what to say."

"Yup."

"Words literally fail me."

"Me too, and for a preacher, that's saying something."

I surmised that the young shirtless men were from his church. They punctuated their work with an occasional respectful question to him.

"You're already cleaning up?" I said.

"Got to as long I've got these young'uns helping out."

I watched the guys churn through the wreckage, seemingly disinterested in what the ash and metal could do to them. Their energy mocked the heat and sun, their resolve apparent, their efficiency amazing. I was too impressed to feel sorry for them.

"Sometimes it helps being an old man," he said. "I guess these gray hairs mean I get to sit here and watch them do all the work. I told them to be careful. Maybe there's something in there I can save."

"Have they found anything?"

"Not yet, but they'll be at it for a while."

"Any idea of what you're going to do?"

"Rebuild."

"I find that hard to believe."

"What choice do I have? I'm too old to start over someplace else. And who would buy this place anyway?"

"I don't see how I could possibly keep living around here. How could I get up every day surrounded by all of this?"

As soon as I said that, I regretted it. While I had personal and financial options, he apparently did not. Or maybe he had fortitude and courage I lacked.

"If you had to, you'd figure out a way," he said.

He must have sensed my pity. "If you're feeling sorry for me, don't bother. I'll get through this. I've already got more help than I know what to do with. And, of course, there's always the Lord, who's looking out for me."

Then he did the most unexpected thing. This suddenly homeless man of the cloth, with few options and almost no possessions, told me a dirty joke. And we both laughed because it was really funny.

"I guess I needed that," I said. "I haven't laughed in what seems like a thousand years."

"That makes two of us."

"Good luck, Reverend. Don't know when I'll see you again. It is my personal goal to leave this neighborhood as soon as I can and never come back."

Like me, he had lost a home he had built himself. When Miranda and I rode our bikes on Park Road 1C, I would sometimes run into him or see him with his horse. His generous smile was so reliable that it seemed etched on his face. In spite of everything, that etching was still visible. I didn't know what to make of it.

A few minutes later, I parked my car just past the red gate and slowly walked down my driveway, past the trees I loved, now dead or dying. Some of the mess on our slab had been removed, and the rest was piled up in heaps. As I took it all in, a malignant thought formed: I am to blame for this.

Why hadn't I made my stand as the fire threatened my home? Why hadn't I stood there with a hose pointed at the house? As the smoke clouds thickened and the embers began to fall, why wasn't I raking away the thick cushion of pine needles that surrounded the deck? What sort of man would allow his home and property to be attacked like this? Someone must be held to account for this unspeakable sight, and who else is there besides me?

With those thoughts, I took my place in a parade that stretches back to the dawn of human experience. Children blame themselves for their parents' divorce, a soldier berates himself for surviving an IED blast that maimed his best friend, the parent or sibling of a suicide victim rushes around looking for the evidence of what they did to drive the beloved to the ultimate act of self-destruction. And the victim of a wildfire castigates himself for lack of an alternative.

As I walked toward what had been a tangle of trees and undergrowth, I saw something so remarkable that it seemed impossible to believe.

I was within a few steps of one of my favorite places on my ten acres before the drought did it in: the small ephemeral pond Gordon dug out to support the endangered Houston Toad. After a good spring rain, the pond filled to overflowing. For days or weeks afterward, as the water slowly evaporated, we would hear an amphibian din as darkness fell. On warm and humid nights, we heard the unmistakable trilling of the males, on the make and looking for love.

The pond dried up early in 2011, and the balmy spring evenings that year were silent. I didn't know whether the Houston toads that I periodically saw near the pond or close to our house had survived. But now I had evidence that at least one had.

At my feet was a perfectly formed but completely dried-out Houston toad. It was like a sculptural hymn to the Lost Pines, every detail minutely rendered, including tiny webbed toes and eyes that still held their pupils. Like any amorous male toad, it was crouched on its hind legs, full of anticipation. I didn't dare touch it for fear it would turn to dust in my fingers.

The last stop on my tour was the large red-brick house on Long Trail where we lived for fourteen years. By this time, I felt like beef coming out of a grinder.

The Long Trail house was a traditional Colonial design. The two chimneys that anchored opposite ends of the house were the only things still standing. How could such a well-built house be reduced to a heap destined for a landfill?

Passing the two dead trees that once held up our old hammock, and where the silver eye screws still poked out, I walked down to the concrete pad where a group of my buddies gathered many Saturday mornings for three-on-three basketball served up with good-natured cussing and trash talk.

There was no trace of the wooden fence I built to keep the ball from rolling into the woods. The netless hoop called to mind a decrepit playground in some beat-down neighborhood. The air barely moved and the sun asserted itself. The scene would have been inconceivable the late winter weekend in 2000 that Hillary and her teammates made one of my dreams come true.

THE LADY TIGERS GO ALL THE WAY

My oldest daughter had been a starter on her high school basketball team since she was a sophomore, about the time she started joining my fellow hoopsters for our Saturday morning games. At first my buddies were apologetic whenever she ran face-first into a screen. They'd let her have an uncontested layup instead of blocking her path and possibly knocking her down. It was easy for her to rebound when nobody put a body on her.

But after I laid into them one morning, insisting that they treat her no differently than they did me, she began to develop the kinds of skills and instincts that could come only from playing against men—people taller, heavier, and smellier than her. They got used to roughing her up, and that only made her play better.

Each year, her team—the Smithville Lady Tigers—made it deeper into the playoffs. While nothing was guaranteed for her senior year, I started to fantasize about seeing my daughter play on the home court of the University of Texas in an arena that seated over sixteen thousand fans.

The Lady Tigers rumbled through the preseason and district play, with most games never in doubt. They had to win four playoff games to get to the Erwin Center, and they did, two by the skin of their teeth. Each game had a different standout player. Hillary was not one of them.

On the day before the state semifinal, I made her an offer: score at least ten points and I'll give you a hundred bucks. Perhaps money could do what her coach's shouting and chest poking couldn't.

The score went back and forth until the fourth quarter, when the Lady Tigers took the Lady Texans of Wimberley High School in an eleven-point run. In the middle of this unanswered run, Hillary dropped off the ball to a teammate and pivoted toward the basket, where a crisp pass found her near the free-throw line. *Swish.* It was a textbook pick-and-roll play that netted Hillary eleven points for the game and a Franklin in her wallet. She ran down the court, pumping her fists. I was the only person in the arena who knew why.

While her point total was admirable, her defense was the difference in the game. Hillary was the X factor in the semifinal, and she landed on the front page of the sports sections in the Austin and San Antonio newspapers. I stockpiled copies in my home office, where I was certain to see them every day.

The Lady Tigers lost in the state final by three points. Hillary's defensive assignment was a UT recruit who would later briefly play in the WNBA. My daughter's performance was a wonderful display of effort and spirit. It was also a complete mismatch. My consolation prize from the championship game was a picture of the future WNBAer launching a jump hook that barely cleared my daughter's outstretched arms. It was taken by a sports photographer for the Austin newspaper who sent me several large prints, one of which I framed and hung near my piano.

During my brief Labor Day trip back to the house, I saved the framed picture but never gave the newspapers or the other photos a thought.

September 29, 2011, 11:30 a.m. Standing on the basketball court, I turned to where the house had been. With my heart in a vise, I knew I would never again set foot on the property where Miranda lost and regained her speech and my daughters turned into young women.

I correctly guessed that Holly would reproach me for making this visit, and in a way she was right when she said it was needless self-torture. But how could I close the book on the Long Trail chapter of my life without one final, sorrowful good-bye to it?

I returned to my car and headed back toward Colovista, passing the place on Highway 71 where the man who crafted our cabinets had lived and worked. I saw him picking through the remains of his shop, his shoulders slumped, his head down, surrounded by an aura of tragedy. His grief seemed so palpable that I briefly pulled to the side of the road, wondering if I should go back and talk with him. But I didn't, because the last thing a broken man needs is another broken man with whom to compare notes.

Late September 2011. For the two weeks we lived at Amelia's, I was regularly at our Cottletown property, keeping an eye on the progress of the debris removal.

Because they had salvage value, the metal roof and appliance hulks were the first to go. Once all of that was out of the way, the mess was dragged and pushed into small piles where it was picked up and loaded into a brown dumpster close to where the carport had been. Most of this was done with a small, noisy loader with oversized back wheels that could do a 360-degree turn from a standing position.

The middle-aged and grizzled man behind the sticklike steering mechanism took little notice of me except to answer my questions. From the look on his face, he could have been cleaning out the holding pen of a dairy farm.

As the work progressed, I couldn't decide what was worse: the house's remains or their absence. With the junk in place, I was reminded what my house looked like. But each time an overflowing dumpster was hauled off, these reminders were swapped for a swatch of bare concrete. Looking at a smooth, hard surface where a room had been drove the point home even more emphatically: the house that Walter designed and I built was turning into a memory.

Nothing worth keeping was found, with one exception. One day, as the job was nearing its end, the loader operator turned off the engine and pulled something shiny out of his pocket.

"Any idea what this is?" he asked.

It was one of Miranda's Special Olympics medals. Of the couple dozen that she had draped over her closet door, and that we were reminded of each time she slammed it, one was left.

"How in the world did you find it?"

"The glare from it almost blinded me when my scoop popped it out of the ash."

"She had quite a few of them. I don't suppose you found any others."

"Nope. Just this one."

"And I bet you found it right here." I pointed to the turn in the wall where her closet had been.

"That's right."

"Thank you. It's miraculous it didn't melt," I said.

"Not only that, there's not a nick or scratch on it."

The job was finished several days before we moved to Austin. I met with the owner of the disposal company on my bare foundation. Several hours earlier, his men had wiped off the remaining ash and dust with large brooms.

"What are you going to do now?" he asked.

"You mean about the slab?"

"Right. Are you going to rebuild?"

"If we do, it won't be here."

"If you want, we can break it up and haul it off."

"I'm thinking we leave it for the time being. If we can talk someone into buying this place, maybe they can do something with it."

"I'm not sure it's any good," he said. "Even if it's not cracked, the drain pipes might be boogered up."

He had a point. I called the man who had done the plumbing. He was the son of the man who did the plumbing on the house Walter, Kevin, and I built in 1986. I trusted him because I trusted his father.

"You're right about the drainage," he said. "Supply pipes aren't an issue because you can always go through the walls. But if the drains are shot, the slab will have to be torn out."

"Is it possible to find out?"

"Yes, and I'm happy to do it for you. I'll be in that area next week and I don't mind stopping by."

"That's really good of you, Jeff. How's your old man doing these days?"

It was a routine question: whenever we talked, I asked him about his dad.

"I guess you haven't heard. The fire wiped him and Mother out."

This dreadful news almost knocked the wind out of me.

"Where are they living?"

"With me. They never threw anything out. Now they barely have their clothes on their backs."

He reminded me they'd been married almost fifty years.

"They're staying with you indefinitely?" I asked.

"At least until they can get back on their feet. She's taking it harder than he is."

"Please let them know how sorry I am."

"They lost a lot of things that can't be replaced. Pictures, of course, but lots of mementos and other stuff like that. When you start to add it all up, it's pretty overwhelming."

The bad news about Jeff's parents was proof—not that I needed it—that the fire was far from finished with me. With seventeen hundred newly homeless families, this kind of conversational jolt would keep happening.

It was probably time to ask for help. But first I wanted to know what I was getting myself into. Amelia seemed a good person to ask because her graduate studies were preparing her to become a mental health counselor.

"You want to know what therapy is like? What happens? How it works?" said Amelia.

"Yes, I guess that's what I want to know."

There wasn't a simple answer, so we stopped talking after a few unsatisfying minutes. My daughter left me with a final thought: "What's the harm in trying it? If you think you need it, you probably do."

I had a choice to make, and to help me make it, I created a list. The list's title was "Do I need therapy?"

Spontaneous outbursts of crying? Check.

Chronic sleeplessness? Check.

A nonexistent libido? Check.

An impulse to use alcohol for reasons unrelated to meals and conversation? Check.

Newfound curiosity about the effects of certain drugs, legal or otherwise? Check.

The list spoke for itself. But there was one more hurdle: what would it say about me if I got mental health services?

In my pre-fire days, when I worked in the executive suite of the state's public health and mental health agency, I had the luxury of pondering mental illness in theoretical terms. It was a disease rather than a self-inflicted condition one snaps out of or defeats through an act of will. Those who stigmatized it were ignorant and unsympathetic.

But now I was on the verge of committing that sin on myself. Nobody would know I was going into therapy except for my family and anyone else I chose to tell. But I would know, and that knowledge might be humiliating and degrading. To make things worse, I felt humiliated by my fear of humiliation because of something I had been told soon after Hurricanes Katrina and Rita hit in 2005.

My posthurricane assignments at that time were making sure evacuees with special needs were taken care of. At our daily briefings, I updated my fellow agency executives on the mechanics of how this was being accomplished. Inevitably, one of my colleagues brought up the subject of mental health services and reminded us that we couldn't focus only on evacuees' physical needs. Whenever he said this, I thought: Whatever. Just don't ask me to do anything that takes my attention away from shelter and medical supplies.

Now, in my fatigued and demoralized state, I would have gladly swapped air-conditioning and my daily three meals for seven hours of uninterrupted sleep and a little inner peace. Turns out my former colleague was right: disaster mental health services are a big deal. But I was having a hard time putting that knowledge to work for myself.

A day after my talk with Amelia, I dug up the e-mail from Mother Lisa that Hillary forwarded to me the night of the Packers game. Without any idea of where it would lead, I called the woman who was matching up burned-out families with a collective of Austin-area therapists willing to donate their time or charge a reduced rate.

Her voice was warm and comforting.

"First, let me tell you how sorry I am about what's happened," she said. "As you know, we have lots of friends in the Bastrop area, as well as family, and many of them are suffering, just like you. I'm glad to play a small part in what will undoubtedly be a long recovery."

"Even though I have no idea what it involves, or what it will be like, I don't think I have a choice but to give therapy a try."

"Of course you have a choice. In fact, the first step is making that choice."

"Let's just say I've decided not to say no to it. So what happens next?"

"The first thing is finding you a therapist. Have you given any thought as to what kind of person you'd like to see?"

She gave me a minute to think. The answer quickly came: an older version of Mother Lisa.

"If it's any help, we won't have to worry about coordinating travel to Bastrop," I said. "We're moving to Austin and I'd prefer to have my sessions there anyway. I'm not thrilled by the idea of running into someone I know."

"Let me make some calls. Once I find a suitable possibility, you will hear from her directly."

"I don't suppose you can tell me what it's going to be like."

"If you want a hard-and-fast description, there isn't one."

"I figured."

"As least you're willing to give it a try. Lots of people are finding it hard to do that."

At dinner that evening, I told Holly, Miranda, and Amelia what I had done. "What do you think?" I asked Holly.

"Time will tell. But I don't see any harm in it."

"Maybe we should do it together," I said.

She said no but Miranda said yes. "I want to go to therapy with you."

"Maybe you should go by yourself," I said. "You're old enough."

"No, I want to go with you."

So it was settled. Father and daughter would enter a world of healing to which I had paid lip service for years. It was a surprise to find that my decision made me feel stronger and more clear-headed than I had been in weeks.

Late September 2011. "If we don't move back to our old place, then where are we going to live?" Miranda asked repeatedly. We could deflect the question while we camped out at the Jensons. But there was no escaping it at Amelia's because Miranda wanted to stay in Bastrop County, and being there reminded her of what she'd miss if we ended up elsewhere. As long as she lived with us, it wouldn't be fair to summarily dismiss her desires.

Having two adult daughters and a grandson in the Austin area meant we weren't leaving Central Texas, even though this was the best chance we'd ever have to move somewhere with a more agreeable climate.

We divided our choice into three basic categories. We could buy a new property somewhere in the Lost Pines that still had life, move somewhere else in the county outside of the burn zone, or relocate to Austin. There was also the question of building something from scratch or buying an existing house and being done with it.

While it was too soon to make any long-term decisions, we also knew that doing nothing would make it almost impossible to look beyond the fire and toward any kind of positive future.

This dilemma became clear one morning as Holly and I walked the dogs across the greenbelt behind Amelia's house. Charlie and the wieners were getting used to their leashes and the lack of continuity in their surroundings. They were more tolerant of other creatures, although yapping and shoulder strains were still to be expected. While our twice-daily walks in Austin had been as enjoyable as a bunion, they were now becoming tolerable and sometimes even comical.

"Just to be clear, we're not rebuilding, right?" I said.

"You've said more than once that you can't go back and live there. And I've seen how your visits affect you. So what is there to decide?"

"That's the way I feel, but how do you feel?"

"I could probably imagine a way for us to stay there, but you can't. So I guess that's that."

"OK then."

"We're pretty raw and exposed right now," said Holly. "Do you think it's wise to be making any decisions beyond that one? Maybe we should wait a while."

"I can see that, but I also wonder if the uncertainty will drive us crazy. Miranda won't leave us alone until we tell her what we're going to do."

"We can't let our daughter push us into doing something we might regret."

"I agree we shouldn't buy anything right away," I said. "But I think it will help if we can at least see what's available while we're out here."

A real estate agent familiar with the Colovista area lived across the street from Amelia. We saw her or her husband most mornings when we walked the dogs. We asked her for help, and she immediately sprang into action. "I can show you some properties right around here. Do you want to try any other areas as well?"

"Let's take it one at a time," I said.

We piled into her car and five minutes later were walking around the first possibility.

"There are dead trees all around here," I said.

"We'll have to get out of the pines entirely if you don't want to see any."

"But there are some places where the fire didn't go."

"Pristine properties probably aren't for sale."

It took less than an hour to look at three properties that left us feeling flat and unmotivated.

"Should we call it a day?" I asked.

"We can if you want. But there is one more place I'd like to show you. Once you see it, you'll understand why I saved it for last. It's literally just over the hill."

"If you don't mind us continuing to waste your time, I'd like to see it," said Holly.

"Looks like I'm outnumbered," I said.

We drove up a one-block street. I had a vague recollection of the place from many years before. I remembered going down the cul-de-sac after a round of golf to see what was back there and being surprised to find land that went down to the river. I wondered who owned such a place and why nothing had been built there. I also remembered being envious of the lucky owner.

As we walked up, the property's graces and beauty were evident to anyone whose mind was open and eyes clear. That group did not include me.

"There's a lot to see here," said Sandy. "Let's start at the top and work our way down to the river."

The fire had ravaged part of the five acres, a ravine with smallish pines and cedars clinging to a steep hillside. The vegetation was burned off and the trees were probably doomed.

We lumbered up a steep incline to a thin strip of cleared land perched a hundred feet above the river. It was a long and skinny rectangle.

"A boxcar without wheels would fit very nicely up here," I said. "Assuming you could hoist it into place with a crane."

"That or a beautifully designed house," said Sandy. "Judging from the house you built for your mother-in-law, I think you and your partner could do something wonderful with it."

Although it was a hot day, a steady southerly breeze kept us almost comfortable. Standing at the edge, we saw the river bend toward the southeast a half mile away. In the other direction, the river shimmered behind a tall stand of trees whose thick canopy of leaves obscured the riverbank. The vegetation on the hillside down to the river was burnt off. But with the exception of a lone pine near the riverbank and an oak nearby, none of the trees appeared to have been damaged.

"It's beautiful," Holly said.

As we followed the trail down to the river, we passed another thin strip of land with a somewhat different river vantage point. Because this view was below the canopy of leaves, we could see the river in greater detail. From this narrow overlook forty feet above the riverbank, we were close enough to notice the gradations of color where the river's depth changed. The final approach to the river was down a narrow path so steep it made our calves burn a bit.

"You realize how unique this is," said Sandy. "Nobody else around here can get down to the river. It's too steep and overgrown. Here, all you have to do is walk."

The temperature dropped noticeably as we reached the bottom, and the breeze made it feel even more comfortable. While there were random puddles of sunlight, most of the ground was in shade. The property had almost five hundred feet of river frontage. We looked straight up through the tops of the sycamores, elms, and cypress trees. They were so tall that we practically had to set our chins at 90-degree angles to our necks.

The smile on Miranda's face told us what she was thinking.

"Since you're showing it to us, I gather it's for sale?" asked Holly.

"It's not on the market, but I believe the owner would be open to selling, even though he likes looking around for arrowheads with his grandson."

Of course there were arrowheads to be found. How could this not be the former domicile of humans over the past several millennia? Everything a small pretechnology community would need was here: water from the river, sandy and loamy river-bottom soil for planting, steep hillsides for refuge in floods and high wind, a natural gathering place high above the river where danger could be spotted miles away, and an alluvial spring that drizzled clean water into a ravine.

While it didn't feel like home to me, I could imagine how it would have to hundreds of people over many centuries.

The two sides of my brain were finding it harder than usual to get along. The left side could see no plausible arguments against this being a suitable replacement for what we had lost. The right side was defensive and antagonistic.

"Should we ask Sandy to make an inquiry for us?" said Holly.

"I guess I don't see the harm in it, so long as she knows we're not making an offer or anything."

Our answer came the next day in the form of a text message. The owner was willing to sell at a price so high it felt like a punch to the gut. I called Walter to tell him.

Less than a month after the fire, Walter and Jeri Nell had already drawn a bead on their new home, a tall building on a busy street corner in Smithville where they could maintain a residence on the second floor and a new business on the first.

"I guess his price simplifies things," I said. "If the offer to sell was reasonable, considering the devastation nearby, we'd have a hard choice to make, since Holly really liked it. But we don't have to worry about that now."

"You don't share Holly's opinion?"

"I know I should. But I'm not there yet."

"I went out there to take a look," said Walter. "I'm on her side."

"Maybe it's my state of mind. The way I feel these days, if the Sharon Stone of *Basic Instinct* appeared to me in a vision, barely clothed and with a wink in her eye, I'd probably be surprised, but that's about it."

"I'm not sure how I'm supposed to respond to that."

"Changing the subject," I said, "I'm kind of amazed that you and Jeri Nell have already decided where you're going to live long term."

"The opportunity presented itself and we took it. I hope it's not a mistake, but at least we won't be worrying about where we'll end up."

"I guess that's something."

"So what are you going to do now?"

"We may look around Bastrop County a little more before we move to Austin next week. I doubt we'll see anything worth considering, but I'm not against being pleasantly surprised."

I was right to be skeptical. The next week, Kenny identified six properties west of Bastrop that seemed as promising on the Web as they proved unpromising in reality. On a hazy and stifling afternoon, we took a tour of a part of the county that showed the effects of the drought in a different way from what we were used to. Instead of dead trees, the lack of rain had turned the miles of ranchland and pasture we passed from green to a crunchy brown.

In better years, a giant hand caressing these fields would have felt something soft and tender. Now that hand would be offended by a gritty, lifeless touch.

As we lurched from one flaming disappointment to another, increasingly frustrated by the marketing misrepresentations we had gullibly swallowed, the odds of us moving back to Bastrop County grew dimmer. By the time we got back to Amelia's house, cranky and sweaty, all we could say for sure was that we would be living in Travis Heights for a while, like Austin tourists who lost their luggage and whose return-trip ticket had been canceled.

CHAPTER 8

October 1, 2011, 8:30 a.m. We relocated for the third time in less than a month on a Saturday. We wondered if the dogs were thinking "Not again!" as we put on their leashes and herded them into Holly's SUV. While we were numb at the thought of another move, we took comfort that it wouldn't happen again anytime soon.

Moving to Austin felt like a milestone. Perhaps that is why I wondered what the future milestones of Bastrop State Park would be as I once again passed its baleful southern boundary. What happens to thousands of acres of forest after a portable crematorium passes through them? What plants, insects, reptiles, and birds will try their luck in a bleak landscape where food is scarce and pollinators are AWOL? What will it all look like when my grandson Ben is pulling up stakes for college and my memory has lost some of its snap?

We pulled our cars into the driveway of our new digs. It didn't take long to carry in our things, distribute them among the rooms we'd inhabit, and unpack. More than once, we took a short break on the second-floor deck that faced across the river toward downtown Austin. There was more greenery around us than we'd seen since the fire.

"I think we're going to be OK here," said Holly near the end of the day as we ate takeout around the breakfast nook table.

"Let's not kid ourselves," I said. "The best we can say is this is where we'll sleep, eat, and get our mail."

"No matter what you think this is, we're going to be here for a while, so let's try to make the best of it."

"Sure. Why not? Who cares that we're an old married couple with three grown kids and no place to call our own?"

"We could think of it as an adventure, right, Miranda?" said Holly.

Miranda shrugged. I supported her ambivalence.

Our first night in Travis Heights, as I lay on my back and stared through the murky light, the ceiling seemed to whisper to me over my wife's barely audible snore: "Who are you, and what are you doing here?"

October 3, 2011, 1:30 p.m. Betty's Bechstein grand piano—now officially *my* Bechstein—arrived from Dallas shortly after lunch. The moving company's owner and his three young employees hoisted the main body of the piano, separated from its legs and pedals, on a dolly and lowered it to the ground with a hydraulic lift. With two pushing, one pulling, and the owner directing them, they wheeled the top-heavy dolly across the driveway, up the cobblestone walkway, over the front-door threshold's bump, and into the living room. Instead of sensibly hiding in the bedroom, I monitored the swaying and wobbling and imagined the hundred-year-old wreckage that would result from a mistake.

They removed the blankets wrapped around the piano and spread them on the floor. With the legs reattached, they turned the piano upright and moved it across the floor by sliding the blankets on which it stood. Five minutes later, I shook the owner's hand and said, "Glad that's over with. Now I can start breathing again."

"Just another day at the office for us," he said. "You wanna know what real work is like? Try floating a piano in a swimming pool."

"Seriously?"

"Did that last month for someone with money to burn. Trust me, this was a cakewalk."

"If you say so. But you can't imagine how I would have felt if something had happened to this piano. It's about the only thing I own at this point that means anything to me."

"How's that?"

"Long story. For now, let's just say I'll be calling you at some point in the future to do it all over again."

"You know where to find us," he said, looking at my piano with obvious admiration.

"You like it, huh?"

"Let's put it this way. I've been doing this for a really long time, and this is the first Bechstein I've ever moved. They don't make 'em like these anymore."

"You mean Bechstein?"

"I mean any piano company. The amount of wood and metal they put in these old beauties is incredible. This thing weighs a lot more than modern pianos that are the same size. Right, boys?"

They nodded their assent while wiping their foreheads with the sleeves of their shirts.

"And anyone who knows anything about pianos knows that Bechsteins are special," he said.

"My piano teacher is partial to Steinway."

"Who can blame him? Your piano isn't necessarily better, but it's definitely unique, and you're lucky to have it."

After the exacting and resourceful piano technician that Anton recommended gave it a major tune-up, my piano's soul emerged like a radiant being woken from a long and productive sleep.

Its refurbished action—the way in which the actual ivory and ebony keys responded to the pressure of my fingers—was light and silky, as gratifyingly responsive as a toddler who never makes a fuss at naptime. The slightly nasal, ringing tone of the middle and upper registers was a perfect match for a Bach prelude or Mozart piano sonata. With the sustain pedal held down, the Bechstein turned into a dreamy and downy bed on which Debussy's sumptuous chord progressions could be laid. If I played a Beethoven sonata with scales or broken chords in the bass register, my piano felt like a growling dog trying to bust off its leash.

Several weeks after the piano was delivered, Anton showed up with a black leather piano stool and an armful of music: the complete piano sonatas of Beethoven and Mozart, selected works of Chopin, some Bach preludes and inventions, and some random pieces he had gathered from his extensive personal archive.

Pointing to the music, he said, "These should keep you occupied for a while." Then, as he set the stool behind the piano, he said, "Your butt will thank me."

A month after the fire stripped me of my former artistic legacy, my mother-in-law and piano teacher jointly laid the foundation for my future one. In fact, they did much more than that. On my darkest days, if the music I made on my Bechstein wasn't the actual means of my survival, it at least felt that way.

How did the heartbroken give voice to their suffering before Bach, Mozart, Beethoven, and the Romantics? With what tools of eloquence did they organize and communicate their feelings in the millennia before humans figured out how to turns sounds into music?

Lucky for me, these questions were only rhetorical. Thanks to Anton and Betty, I had the means and the growing ability to channel my swirling emotions into the music stacked next to my bench.

A gnawing question sometimes posed itself at the end of a practice session: should I give thanks to the fire for the great gift of this piano?

October 3, 2011, 10:30 p.m. As we would do for many balmy evenings that we lived in Travis Heights, Holly and I carried a bedtime drink to the second-floor deck and sat on cushioned metal chairs under the branches of a venerable live oak tree, looking north to the tall buildings of downtown Austin.

The handful of families that had lived in this house since the Depression era had a front-row seat to the evolution of Austin from a sleepy and segregated state capital in the 1940s and 1950s to a college town bursting with the counterculture vibe of the 1960s, to a nationally recognized country and rock music incubator in the 1970s and 1980s, to the high-tech and hipster magnet of the 1990s and early 2000s, to the too-much-traffic and too-expensive global city it was now.

Between the day we arrived in Austin in late August 1979 and this pleasant October evening—the sum total of our possessions being roughly the same—the population of the Austin area had more than doubled, and nothing captured this fact better than what we were looking at: a combination of high-rise apartment and office buildings, an urban landscape that would have been hard to picture on the night I rushed Holly to the hospital for Miranda's birth.

Although we couldn't see it, we also knew that just to our west was a neighborhood that had been transformed from the embodiment of seediness—a hive of prostitution, drugs, dilapidated apartments, rundown houses, an old-school porn theater, and nominal law enforcement—to an overpriced, defiantly gentrified enclave of hip restaurants and stores, upscale condos, and refurbished one-story houses.

All of this progress—although some longtime Austin residents might have had a different word for it—was now on view to us because the other views to which we had become accustomed no longer existed. Brightly lit, multicolored, metallic, and highly vertical downtown Austin was now our visual horizon instead of the Lost Pines, which also looked very different from what we saw that September 1979 afternoon when Holly and I came upon the western edge of Bastrop State Park for the first time.

As long as we lived in this house, we'd take in the bittersweet view from the second-story deck. An unsympathetic critic of our ambivalence could have said the same thing about our children or our income or our increasingly uncooperative bodies: all were touchstones of the same inevitable and jarring passage of time. But there was something about the two competing landscapes—a vibrant downtown with a few construction cranes and the deathly Lost Pines—that drove the point home in a way that oppressed me.

"Feeling old?" I asked.

"Of course," said Holly.

"This just seems so unbelievable, us sitting here, looking out on all this, about to go to sleep in someone else's bed."

"I know."

"How long before it starts feeling normal, I wonder, not that I even could tell you what that word means at this point."

After a few minutes of silence, I said, "Maybe I can sort all of this out in therapy. Miranda and I start tomorrow."

October 4, 2011, 3:30 p.m. The Tuesday after we started receiving our mail in Austin, Miranda and I found ourselves in a small, two-story wood-framed house a few blocks northwest of the Capitol where a couple of therapists shared office space. We had arrived early for our first session so we could fill out the necessary paperwork. Clad in shorts and T-shirts, we sat elbow to elbow, on a small light-colored sofa with classical music playing quietly from a radio.

"Do you want me to fill this out for you?" I asked Miranda.

"No. I want to do it myself."

I finished quickly and then helped Miranda with a few questions she didn't understand. We had ten minutes left before our 4 p.m. appointment. "What do we do now?" she said.

"Nothing. Maybe look through a magazine." We riffled through a pile of them on the low-slung table in front of the sofa.

"Look at that one," Miranda said. "It's Bastrop."

She was right. It was the cover of *Texas Highways* magazine. The October 2011 issue featured a long story on Bastrop State Park, with many photos. A pictorial homage to one of the state's most popular and heavily visited parks was now an inadvertent epitaph. My cheeks felt hot as I leafed through the article, and my forehead was sweaty. I fought back tears while Miranda watched me.

"What are the odds of this?" I said. "We're here to talk about the fire, and the first thing we see is a magazine reminding us of what the park used to be like."

"That's weird."

One of the interior doors opened and a smallish, thin woman with a warm smile greeted us. Introductions were made and we shook hands. If I was look-ing for an older version of Mother Lisa, my order had apparently been filled, at least physically.

"Look at what you had on the table here," I said, and handed her the maga-zine. "Quite a coincidence, wouldn't you say?"

"Oh, I'm so sorry. I don't put those there, but that's no excuse for exposing you to something like that, especially on your first visit."

"I'll get over it," I said, with a weak smile. "Maybe with your help."

She ushered us into a small, stuffy room where the late afternoon sun slanted through a window. I looked around the little room. The carpet was a little threadbare. She had a few books and some papers on her desk, and there were a few small pictures on the wall as well as a framed copy of her professional credentials. The walls were painted a neutral shade of white. There were doors on two sides of the room, one leading to the waiting area and the other to a small kitchen and bathroom. A digital clock with a large display was positioned so that we could all see how much time was left.

All that I knew about the physical trappings of therapy came from the movies and TV. Judging from her office, this counselor definitely had more in common with Tony Soprano's therapist than with the shrinks in a Woody Allen movie.

"Would you like some water?" she said.

"Yes, please. And if we could pull those curtains shut, it might get a little more comfortable in here."

"I'll also turn the thermostat down. Some of my clients like it on the warm side."

After getting chilled water for us in small paper cups, she sat on a swivel-type office chair facing us. Miranda and I sat opposite one another in comfortable armchairs.

"I know we talked about it on the phone," I said, "but I just wanted to make sure you're still OK with my daughter being part of this."

"It's unusual. But I'm fine with it if you are."

Miranda and I both nodded and then I launched into my prepared remarks, aided by a few notes. I told her about my time as the chief operating officer of the Texas public health agency. I reiterated my belief in mental health services as well as my functional ignorance of them. After a few minutes of this, she gently cut me off.

"If you don't mind, can we use the time we have today to talk about your situation? There will be plenty of time later to discuss the hows and whys of therapy. For now, I'd like to learn how you and Miranda are getting along."

"You're the boss," I said. "Before we talk about that, can I ask you a question?"

"Of course."

"Actually, two questions."

"Yes?"

"How will I know it's working? And how long will it take before I know?"

I knew my questions were unanswerable as well as obnoxious. But it felt good to say the sort of get-to-the-point thing for which I was famous in my pre-fire professional days. Maybe this was one way therapy could help: by giving me a place where I could pretend I was still the person I wished I were.

Her reply was what I expected, but I was surprised at how patiently and kindly she delivered it. Then, leaning forward a little and looking only at me, she said, "Please tell me how you're feeling these days."

I glanced at Miranda. She was sitting very still in her chair, looking at me with great concentration and interest.

"Not good. Not good at all. I feel depressed most of the time, except when I'm pissed off at the feel-good new stories that seem to be stalking me. It seems like every time I turn on the TV or read the newspaper or go online, there's some smily-faced fire victim who is dying to tell the world of some wonderful thing that has happened to them. Do you know what I'm talking about?"

"Yes, I've seen one or two of those stories."

"Do you think these people really feel that way? How could anybody in a situation like ours act like that?"

"People respond to traumatic events differently. Some of these people may really feel OK now but hit a wall in six months or maybe even a year. Almost everyone who goes through a loss like you and Miranda have suffered will experience grief and shock and sadness."

"So their time is coming? Is that what you're saying?"

"Perhaps so."

"One can only hope."

I asked her why there weren't any stories about people like me, and she suggested I step forward and set an example. She wasn't being snarky or trying to call me out, but I still felt like a hypocrite. Cornered by my own complaint, I changed the subject.

"You have to understand that we didn't lose just any old house," I said. "It was a house that my building partner designed and I built. It was exactly what I wanted at this time in my life. I intended to live in it until the day I died."

"And now you're grieving over it, as you should."

"I know I should be glad that nobody was hurt or killed, even though one of us could easily have been. And our needs will be taken care of. But I still feel awful."

"Miranda, do you feel the same way as your dad?"

"Sort of."

"I'm not sure that's actually true," I said. "She's only cried twice that I know of. The first time was when we told her what had happened. That also happened to be her twenty-first birthday."

"Oh my goodness," said our therapist.

"The second time she cried was at church when our priest prayed for a group of fire victims, including us."

"Dad's been crying a lot," said Miranda.

"And this is unusual?" asked our therapist.

"Very. My kids told me a few weeks ago that they'd never seen me cry before. They're wrong, but I think you see the point."

In response to a couple of simple questions, I let loose with a soliloquy (or was it a confession?) about my feelings that lasted at least ten minutes. It felt both a self-indulgence and a relief. Several times I tried to engage Miranda, but she didn't bite. I began to wonder if her idea of therapy was watching her father emote.

Then, without knowing exactly how it happened, I flipped from self-pity to self-blame.

"There are so many people we know or we've heard about who are staying with family or friends or in a motel. Maybe some of those who got burned out are even living out of their cars. And yet we're camped out in a place with a historical landmark on it. You want to know how I've started describing our situation, mainly to myself?"

"Yes I would."

"We're the most blessed among the afflicted."

I told her about the e-mail I received from my disaster relief friend in which she compared our situation to the families she helps. "She meant well, but the underlying message was obvious to me," I said. "How can I feel bad about what happened to us knowing that millions of other people around the world are left with literally nothing? Among all of the world's disaster victims, why are we the lucky ones?" I took a deep breath and sighed. "So there you have it."

"Miranda, how do you feel?" our therapist said.

"I want my dad and Walter to build another house so I can move back to Bastrop. I want to be near my school. I want my own room."

"You have a room, Miranda," I said. "With maybe the best view in Austin."

"It's not mine. How long before we move back?"

As Miranda and I drove back, I thought about what had just happened. Nothing felt unique or like something I couldn't do on my own. If the first session was a sign of things to come, it seemed like therapy would mainly consist of talking to myself, out loud, with two other people eavesdropping, neither of whom had any advice to give or insights to reveal.

Because I paid for it and it was called therapy, all of my self-involved yakking was legitimized. If I went on and on like that at home, or with a friend, or in a group, it would be narcissistic and obnoxious. If I did it alone, then the men in white jackets would eventually show up to haul me off. But in a stuffy room where someone had hung a diploma and professional credentials, and where I would place a check on the desk at the end of the hour-long session, it was officially declared to be a good thing.

I decided to stick with it for no other reason than it felt good to have someone egging me on to complain and be pissed off and feel sorry for myself. There also seemed to be a certain symmetrical logic to having Miranda there. I had tried to be her rock when she had suffered. Maybe it was time for her to return the favor.

October 2011. Our Travis Heights neighbors didn't know what to make of us. None of them knew that the historical home had changed from overnight accommodations for tourists with too much disposable income to a temporary home for a dislocated family with an equal number of humans and dogs.

For the first couple of weeks, it wasn't unusual for someone to look at us warily as we walked the dogs. We could imagine what they were thinking: "Since when can people stay there with animals? And how do grubby and unkempt people like them get to stay there for days on end? What's going on? Are they legit? Should we call the cops?"

We could have introduced ourselves and explained our situation, but we didn't. I didn't want to become friendly with anyone who lived near us, because that would be the first step in sinking our roots into Travis Heights. The less people knew about us, the better.

I made one exception to this rule. We lived less than a block from an elementary school. If we timed our morning dog-walk with the arrival of the schoolchildren, something wonderful happened that got better with each passing week. While the wieners were their usual yap-happy and obnoxious selves, Charlie craved and sought out the attention of the youngsters, who were at first scared by him, then amused, and finally smitten.

For fifteen minutes each morning that school was in session, laughing and jabbering children would walk to school by themselves, in small groups, or hand in hand with a parent or grandparent. Many of them learned Charlie's name and made a point of intercepting him as he walked in the opposite direction of them. Charlie devoured their pats, strokes, squats, and giggles. He would show his gratitude with loud pants and sometimes a spray of slobber when he shook his jowls.

Getting him out the front door and on to the street was a battle. But the battle was won when the children came into view as we turned the corner. As soon as he saw them, his listlessness and resistance was replaced by a light step and a trot, which for an English bulldog is like a sprint.

It was a felicitous situation. The children enjoyed the dog and I enjoyed them. And the energy Charlie gained from walking against the grain of the children as they ambled and skipped toward their school powered him up the steep stone steps that took us back to the house.

"Why do you like that so much?" Holly asked me one morning as we finished our walk.

"You really have to ask? Those children are goo-goo-eyed over Charlie, and he feels the same way about them."

"I know how he feels. I'm asking why you like it so much. On some days, it's the only time I see you with anything resembling a smile."

"They're beautiful and happy and they know nothing of our situation."

One clear and comfortable Saturday morning in late October, a pleasant-looking gray-haired woman we sometimes saw on our walks approached us and introduced herself. She was at least ten years older than us and had a gentle air about her.

"I've seen you around here for a while now." She pointed to the top of the stairs and asked, "Are you staying there?"

"We're renting it," Holly said.

"I had no idea it was available for rent."

"It's an unusual situation," I said. "We sort of stumbled into an arrangement with the investors who own it. We'll probably be here for a while."

"Really?"

"Yup. It's kind of complicated," I said.

"OK."

Silence.

"What's it like?" she asked.

"What do you mean?" I said.

"I've lived in this neighborhood for many years and I've always admired that house from a distance. Lots of us have. I've always wondered what it's like inside and how it's furnished."

"Do you want to see it?" said Holly.

Her eyes widened. "Could I?"

"Sure," I said. "Why not?"

With the dogs in tow, we climbed the stairs, showed her around the perimeter of the grounds, and then gave her the full tour.

"So now I know," she said as we wrapped up her short visit. "Thank you so much for showing it to me. I guess I don't need to tell you how lucky you are to be living here."

Holly looked at me as if to say: Please don't take the bait.

"We know that," I said.

"I would love to switch places with you for a day or two," she said. "Of course, I don't mean that literally."

I held my tongue.

October 13, 2011, 9:30 a.m. One morning an unfamiliar number popped up on my phone. The caller was an elderly woman I knew from church. Helen and her husband, Ed, sang in the choir when I was the organist. They had married on Christmas Day in 1940, and it was impossible to think of one without the other. An elfin couple, they always sat in church on the first row next to the aisle, Helen's wavy gray hair barely visible above the pew.

"We heard what happened to you and your family," she said. "We have a sofa we'd like to give to you. Would you have time to come by and take a look at it?"

"We're living in a furnished house in Austin right now, Helen, so we wouldn't have a place for a sofa or any other furniture."

"But you probably will at some time in the future. Ed and I would be honored to give it to you. We can keep it here until you're ready to take it."

Holly and I took turns driving Miranda to school in Bastrop several days a week. I had no excuse not to at least look at the sofa. She gave me her address and we settled on a time. I arrived just after lunch. Both of them came to the door, Helen pushing Ed in a wheelchair. Helen wore a dress, and Ed wore an untucked open-collared shirt with comfortable, loose-fitting pants.

"What happened, Ed?" I said.

"You mean the wheelchair? I'm ninety-five years old, that's what happened." Ed spoke softly but clearly. Helen's sharp wits were on full display, and her eyes lit up behind her glasses.

"It's in here," said Helen. She showed me into a sunroom. The sofa was dark brown and roughly the same size as the leather sofa that used to sit in our family room.

"Holly and I want you to know that we really appreciate your generosity in offering this to us. But we think you should find someone else who needs it now. Maybe Mother Lisa knows of a family that didn't have insurance."

"But we'd like you to have it," said Ed.

We talked for another minute or two and then agreed that the Fritz family would not get the sofa. We went back into their living room, where a baby grand piano sat next to the curtained windows facing the street. It occupied about a third of the room, and its top was up.

"That looks like a smaller version of the piano I lost," I said.

"Are you going to get another one?" Ed asked.

"Right after the fire, my piano teacher started looking for something to take its place. And then guess what happened? My mother-in-law gave me hers. I can't begin to describe what it means to me."

"We're so glad," Helen said. "We know how much your music means to you. We always enjoyed your playing when we were in the choir."

"It's a little different now. My teacher, who is quite a virtuoso, is working hard to break me of some very bad habits I developed when I played the organ. I think we're making progress, but it's slow going. You mind if I take a quick peek at Ed's piano?"

The first two pages of "Clair de lune" sat on the piano's music stand.

"Ed, is this what you're playing these days?"

"I don't play much anymore. But when I was, that was a piece I tried to learn. I never got past the first page."

"It's not easy, that's for sure," I said.

"Do you know it?" said Helen.

"I've been playing it since last May. In fact, it was the last piece I played the day we evacuated." I guessed what they were thinking. "Would you like me to play it?"

"We'd be honored," said Helen.

"I don't have all the music up there," said Ed. "I'd have to look around to find the rest of it."

"No need. I can play it from memory. Or at least I hope I can."

Helen took a seat next to Ed, and I played a few scales to warm up.

"Here goes," I said.

For four minutes, I went someplace where the fire hadn't happened. I saw my fingers move and I heard music. But it wasn't me playing, or at least it wasn't a nervous and sleep-deprived person fearing a memory lapse. Claude Debussy's music was where my brain had been, his notes where my fingers were, the music coming from a place I was unfamiliar with. I finally remembered where I was and what I was doing as the D-flat major arpeggio that ends the piece lingered while I held down the sustain and soft pedals. I had never experienced anything like it.

I turned around. They were holding hands. Ed's eyes were closed and Helen's face could have been mistaken for a saint's.

I laughed. "So I guess it sounded OK?"

We exchanged hugs and I left. I immediately called Anton and left him a voice mail about how time had just stood still for me. Later that evening, I received his e-mailed reply:

I want you to know that I was first of all amazed to find a message from you on my phone, talking in a more excited voice that I've heard you use for a long time. It seems that you had a taste of what I often experience, and never tire of: knowing that you have just supplied people with a whole lot of pleasure and moved them in an unexpected way. Isn't it wonderful? And how lovely it is to have this ray of goodness in the middle of the darkness.

October 14, 2011, 1:15 p.m. My Cottletown Road visits were counterproductive and justified by the flimsiest of logic. But on this day, I set out with a purpose I could actually defend: to meet with a structural engineer who would evaluate the physical integrity of our concrete slab.

Our plumber Jeff had confirmed that the drainpipes hadn't melted. Now we needed to know if the slab was worth keeping, possibly for some family in the future to build on.

I arrived early for the 1:30 p.m. appointment. The calendar said it was fall and the weather almost agreed, with temperatures in the low 80s, a pleasant breeze, and a sun that bordered on amiable. Holly's walkway flowerbeds were well on their way to making their comeback. The hints of green that I had seen several weeks before were now shoots at least an inch high. The Lazarus-like potato sprouts in my garden had full-fledged leaves, and a few of the morning glories had sputtered back to life. Several of the skinny pine trees in front of the house had fresh needles, and there were splotches of green on an adjacent oak tree.

I had mixed feelings about these rejuvenations. Had my fatalistic view of our land been a rush to judgment? Should we reconsider a decision that had been locked down for over a month?

If I was looking for an excuse to stay the course, I found it with my favorite tree, the formerly ravishing pine that twisted upward from the side of our creek-bed. This gravity-defying marvel had turned brown and lifeless. In a few months, I surmised, it would be officially dead, and in a year or two, broken in pieces and lying on its side. With a guilty twinge, I almost felt relieved that we could stick to our plan.

As I walked back to the slab, I passed the frame of our trampoline. There were splotches in the metal where the burned-off leather had rested on it. I remembered the day Holly and I assembled it and the conversation we had.

"I guess the fact that we're doing this means we're now officially open for visits by our grandson," I said.

"Now Benjamin will always have something to do when he comes to see us."

"Hopefully, that won't include doing somersaults and breaking his neck."

"That goes for him and all his future siblings and cousins," she said.

I called the disposal company that had carted off everything else and reminded them that one more forlorn relic of our past life still had to be picked up.

The structural engineer arrived, wearing khaki pants, a short-sleeved shirt, comfortable shoes, and no cap. He shook my hand and got down to work, clinking a small hammer on the edge of the slab and at various points in the middle and talking softly into a digital recording device.

"What kind of reinforcement do you have in the slab?" he asked.

"Rebar."

"That's good. Rebar holds up in a fire."

"What else could there be?"

"High-tension wire. That wouldn't be good in this case. What I'm seeing so far gives me confidence, but I need to check on a few more things."

I sat on the edge of the small concrete patio that bordered our former bedroom. With the exception of some stray pine needles and dirt that had blown on it, the slab was slick and clean, the soot washed off by a recent rain. If it wasn't for the anchor bolts that the guy who cleared our slab had accidentally bent with his front-end loader, and the lack of any stubbed-out plumbing, it could have passed for a new slab ready for the framing carpenters.

Our house looked now like it did at the beginning: an outline on the ground, full of the promise of Walter's design. I could have seen it as an opportunity for rebirth. Instead, it brought to mind an old man who is reverting to the helpless condition of a newborn.

The movie in my head about my last visit to the house kept playing, but a new plot twist entered the script. Everything I had gone through in the past month, and everything I'd face in the coming months, could have been avoided if I had lingered long enough for the carbon monoxide to work its fatal magic.

From what evil place were these thoughts gurgling up? And what did they signify? I was afraid to know. I put my head in my hands and sobbed without relief.

After a while, I looked up to see the engineer putting his tools back into his car. Whether from respect or embarrassment or indifference, he ignored me. He probably would have left without saying a word or looking in my direction.

"You're leaving?" I shouted at him, wiping my eyes and nose.

"Yes. I've got everything I need. I'll mail you a certified report."

I stood up, wiped my face with my dirty hands, and forced myself back into the moment. "Sorry about the outburst."

"No problem."

"So what's the verdict?"

"The details will be in the report, but the long and short of it is that your slab is OK structurally. I don't know about the plumbing, though. You'll need to get another opinion on that."

"I already have," I said. "It's fine."

"In that case, you don't need to tear it out."

"I guess that's good."

"Well, at least this way you have options. If you want to rebuild, you can."

"I can promise you that won't happen."

He nodded, got into his car, and was gone. I took a valedictory walk around the slab. With my unsteady walk and crimson face, someone at the top of the hill would have mistaken me for a drunk.

CHAPTER 9

October 16, 2011, 11:15 a.m. When we first moved to Austin from Chicago in 1979, we occasionally went to an Episcopal church in downtown Austin. St. David's was an intriguing mixture of the old and new, with a traditional Sunday morning Eucharist in the large first-floor sanctuary and an informal service upstairs with modern music and jazzed-up prayers.

We thought of this place as we tried to decide whether to ditch church-going for a while.

On the one hand, it seemed hard to imagine weeks or months without any formal spiritual sustenance and practice. The other side of the argument was the idea of emotional wrecks trying to keep it together in the presence of people who couldn't help pitying them.

We decided to give the informal service a try because, at the very least, we'd probably enjoy the company of the young children and the guitar music. If it didn't suit us, we'd have extra free time on Sunday mornings for the foreseeable future.

"That wasn't so bad," said Holly as we filed out on our first Sunday.

"You're right," I said. "I'm not against giving it another try."

"You still cried," said Miranda.

The only way out of the chapel was past the church's rector who was shaking hands and making small talk. He had shed his vestments, and his collar was the only visible sign he was a priest. I later learned that my initial assumptions were correct: his age and Wisconsin upbringing were almost identical to mine. Absent the rot growing inside of me, we could have been natural-born buddies. Holly made the introductions.

"Are you new to Austin?" he said, not realizing he had posed a trick question.

"We've lived in the area for many years, almost all of them in Bastrop," said Holly. "We lost our home in the fire, and we're staying in Austin for the time being."

He grabbed our hands and looked us straight in the eyes. "I'm so sorry," he said with self-evident sincerity. "I can't imagine what you're going through."

"You're probably right about that," I said.

"Is there anything I can do to help? Or anything St. David's can do?"

"Do you have a time capsule?" I said.

An explanation was in order, given his confused look. "If you have a way to send me back in time, then yes, you can help. If not, then I doubt it."

Holly and Miranda were embarrassed and the line was starting to back up, so I summed up my argument: "All I want is to have things go back to the way they were. Other than that, forget it. Although it is nice of you to ask."

I didn't wait around for him to fabricate an appropriate response, assuming there was one. As we walked down the stairs, Holly said, "You almost sounded angry at him."

"I probably was."

"Why would you be mad at him?" said Miranda. "He didn't start the fire. He didn't make us move."

"I'm angry because I am. At least give me credit for being honest about how I feel."

"We all feel bad," said Holly. "But that's no reason to treat people who want to help us like that."

"I'm pretty sure his job description includes having his good intentions thrown back in his face," I said. "I doubt that he gave it a second thought."

"You don't think you did something wrong?" said Holly.

"I'm not saying that."

As we drove back to our so-called home, I began to regret what happened, but not for the reasons Holly or Miranda would have guessed. It wasn't what I did that gnawed at me but what it implied. After a Google search confirmed my recollections about the five stages of grief, I ruefully realized that I had lashed out because that's what my rewired brain was programmed to do.

I was now firmly in the grip of anger, having quietly and predictably graduated from the denial stage. No longer the renegade or outlier, I was apparently becoming a psychological cliché.

October 17, 2011, 7 p.m. A major disaster spawns philanthropic impulses that are often channeled into a grand gesture involving celebrities and high-profile do-gooders whose goodwill, I was to learn, does not necessarily translate into a positive experience for the people they aspire to help.

The wildfire's grand gesture was a benefit concert featuring a gaggle of well-known country and rock musicians, including a couple of national headliners. While paying ticket-holders filled most of the eighteen thousand seats, those who lost a home in the fire got free tickets in a designated corner of the University of Texas basketball arena where the concert was held. These included Holly and Miranda, who wanted to be there, and me, who showed up under duress.

It didn't take long for me to realize I had made a mistake in coming. Video snippets of the fire played on large screens between musical acts, presumably to remind everyone why they were there. While some of the videos were distant shots of the smoke roiling up into the atmosphere, or close-in post-fire panoramas of destroyed properties, the ones that twisted my stomach and dried my mouth were of the fire leaping from tree to tree, incinerating mature loblollies in a roar of flame and sparks. Whoever had shot the videos got close enough to have risked his or her life.

Would anyone make the victim of a bombing repeatedly watch a video of the device going off, except perhaps as a form of enhanced interrogation? So why expose us to this?

With equal parts self-righteousness and anger, I kept a mental list of the benefit's manifold transgressions and insensitivities. One of the organizers, a well-known Austin entertainer, incited the crowd to roar their approval of his idea to plant a million trees to replace those that had died. This was a fatuous commitment, in my opinion, as easy to make as it would be to quickly forget.

The singers and bands riffed on twin themes of "We'll all get through this together" and "It's not an end but a beginning." All I could say to that was: How would you know?

"I can't believe I let you twist my arm into coming to this," I shouted to Holly over the deafening music.

"I didn't make you do anything," she said.

"You kind of did."

"Don't talk so loud," Holly said. "People will hear what you're saying."

"I'm talking loud because the music is loud. How can they hear me when I can barely hear you?"

"I don't know. But some of them are looking at you."

"So what?"

"Why can't you just be grateful for all these people who showed up to support us and our friends?"

"These people came to hear George Strait and the Dixie Chicks," I said.

"They're here for us."

"No they're not. They're here for the music."

"We need to leave if you're going to keep talking like this. I'm not offended, because I've lived with you for the past month. But others might not feel the same way."

"Why can't we stay?" asked Miranda as we pulled her out of her seat.

"It's too hard to explain," I said.

"Why do we always have to do what you say? And why are you always grumpy and mad?" she said.

The next day, with Miranda as witness, our therapist made it official: I was recycling my grief into a glowing blob of anger.

"All that Elisabeth Kübler-Ross stuff just seems too simple for what I'm going through," I said. "Or is that just me still stuck in the denial stage?"

"What we think we know about how people respond to grief is backed up by a lot of human experience," she said. "But I'd be the first to agree with you that there's nothing simple about what you're experiencing."

"I know some of what I'm doing these days is bad. Sometimes I think my wife expects me to simply make a decision to feel better. Do you think it's possible for someone like me to choose a different path?"

"If I answered yes, would you believe me?"

"No. Just like I wouldn't believe you if you said the opposite."

"There are clinical descriptions for what you're going through," said our therapist, "and you probably have plenty of company in how you're feeling right now. We'll talk about this more next week."

October 21, 2011, 8:30 a.m. Hillary and Jared dropped off one-year-old Benjamin on their way to the airport for a weekend romp in New Orleans. In our pre-fire days, three days with our grandson meant nonstop ruckus and fun except for when he was sleeping. Smiles and giggles vastly outnumbered tears and pouts. At the end of the day, I would be rewarded with a half hour of bliss: reading to him several of the now-decrepit children's books that we had read to our daughters many years before.

In our post-fire world, the deep-down fatigue Holly and I felt and our growing irritability with one another meant Ben's visit took on the character of a low-grade domestic disturbance.

Our failing performance as grandparents was the initial topic of discussion as Holly and I sat on the second-floor deck after we put Ben to bed.

"This isn't going so well, is it?" I said.

"Not really."

"At least Miranda is doing her best to keep him occupied."

"I don't know where she gets it, after all we've been through."

"How much longer do you think we'll be like this?" I asked.

"Who knows? It hasn't even been two months since the fire."

"It feels a lot longer than that."

"In some ways, that's true," said Holly. "But it also feels like a blur."

"I guess after this weekend, I'll have even more to talk about in therapy, the benefits of which I have yet to see."

"I wouldn't know."

"Speaking of therapy, Miranda doesn't say much there. But when she does, it's always about getting her own room."

"You've told me that."

"I know I have. But I'm starting to wonder whether she's right that we need to decide where we're going to live long-term."

"We've already agreed we shouldn't rush into things. It's too soon and we're too raw."

"But being in limbo isn't helping either. If we keep going downhill, who knows where we'll end up?"

"What are you suggesting?"

"I don't know, other than we can't keep up like this."

When Ben went down for his nap on Saturday, after a morning that got worse as it crept along, Holly and I picked up where we had left off on the deck.

"I've been thinking that maybe we should take a drive around Travis Heights to see what's for sale," I said. "I know Kenny has a few properties on the market around here. Maybe we should check them out, since his taste is similar to ours."

"For what reason?"

"To see what our insurance money might get us. We're stuck in Central Texas because this is where our daughters and grandson live. And if we're staying, I can think of a lot worse places than Travis Heights."

"OK. I guess we can do that."

"I'll make up a list while Ben is sleeping."

After his nap finished, we strapped our grandson into his car seat and headed with Miranda to the first house on the list, a modern design with a metal roof. An hour later we gave up, discouraged and gripped by regret.

"It's hard to believe that out of that many expensive houses, we didn't like a single one," I said.

"I liked certain things about a couple of them. But you're right. I wouldn't want to live in any of them, much less pay anything close to what they're asking."

"Doing this was a mistake."

"Probably."

Silence.

"Listen to us," I said. "Even though we've got nothing of our own, we're too good for houses that most people would be thrilled to live in."

"All I know is that I'm not going to buy something just because we think it will stop making us feel miserable. Or because anyone else would be glad to live there."

"I hate this. I hate how we're reacting to the mess we're in almost as much as I hate the mess."

"You get no argument from me."

All of this was said as Miranda cheerfully attended to Ben. Our talk soon fizzled and the evening passed devoid of smiles. Walking the dogs bordered on agony, and reading to Ben felt like a chore. Holly and I ended the evening on the deck, nursing a dessert wine and hardly talking, with Miranda hunkered down in her bedroom.

The next day, after Ben was asleep, we gathered on the smallish downstairs deck for lunch.

"You're not helping much with Ben," said Miranda.

"I'm doing my part," I said.

"Not really," said Holly.

"And what about you?"

"I could be doing better," said Holly.

"Is it really necessary to pay attention to him every minute that he's here?" I asked.

"Are you serious?" said Holly.

"If I'm not mistaken, we didn't act like this when our kids were Ben's age. If we did, we would never have gotten anything done."

"He's barely one year old."

"I know that."

"I'm sick of you guys always fighting," said Miranda. "I'm going inside."

"Stay here," I said. "We're not fighting."

"Yes you are," said Miranda.

"Yes we are," said Holly.

"You call this fighting? We're having a discussion."

"We're fighting," said Holly. "Just like we've been doing for weeks now."

"Mom's right," said Miranda. "And I'm sick of it. If you don't stop, I'm going to leave."

"And where exactly would you go?" I asked.

"To Hillary's. Or Amelia's. Just not here."

"That's ridiculous," I said.

"Please don't talk to your daughter like that," said Holly.

Our lunches sat on our plates while we stared at each other. I wanted to apologize, but I couldn't because I believed the circumstances justified my behavior. I also wondered if they owed me an apology for making me feel ashamed. The eddy of emotions that began gathering when Ben was dropped off had finally organized itself into something full-blown, bent on destruction.

"You're right, Miranda." I said. "It's not fair to put you in the middle of Mom and me."

"I don't know how much longer I can take this either," said Holly.

"Are you blaming me?"

"Mostly I am. You've been a lot harder to live with these past few weeks than I think I have."

"Seriously?"

"I think if you asked any of your daughters, they'd agree with me."

"So now we're picking sides? All of you against me?"

"Mom's right," said Miranda.

"Great. So everyone but me has forgotten about the fire?"

"The fire happened and we have to live with it," said Holly. "You can't keep using it as an excuse for everything you do."

"It's not an excuse," I said. "It's a fact."

"Whatever. I just don't want to keep living like this. I can't."

"A couple days ago you reminded me that it's not even two months since the fire. Now you're saying you're at the end of your rope?"

"I guess I am," said Holly.

"So it's hopeless?"

"Maybe."

"You're asking me to do something I can't."

"You have choices, just like we all do."

"I'm not sure I do. This is a regular topic with our therapist. Just ask Miranda."

"Hmmm," said Miranda.

"We're not talking about your therapist. We're talking about you and me. And Miranda. And I say you have choices."

I felt overwhelmed. I couldn't remember feeling this overwhelmed before except when Miranda's speech was slipping away from her.

"I don't know what to do anymore," I said, staring at my feet. "I feel awful and I feel powerless to do anything about it. I know I've been like this for weeks, but it got even worse after our drive around the neighborhood yesterday. How can I have choices when there is nothing in the future we can look forward to? Everything we had and know has been stolen from us and there is nothing to take its place that I want." I kept other, more sinister thoughts to myself.

Holly and I instinctively knew that we were close to crossing an irreversible line as a family. Because we didn't know precisely where the line was, or what was on the other side of it, we sobbed, and then the three of us hugged.

When Ben woke up, Holly put him into his boxerlike swim shorts. Miranda and I wheeled him in his stroller to the Stacy Park pool, two blocks away. Like almost every day since early spring, the mid-October afternoon was warmer than normal. The Central Texas sun still had to be the center of attention.

Perhaps because it was NFL Game Day, we had a good chunk of the pool almost to ourselves. The cool, clear water put Ben in a giggly mood that I was unable to completely resist. Miranda and I took turns spinning him in circles by holding his ankles while he rested on his back with his face pointed to the sky. With Miranda's help, my grandson held on to my neck as I swam with him on my back.

"What a cutie," said an elderly woman who was sunning herself on the edge of the pool in a one-piece bathing suit.

"No doubt," I said.

"Must be nice to have a grandson as adorable as him."

"It is."

"Looks like you're having fun."

"I guess I am."

Unlike playing my piano, swimming with Miranda and Ben didn't take me outside of myself. Everything that had happened that weekend was lurking in my mind as the time we spent in the pool ticked away. But Ben's laughter and nearly perfect beauty were a counterbalance. In that moment, Holly's point about me having a choice was true. I could let grace envelop me or I could fight it.

After we toweled off and changed, Miranda went to her room and I sat on the living room sofa with Holly while Ben rolled around on the floor, pestering the dogs.

"Looks like that swim did you some good," said Holly.

"I feel better. I admit it."

"While the three of you were gone, I thought about why I hated all those places we saw yesterday," Holly said. "I think it's because we've lived for most of our marriage in houses we designed and built ourselves. We know what we like and that's what we've given ourselves."

"But where would we build?"

"I can think of a place."

"That one on the river?"

"Yes," said Holly. "I think you should give it another chance. I know how important water is to you."

"But what about the price Sandy quoted to us?"

"And what about the prices of those houses we looked at yesterday? We have insurance money, and we should spend it on what we need to stay a family."

"I need to see it again."

"Just please don't go out there when you're in a bad mood."

"So I should wait a year or two?"

"You were smiling a few minutes ago."

"There's still the question of building, and I don't have the strength or brainpower to do that. I can barely pull myself out of bed in the morning, much less ride herd over a bunch of subs. And even though Walter said he'd do it, do you really think he has it in him to design a house for us?"

"I don't know. But I'm pretty sure we'll only be happy in a house that we build for ourselves."

Sandy confirmed that we could still have the property at the stated price but not for much longer. With a knot in my stomach, I placed a call to the man who had framed the Cottletown Road house. The work he did for me three years earlier had proved that he was skillful, trustworthy, and reliable. I also liked him personally.

"Randy Fritz?" he said. "I haven't talked to you in ages."

"You know what's happened to us, right?"

"Yes. I ran into Walter and he told me. I went by and saw it for myself. I'm very sorry for you. I know how much you loved that place. It was really something."

"Thanks to you," I said.

"And Walter."

"Yes. And Walter."

"You doing OK?"

"Not that great, I'm afraid. We're living in Austin in a nice place, but it's been hard. Maybe someday we can pop a cold one and I'll give you the whole story. But dumping my problems on you isn't why I called. I have something to ask. It's something big."

"I'm listening," Jeff said.

"Holly and I have decided we need to build something of our own rather than buy a house."

"On your land?"

"Absolutely not. I could never live there again."

"So where would you build?"

"Holly likes a place in Colovista. But no matter where it is, I can't be the general contractor like I was on the house you framed. I'm too tired and brain dead."

"You want me to do it?" Jeff said. "Line up the subs and keep an eye on them?"

"I basically need you to manage the whole thing. I can't trust myself with any of it. You'd also have to do the framing."

"I figured that."

"I need someone I can put my total faith in, and there's no one else but you."

"And Walter."

"The most I can ask of him is to design it, if that's even possible."

"We'd be a team."

"That's true. But you'll be the glue that holds everything together. Once you spend a little time with Walter or me, you'll appreciate what I'm saying."

He laughed. "I kind of feel like I've been put on the spot."

"I know this is coming at you out of the blue. And I'm not trying to guilt you into anything."

"But I also think you're saying you've got no backup plan."

"You're right. There's no Plan B."

"I guess that means I have to do it then."

"Why don't you think about it for a day or two? This is a big commitment."

"I know what I'm agreeing to. I've been building things for a long, long time."

"I just don't want to take the chance that you'll change your mind later. If we do this, you have to be all in."

"I'm all in," he said.

Once I heard those words, I could finally breathe again.

Next I called Walter. "I told Holly I'd take a second look at that river property," I said. "I need your advice as to whether it's a suitable building site, sitting way up there on that ledge."

"You're going to do it all over again? Be the builder?"

"I've asked Jeff to do it and he's agreed. So that leaves you as the other big piece of the puzzle."

"I want to do it. I guess we'll find out if I can."

"I think there's enough of the old Walter left to get the job done. And maybe the new Walter has tricks up his sleeve that the old one didn't."

"How much do you want me to do?"

"Same as last time. Why don't we meet out there in a week or two and walk the place?"

"Deal," said Walter.

My last call was to the man who did the masonry and stonework on all the houses Walter and I built together. I felt a special bond with him because of how my grandfather made his living, mixing up mortar, laying brick, and supervising a crew. I thought of him as an unofficial member of my grandfather's extended professional family.

"I don't know if you've heard," I said, "but we got burned out."

"Yup, just like I heard about Walter."

"All that work you and your guys did, it's buried somewhere in a landfill now. But I didn't call to talk about that. I wanted to let you know we might be building a new place somewhere in the area, and I hope you'll be there for us when the time comes."

"You betcha," he said. "You and Walter are my favorite customers. But even if you weren't, I'd still do it because Lord knows I need the work. I'm an old guy that's pretty much starting from scratch again."

My eyes started filling up as he described what happened to him in the fire's northern boundary. Unlike Cottletown Road, where there were many more losers than winners, he drew one of the few short straws in an area that burned when the wind suddenly changed direction and the fire got slammed into reverse. Like some of our other self-employed friends, he made his living with tools and equipment that he stored next to his home. Little of it remained.

"I don't get it," I said. "The wind blew south the entire time."

"Except for when it went the other way just long enough to get me."

He chuckled. It was a mirthless and brittle sound. "No point in getting my blood pressure up, right? I keep telling myself that."

"Where are you living?"

"On my land."

I didn't press him for the details. "This is really terrible news. It never would have occurred to me that you'd be wiped out too."

"Me neither. You don't think about something like that until it happens."

"Seems like every time I think I've heard the last of the bad news, there's more of it."

"Ain't that the truth?"

Several days later, Jeff and I met halfway between Austin and Bastrop. We spent fifteen minutes in his large pickup working out the details while Miranda sat in my car listening to the music on my iPad. It felt good to sit next to a man entirely in control of his faculties.

Because Jeff is a man's man, I knew a hug was out of bounds. I hoped he understood that my strong grip on his rough, calloused right hand and my sincere smile meant I was turning my future over to him with confidence and thanks. I was glad my eyes stayed dry until I was back in the car with Miranda, the family's official guardian of my emotional state.

"It's done," I told Holly as Miranda and I drove back to Austin.

"Thank heaven," she said.

"I feel like a great load has been lifted from us by Jeff agreeing to do this. We may not have land yet, but at least we have a builder. The first piece of our future is finally in place."

October 25, 2011, 4:15 p.m. "I told Amelia that we were going to talk about clinical stuff today," I said. "She suggested that I ask if you've come up with a diagnosis yet."

With her legs tightly crossed, our therapist looked at me intently and leaned forward a little. "I generally don't like to have this kind of conversation early in therapy. But you know more than most people about mental illness, and you have a daughter in the field. So I'm comfortable talking about your experience within that context, although I don't want it to affect the work we have to do together."

"Duly noted. So what do you think?"

"Right now, I would say that you have post-traumatic stress disorder. In fact, I'd say you're almost a classic case of it."

"I wondered if you were going to say that."

"Why?"

"That term is everywhere these days. A trendy acronym for people who are depressed or can't sleep."

"It's a serious illness," said my therapist.

"I suppose it is. But I think you get my drift."

"PTSD is a medical condition that develops as a result of a traumatic event. There are many things that can happen to people that trigger it. A wildfire is certainly one of them."

Even though I expected this diagnosis, it still unleashed a wave of ambivalence. On the one hand, saying I had a disease theoretically meant there was a treatment. It also meant I wasn't alone and my sour mood wasn't entirely my fault.

But equating what happened to the Fritz family with the trauma of war felt like an overreaction and an insult to those whose conditions warranted the clinical diagnosis. I hadn't watched my buddies die, and I didn't kill anyone. Surely what applied to veterans trying to find their place in a newly alien world shouldn't be applied to me. I wasn't worth it.

"PTSD is a condition in the brain," our therapist said. "It's biological and chemical and a little mysterious as well. We know more about the brain today than ever before, which is why I don't think there's anything wrong with talking about it as a physical condition or giving it a technical name."

"As opposed to saying I've chosen to be hard to live with?" I looked at my youngest daughter out of the corner of my eye. As usual, she said nothing and sat perfectly still. Just having her there was a comfort.

"Anxiety and its related emotions are natural and necessary reactions to life-threatening events and situations. You and Amelia had a close call with death. You visited your land almost immediately after it was destroyed. You see dead and dying trees every time you go back. Of course your brain is reacting to all of this. How could it not?"

Now I looked directly at Miranda. She had already proven to me that the brain sometimes goes its own way, for good as well as ill. While most people could multiply and divide three-digit numbers or shoot a free throw, she could focus intently and patiently on little children long past the breaking point for almost anyone else and still let loose a smile that charmed even the grumpiest of grumps. Miranda had something to teach me.

"Do you want to say anything about this?" I asked her. She shook her head.

"I also think you're in a state of bereavement," said our therapist. "Grief brings its own set of symptoms and issues. They can be similar to PTSD, but they're not exactly the same."

"Given what I think I know about mental illness, I want to believe you," I said. "But it feels like we're just slapping a label on something that continues to make no sense to me."

"While I could sit here and explain some of it in technical terms," said our therapist, "I don't think that will serve any therapeutic purpose. Mental illness and its treatment are a mystery in many ways, and I'm not ashamed to admit that I don't know why therapy works for some people and not for others. I'm not even sure that saying 'it works' is the right way to put it."

"Do you think I need drugs? Although the thought of taking a pill for what I'm going through seems weird, to say the least."

"I'm not professionally credentialed to answer that question. But I don't think it would hurt for you to consult with a medical professional you trust."

"Would pills help me sleep?"

"That's not a question I should answer," she said.

As Miranda and I drove back, it occurred to me that having PTSD could be a giant "get out of jail free" card for my many transgressions and shortcomings. Perhaps I could get a tattoo on my forehead: "It's not my fault: I have PTSD."

But that juvenile humor was more than offset by the implications of our therapist naming my condition. When I got back, I did what any twenty-first-century man would do: I logged on to Google.

In less time than it takes for a major-league fastball to reach home plate, I received more than 25 million results to my "What is PTSD" search. I started with the first ten, and over several hours I read about the symptoms, possible treatments, and anecdotal tales of PTSD victims or patients or whatever noun is most appropriate for that condition.

Our therapist was right about the mystery part. The more I learned, the less I knew. And the less I knew, the more I understood.

The brain is an organ that can be analyzed with tools and tests, the existence of which shows how far human beings have come since the invention of the wheel. But there's a limit as to how much we can, or perhaps even should, connect the biology of the brain and eyes to a middle-aged man who has suddenly gone weepy. At what point is it counterproductive to mention neurotransmitters and MRI readouts in explaining why someone with PTSD can't think straight or suddenly has an angry streak? Who cares about the "fight or flight" reaction in the dead of a wakeful, agonizing night?

Where did my soul—whatever that is—factor into all of this medical information? If I wasn't in control of the things happening in my head, then who or what was? Were my PTSD symptoms the problem I needed to solve or merely the signs of a larger, even more implacable one?

I wondered whether the PTSD tribe—of which I was a new initiate—was proud or shameful. How would my burned-out friends react if I told them, "I think you have PTSD, just like me." While I wouldn't hesitate recommending an orthopedist to a buddy with a torn ACL, could I refer my therapist, or someone like her, to an acquaintance whose mind seemed as off-kilter as mine?

These were questions with no answers, and I was surprised that I didn't mind that. Perhaps the schematic of my post-fire mind included new circuitry for the acceptance of ambiguity.

My PTSD research ended with three conclusions: I need my therapist even more than I thought. I must see Robb because I'm sick. The awareness of ignorance is knowledge.

November 3, 2011, 8:45 a.m. The last time I saw my longtime friend Robb was at a racquetball game several weeks before the fire. In his professional capacity as a physician's assistant, he had been our family's medical go-to guy ever since we moved to Bastrop County. I sometimes joked that a new patient would quickly realize he wasn't a doctor because nobody with an MD is allowed to have such a caring and engaged bedside manner.

I got to the clinic—a one-story nondescript building that had seen better days—ten minutes early to fill out the paperwork. I gave a noncommittal answer to the receptionist's "What are we treating today?" question. After taking my weight, a nurse led me into a small room with some industrial-style chairs and a sawed-off bed, then took my pulse and blood pressure. Both were worse than my usual tip-top results.

In another departure from the normal medical world, I didn't have to wait long for Robb to show up. He came in looking like he always did at the office: a full head of white hair set off with glasses, a white-shirt uniform with a stethoscope slung around his neck, and a clipboard in his hand.

After every periodic physical he had done for me over the years, he would say something like "You're healthier than anyone your age has a right to be." On the morning I saw him for my alleged PTSD, he came to a different conclusion.

"We've been friends long enough for me to lay it on you straight," Robb said.

"Knock yourself out."

"You look bad," he said, as he slid his chair close enough to peer into the usual orifices. "Probably worse than I can ever remember."

"It's that obvious, huh?"

"Your eyes are puffy and your whole body looks slumped. Are you feeling depressed?"

"My therapist says I have PTSD."

"You're in therapy?"

"That's why I'm here. To see whether I need some kind of drug to treat the affliction she says I have."

"Is she recommending something?"

"She can't. No license to do that."

"How are you sleeping?"

"Terrible. If nothing else, I hope you can give me something for that. Maybe if I start sleeping again, half my problems will go away."

"Lack of sleep can make a lot of things worse. But better sleep isn't a panacea for PTSD."

With his usual patience and attentiveness, he went about his business, explaining everything he did. After he asked some questions about my physical and emotional health, he told me about several more mutual acquaintances who had lost their homes.

"I keep thinking my personal list of fellow fire victims is complete and then someone like you comes along with more names," I said. "That's partly why I'm glad we're living in Austin. There's almost no chance I'm going to run into any of them."

"Why wouldn't you want to do that?" asked Robb.

"It's hard to explain. Part of it is guilt about where we're living compared to others. But I guess the main thing is I hate it when people feel sorry for us, and I'm afraid that's how I'll react to them. You'd think I'd know better than anyone how to talk to a fire victim. But the opposite is probably true. I know too much."

"Well, unlike you, I see them in the clinic practically every day. A lot of it is anxiety-related. People with chronic conditions are especially vulnerable."

"Well, let's talk about me and my anxiety. Do you think I need something?"

"Yes. Your therapist was right to suggest that you see me."

He prescribed a psychotropic drug and ordered up a blood test to make sure I wasn't at risk for any nasty side effects. We gave each other a quick hug and mutual slap on the back and I said good-bye for the foreseeable future.

I took my prescription to the drugstore just down the street. The pharmacist on duty was a man I had known for most of the time we'd lived in Bastrop County. He was someone who fit in that category of not-quite-a-buddy but also more-than-an-acquaintance. He had filled Miranda's prescriptions in the dark days when her condition was at its worst.

He greeted me with a pleasant smile and an outstretched hand. While I was embarrassed by my prescription—official documentation that I was cracking up—I was even more embarrassed by my baseless fear that he'd pass judgment on me. I sucked it up and handed over Robb's little piece of paper.

Ever the professional, he looked at it without any reaction, went in the back, and came out a few minutes later with a small plastic container in his hand. He started to give me the standard consultation that goes with a serious drug.

"You can skip all that," I said. "I know how to read."

"You sure?"

I glanced at the women who were milling around, a mix of employees and customers. Nobody was paying attention to our conversation, but I wasn't about to take any chances. The world didn't need to know what I was buying.

"Absolutely."

I thanked him and walked out. In the car, I twisted open the childproof container and looked at the small white pills, shaking my head with a combination of wonder, disgust, and worry over whether they'd help me sleep. I scanned the laundry list of side effects with the same interest I'd give a tax form. Then I called Holly.

"I got my pills," I said. I told her what Robb had prescribed. "It sure felt awkward signing in at the clinic and having Gary fill the prescription. Nobody said anything, or gave me a funny look. But God only knows what they were thinking."

She gently reminded me that I was not the object of anyone's fixation.

"Never in my wildest dreams could I have imagined needing something like this," I said.

That night, I swallowed the first tablet with a gulp of water and went to bed, not knowing what to expect. I briefly woke up at my usual wee-hour time but then quickly went back to sleep.

"How did it go?" asked Holly as we both lay in bed with the first hint of daylight.

"Best night since the fire. Not perfect, but I'll take it."

CHAPTER 10

November 4, 2011, 10:30 a.m. I arrived at the river place a half hour before Walter. It was a nearly perfect Central Texas fall day. The clear sky was a deep blue. The temperature was in the upper 70s, and a gentle, balmy breeze blew out of the south. I intended to walk it by myself before Walter arrived to size up its potential as a building site.

Thanks to my first decent night of sleep in two months, my eyes were clear and my mind open.

Several recent soaking rains had turned September's brown grass green. On my way to the river, I walked under two very old oaks, each of which curved upward and to the right, like a half-completed arch. A steady stream of clear water from an alluvial spring dropped fifteen feet to the bottom of a ravine that channeled it into the river. It was a never-ending sound, something lovely and soothing that would always be heard by anyone standing underneath the oaks. Ferns grew at the bottom of the ravine.

I paused at the flat, midlevel strip of land and considered its possibilities. It was too small for a building, but there was plenty of space for a vegetable garden at least as big as the one we lost. Standing at the edge of the strip, I looked across the river. Though it had a slightly brown hue, it was clean and beautiful, sparkling and glittering in the late morning light.

The river jolted loose a memory from the last weekend of August, when the Fritz family convened at a local resort for a two-day celebration of Miranda's upcoming twenty-first birthday. The summer's hateful climax happened during our stay, with consecutive record-busting days topping 110 degrees, the prelude to Tropical Storm Lee's formation in the western Gulf of Mexico.

By that point in the summer, nothing the sun and suffocating air dished up could depress me any further. Despite my demoralized and sour state, I decided to get up with the sun and take a walk along the Colorado River by myself.

With everyone else still asleep, I walked down to the river and followed its southeastern flow, its glassy surface mirroring the trees that grew over it.

The shade and the breeze blowing over the water made the air temperature a few degrees cooler. The brownish ribbon of water, bounded by sycamore and cypress trees, dampened the discontented rattling in my head.

The drought had turned the idea of rain into a frustrating abstraction with a mythic, unattainable quality. It was something wonderful that used to happen but now didn't and perhaps never would again. But the river was proof that rain in Central Texas wasn't a lie after all. Before me, an innumerable army of freshwater molecules passed by on their long march from the place where they had deployed as precipitation to the place where they would enter the Gulf and wait for their next mission in the endless cycle of evaporation and condensation.

As I walked on that Sunday morning, a week before the fire, I couldn't help wondering how life would be different if Holly and I had originally bought land on or near the river instead of in the Lost Pines. It was hard not to fantasize a different situation, one in which the shimmering and moderating effect of gathered and flowing rainwater would always be close at hand, along with the trees that prospered in that kind of place.

Now Holly, Miranda, and I had that choice. The river invited a closer look.

The autumn sun was lower in the sky than it had been during my last visit, and the light was richer. A turtle sunned itself on a large reddish rock a few feet from the riverbank. It plopped into the water and invisibly swam away when it heard me shuffling through the grass. Cardinals and warblers sang, a pileated woodpecker tap-tapped, and a heron flew away with a squawk, apparently taking issue with my intrusion into its personal space. A group of buzzards rode the thermal currents of the wind, up and down. They were quick-change artists that went from thrilling in flight to creepy when still.

There were fresh deer tracks in a sandbar that jutted fifteen feet out from the bank. I imagined a doe and her fawns having an early morning sip, or maybe a group of larger deer gathering at sunset for Happy Hour. I took care not to twist an ankle in little potholes where nocturnal critters—armadillos, perhaps, or possums—had been laboring.

Keeping an eye out for snakes, I walked along the riverbank. The river's summertime brown had been swapped for a less turgid sandy hue. A solid line of trees stood along my side of the river up to the bend at least a mile away. It was more open on the other side, and the river's bank was less pronounced. In some spots, on that side, the ground melted into a grassy sandbar that seamlessly slipped under the water's surface.

I could picture myself sitting near the riverbank on a balmy morning or sublime evening, trying to focus on a book rather than the cypress, sycamore, and elm trees above me. But would it be fair to live among trees like this when our Cottletown friends and others we cared about planned to rebuild in a scarred and mutilated landscape?

The combination of water and rich river-bottom soil meant there was far more life here than any other place we had called home. I was starting to come around to Holly's point of view.

My last stop was the property's signature spot: the high point overlooking the river's southward bend. The current owners had dug out a deep, circular fire pit just to the right of a large and sinuous oak tree anchored as close to the edge as physically possible. Plastic and wooden chairs were arrayed in a semicircle around the pit in the direction of the sunset. I imagined the owners and their friends one-upping each other with beer-drenched superlatives to describe the sights in front of them.

I sat in one of the red wooden chairs and took it all in: the curved river, the meadow on the river's far side, the prodigiously leafed-out trees, and the steep hillside. It was a view as uniquely exceptional as a truthful politician or a grateful and serene teenager.

In the middle of all this was a solitary loblolly, at least seventy-five feet tall, a lost pine at the southern extremity of the Lost Pines. While its top was green and lustrous, the bottom looked bad. The fire had scuttled down the hillside, gobbling up the vegetation. It torched the pine's base before reaching the river's edge and giving up, leaving the other trees unmolested.

My reverie was interrupted by the sound of Walter's pickup as he pulled up and parked at the bottom of the ridge. He was wearing jeans and a comfortable, long-sleeved shirt.

"I'm up here," I shouted. I met him halfway down.

"So I take it you're giving this place a second chance?" he asked.

"Have to. Nothing else seems remotely plausible at this point."

"You could do a lot worse."

We climbed back up to the top. I pointed at the lone pine. "You think that one is going to make it?"

"Hard to say. It might be a year before you know for sure."

"Great," I sighed.

We caught up on what each of us had been up to in the month since we last talked in person. We had a lot in common. In each of our families, the men seemed to be doing worse than the women. From a sociological perspective, it was counterintuitive and refreshingly contrary to the myth of a modern man. From a personal perspective, we agreed that it sucked. Then it was time to talk business.

"So what do you want to know?" he asked.

"Is there any risk of building up here? And do you think you can design a house for this site, given how skinny it is, with zero margin for error?"

"I can certainly design something. The real question is whether you'll like it. These dimensions are tough."

"If you can keep it from looking like an oversized storage container, that'd be a good start."

"As for risk, you won't have to worry about flooding. All of Central Texas would be underwater before it ever gets up here."

"Given all we've been through, a flood doesn't sound half bad."

"So I guess the main question is whether this ridge is solid. I think it is, but we need to go down to the bottom and take a closer look."

Walter and I walked the five-hundred-foot length of the bottom facing the opposite direction of the river and scanning the breadth of the hillside. Everywhere we looked, enormous red sandstone rocks peeked or poked out.

"With those boulders, it's safe to say this ridge isn't going anywhere. It's been here a long time, and it will be here long after we're gone."

"Those rocks will keep the foundation stable?"

"Definitely."

"What about when the river rises thirty-five or forty feet, like it did during the last flood, when I was judge?"

"Something like that probably happened regularly before the dams were built. When the river goes up like that, it turns into a lake instead of a raging torrent."

"What about erosion?"

"I think most of what burned off will come back. But you probably should plant some perennial rye grass near the top to keep the dirt in place before it comes back to life next spring."

We walked back to his pickup. "You can build here," said Walter. "It won't be easy, but if anyone is up to it, it's Jeff."

"And you," I said.

"Maybe."

"How does it feel to be living in town?" Walter and Jeri Nell were now in what used to be Holly's old dance studio.

"Jeri Nell likes it a lot."

"And you?"

"It was the right decision to buy it. And having an elevator already in place for Jess is a real blessing."

"You have an elevator?"

"That's right. The previous owners put it in for an elderly family member."

"So I guess it was meant to be," I said.

"But I'm not giving up on our land. We're keeping our dogs out there, and one of us has to go back at least every other day to feed them."

"How can you stand that?"

"It's better than staying away. I need to be in the woods."

"But the woods are gone."

"Not all of my trees are dead."

His commitment to his devastated land was as admirable as it was incomprehensible. But it felt wrong to say anything that might change his mind.

"So what do you think you're going to do about this place?" he asked.

"I have to sleep on it. But right now, it's this or nothing."

"Well, let me know. If you pull the trigger, I certainly won't mind coming out here regularly."

Holly, Miranda, and I took the weekend to make a decision that finally felt inevitable. Besides getting to live in another Walter-designed house tailored to our aesthetic tastes and personal needs, each of us would receive a specific bequest from the fire. For Miranda, it would be a room sufficiently isolated from her parent's bedroom that she could one day describe it to her paternal grandparents as "her apartment." For Holly, the property's verticality meant a view she would never take for granted and numerous garden terraces where she could pour her love of growing things. For me, it was the water and the riverbank trees.

The weekend of Ben's visit, my marriage to Holly was probably at its greatest risk since our first years together, when—like most new couples—our tenderness to one another was more than canceled out by the many innovative ways we found to annoy or frustrate each other. An irreversible disintegration of our family was not inconceivable.

But the mutual sense of hope that our decision gave us ended the possibility that our dependent daughter's adult life would have to straddle two alienated and undone parents. First thing Monday morning, I called Sandy.

"Time to draw up the papers," I said. "We're buying it."

November 21, 2011, 2 p.m. Holly, Sandy, and I walked into a Bastrop title company three days before Thanksgiving with a cashier's check in Holly's purse and certainty in our hearts. The offices were on the second floor of a new bank building. Everything was spic and span and orderly, including the perfectly arranged magazines and newspapers on a small end table. After waiting a few minutes, we were escorted into a brightly lit conference room with a long table and twice as many chairs as we needed. The closing officer sitting across the table from us was Judy, our former Cottletown neighbor and my companion at the overlook while the fire was happening.

Each of us was an Eisenhower or Truman baby. Judy and Sandy were nicely dressed, while Holly and I were our usual ragamuffin selves. I had a two-day growth of beard and wore my post-fire warm-weather uniform: khaki shorts and a cotton T-shirt that one of my work colleagues had given me a week after the fire.

I reached across the table to shake Judy's hand and said, "We're seeing each under better circumstances than the last time."

She nodded and smiled.

"Where are you living these days?" I asked.

"In town."

"Did you buy something?"

"Renting now, but I'm about to close on a house."

"Please don't tell me it's in the fire zone."

"I'll be a block or two from where the fire stopped."

"Just like us," I said. "We pass a lot of damage to get to the property we're buying. But once we're there, we can sort of forget about it. At least that's what I'm assuming."

"You and me both."

"What about your place on Cottletown?"

"Still own it."

"Same as us. Some days I feel like just putting out a sign that says 'Free to the first taker.'"

"I'm not sure what I'll do with it, but I'm keeping it for now," she said.

"At what point did you find out what happened?"

"Right after they let everyone back in."

"So you went a whole week without knowing?"

"From what I'd heard, I sort of knew better than to hope. But it was still a shock to actually see it. What about you?"

"I snuck in very early the morning after it went through," I said. "I kind of wish I hadn't now. I've thought about our conversations on the overlook more than once. I guess we were deluded."

"That's true," she sighed.

"But you've been doing OK?"

"A lot has happened since then. I'm doing my best to stay positive."

There was so much I wanted to ask her. Was she having trouble sleeping? What about therapy? Did she obsess about the past? Most of all, since she was single and living alone, how did she summon the strength to get up every morning?—some days the only thing that kept me going was my family obligations. I wondered if she had had any thoughts like I did as I watched the structural engineer tap away on our slab.

"I'd love to keep talking, Judy, but I think we're starting to try Holly's and Sandy's patience. Let's do this thing."

A half hour later, we were in the parking lot with a thick plastic envelope containing a bunch of legal papers that meant we now owned just over five acres of land on the river. Holly and I shared an emotional hug.

The next day, I told Miranda and our therapist all about it, including the brief visit Holly and I made to our new property.

"Your mom and I stood at the top and started discussing where we thought the house should be," I said. "You'll have your own room and bathroom, probably on the second floor looking out over the river just like your mom and dad underneath you."

Miranda nodded and mumbled, "Mm-hmm."

"You don't have anything to say?" I asked her. She shrugged. "But this is what you wanted." Her face was blank and she didn't move.

Hoping for reinforcement, I looked at our therapist, who gave me a gentle but firm "Don't go there" look.

"OK, OK. It's obvious I need to change the subject." I turned to our therapist. "Something has been gnawing at me. Now that this has happened, I'm wondering when it's OK to start feeling better. Any thoughts?"

Our therapist gave the nonanswer I expected.

"We've spent a lot of time talking about guilt," I said. "Maybe it's more accurate to say I feel morally ambivalent that we now own a beautiful property, much of which escaped the fire. I know there is no chess master in the sky, moving the pieces around, arbitrarily picking winners and losers. We didn't do anything to deserve the good fortune that has come our way just like we didn't deserve what the fire did to us. But many others are still waiting for something good to happen. Maybe for some of them, it will never come. Why us and not them?"

"You have nothing to be ashamed of," said our therapist, "and much to be thankful for."

It was a rare outburst of actual advice. I gulped it down.

On the way home, I fought the urge to force Miranda to thank me or do something to acknowledge that the only thing she talked about in therapy was now going to happen. But I finally couldn't stop myself.

"You don't care about what's happened?"

Silence.

"This doesn't make any sense, you not saying anything back there or now in the car."

"Leave me alone," she said. I could see her eyes starting to fill up.

"You're crying?"

She slapped my words away with her right hand and turned away.

"What's wrong?"

She kept sniffling and I shut up. Just before we got to our rental house, without looking at me, she said, "I don't want a new room. I want my old one." She wiped her nose with her shirtsleeve. "I wish none of this had happened."

Several days later, she announced she was finished with therapy. Her goal had apparently been achieved.

December 5, 2011, 9:30 a.m. My smartphone lit up with the number of the FEMA contractor in charge of private property tree removal. Some of their workers had marked the trees on our land that were a safety hazard. Now they needed our consent to remove them.

"What do you need us to do?" I asked.

"Go out there and make sure there aren't any marked trees that you want to save. Put yellow tape around the keepers so the guys leave them alone. Once that's done, we'll get started."

"How long will it take?"

"Not long," she said. "They go out there with bulldozers and chain saws and really have at it. A couple of days at the most." That seemed reasonable. After all, how many could there be?

"What happens to the trees?"

"Everything gets dragged to the side of the road and then gets picked up."

"OK. My wife or I will be back in touch soon."

I told Holly about the situation. "Don't you think I should go out there instead of you?" she asked.

"What would I see that I haven't already seen?"

"I don't think it's a good idea."

"As long as we own it, we can't pretend it's not there. We'll need to do some upkeep, or at least pay someone to do it."

"I can see you've already made up your mind," she said.

As I drove past the Highway 71 burn zone, I had a hard time keeping my eyes on the road. Things looked worse than they did a month ago. Trees that were in shock before were now brown and definitively dead. Some of the blackened bark was peeling or falling off. The company that had been hired to haul off the debris had cleared an enormous area on the south side of the highway, where it was systematically gathering the mess into an enormous pile. This was where my beloved trees would end up. It was all very depressing.

I parked my car just past the red gate and got out. The low, benign December sun was nothing like its malevolent summer twin. It was cool enough that I needed a light sweatshirt. The first thing I saw was a dead oak with a three-digit number spray-painted on its trunk. I walked down the driveway toward the slab and noticed numbers on every tree.

The more I looked around, the less sense it all made. I called the FEMA contractor woman and identified myself.

"Are we good to go?" she asked.

"Not yet," I said.

"So what's up, then?"

"There are a bunch of trees with red numbers painted on them," I said.

"Right. Those are the ones you need to double-check."

"But here's the weird thing. Some of them are numbers in the two hundreds. I'm looking at a pine tree right now with the number 203 sprayed on it. I just passed 220."

"So what's your question?" she said.

"What do the numbers mean?"

"You don't get it?"

It was an immensely annoying response. "I wouldn't have called if I did."

"The guys went through and numbered every tree that's gotta come down. If you passed 220, then you have at least that many trees that need to go."

I was speechless.

"Hello?" she said.

I still couldn't say anything.

"Are you there?"

"That's not possible," I finally said. "Are you sure they didn't start at a hundred?"

"They started at one. Just walk around if you don't believe me."

Feeling dizzy, and with my head pounding, I walked the entirety of our ten acres. She was right. I located the tree marked "1" and most of the others in between. The highest number I found was 235.

The numbered trees were only those that the FEMA contractor believed posed a safety threat, which meant there were hundreds more that hadn't been counted. It was bad enough to know that most of my trees were dead. But quantifying that fact made it much worse.

I called Walter.

"You're not going to believe what I just learned," I said.

"What?"

"That FEMA bunch wants to cut down and haul off at least 235 trees. Can you imagine what our place will look like after they're done?"

"I don't have to imagine," he shouted. "I'm looking at it right now."

"Why are you talking so loud?"

"It's the bulldozers. I'm out here to keep an eye on them, but there's nothing I can do at this point. It's awful and getting worse by the minute."

"How many trees are we talking about?"

"Four hundred, more or less."

I was stupefied. "What are they doing with them?"

"They're pulling or pushing them to the right-of-way. And tearing up everything in their path as they go."

"Four hundred trees just around your driveway and where your house used to be?"

"That's right," he shouted.

"And how many dead ones do you think you have on the rest of your forty acres?"

"Tens of thousands."

"I can't believe you're there, watching it," I said. "It's like witnessing a murder."

"The murder happened three months ago. All they're doing now is hauling off the bodies."

For the good of both of us, Walter ended the call. I tried to picture the scene unfolding a quarter mile away, but I couldn't. I considered going over to see for myself, but I didn't. I thought about calling Holly but couldn't imagine any good coming of it. I knew a call to my therapist would go straight to voice mail. I sat in my car for a while, trying to calm down enough to drive. My one consolation was that I had therapy the next day.

Finally, I got out and leaned against the red gate's pipelike post, halfway standing, halfway sitting. I had exposed myself to this without accomplishing my assigned task: identifying the trees we wanted to save. Holly would have to do that another day.

I scanned the flat part of our land and marveled at what a couple of minutes on Labor Day had done. How could such a fleeting moment produce something so seemingly permanent? Four years of work and the plans we had for the rest of our life, undone in a cosmic eyeblink. I drove off, knowing with absolute conviction that I would never again set foot on the benighted property

that Gordon and his wife had sold us on a late fall day in 2007. That smile-
and laugh-filled occasion no longer seemed real.

Several days later, Holly wrapped yellow police tape around a still-alive oak
in our circular driveway and some pines that ringed the slab. Then I gave the
FEMA contractor woman the OK to start knocking them down.

"Someone has to be out there while it's happening," she said.

"I've been talking to one of my friends out here about how this is probably
gonna go. Are they going to leave our place a godawful mess?"

"They try to be careful," she said.

"That's not what I asked."

"I can't make any guarantees, if that's what you want."

The next day, Holly took Miranda to school in Bastrop and then went to
the Cottletown property to meet the agents of destruction. Around noon, her
name popped up on my phone.

"How are things going?" I asked.

"It's horrible," she said, her voice cracking. "I can barely watch it."

"You sound upset. Are you crying?"

Silence.

"Holly?"

She coughed a little. "What do you think?"

"Are they ripping everything up?"

"They're doing the best they can. But, yes, it's unspeakable, just like you
predicted."

"I'm sorry you have to see it."

"I guess now I'm the one who's upset."

"Do you really have to stay out there?"

"They're going to let me go soon. We're on the same page about what needs
to be saved. There's no reason for me to keep watching them do it."

The sniffling stopped.

"There is one wonderful thing, though. My flower gardens are green. They
survived. My plants are going to make it."

OUR GARDENS

When Holly and I first moved to Central Texas, we grew our own food out of
economic necessity. Besides feeding our family of two, our garden produced a
small cash crop at a time in our life when literally every dollar counted. Our first
summer in the Lost Pines, we carted oversized bags of our tomatoes, potatoes,
and squash to a just-opened Austin grocery store a few blocks north of the river.
The people who stocked the produce aisles at the original Whole Foods, and

who found much to like in what we brought them, had tattoos galore, nose rings, and unnaturally placid demeanors.

But money had nothing to do with the gardens we dug, composted, mulched, and tended to on an almost daily basis at the Cottletown house. In a very real sense, they were priceless to us.

Holly and I split up our gardens into the utilitarian (mine) and aesthetic (hers). My fenced-in vegetable garden was six hundred square feet of sandy loam soil divided into a set of parallel and perpendicular raised beds enriched with compost and local manure.

The cycle of planting, watering, weeding, and harvesting was gratifying and enriching to me in ways that few prior personal undertakings had been. Each month brought new possibilities as well as the end of others. About the time spinach was going to seed and the radishes were picked over, my heirloom lettuce was at its peak. When that petered out, I began digging up new potatoes. Then it was on to scores of tomatoes and just as many peppers. Melons kept coming throughout the summer, and the mild Central Texas fall and early winter brought a bonus harvest of tomatoes and peppers, a reward for the watering and weeding I soldiered through during the dog days. The cycle started again in January.

Holly's flower gardens were close to the house, terraced and framed by the limestone left over from building the house. Taking the long view, she favored perennials. While a smattering of annuals inevitably showed up—the plants that begged to be adopted whenever she paid a visit to the neighborhood nursery—the flower gardens around the house and curved walkway were mainly set up to get better with each passing year, which they dutifully did in our first two years. On both sides of the walkway leading to the front door, and in the garden she created inside of the circular driveway, she cultivated daylilies, Indigo Spires, daffodils, tulips, and blackfoot daisies. Outside our bedroom, she grew gardenias.

Holly began most mornings by walking among her seedlings, flowers, and bushes, coffee cup in hand. On balmy April and May evenings, with warm breezes blowing, we opened our windows to carry the delicious odor of the gardenias into our bedroom, a month-long perfume factory that ended just as Miranda's vocational program was letting out for the summer.

On the morning of the fire, Holly watered her gardens as Tropical Storm Lee blew in. While the leaves and most of the stems burned off, the wet ground kept the roots alive. By the time the bulldozers knocked down and hauled off the dead pines and oaks, their tiny plant-world cousins were above ground, bringing a bit of hope to the woman who had planted and nurtured them.

December 15, 2011, 2:30 p.m. The week after Thanksgiving, Walter and Jeff and I began a twice-weekly ritual at the new property where we discussed Walter's conceptual ideas and Jeff's practical ones. While we had faith in Walter, we weren't sure how he'd avoid the boxcar look everybody feared and nobody wanted.

But the problem was solved when we acquiesced to Jeff's insistence that the garage be built into the north-facing hillside, with part of the house resting on top of the garage. This split-level design liberated Walter's aesthetic instincts because it was more rectangular.

Our get-togethers began at the end of the cul-de-sac after I dropped Miranda off at her vocational school. Each of us had a uniform and standard equipment. I wore sweatpants, tennis shoes, and a T-shirt under a dirt-spackled sweatshirt. My smartphone stored the notes and questions that randomly occurred to me. Jeff sported steel-toed boots, jeans, a work shirt, a gimme cap, and a tool belt cinched around his waist. He was the only one with tattoos, but they weren't the hipster kind. Old school through and through, he kept his pencil-made notes and drawings in a plain manila folder with an organizational method known only to him. Walter was decked out in tennies, jeans, and a flannel shirt. His main tools were a tape measure and printouts from his architectural software.

Jeff's mind was turbo-powered, which more than made up for the misfiring cylinders in my mental engine. Walter was somewhere in between. The property's verticality dominated most of our initial conversations, and almost all the topics were interrelated. We couldn't talk about foundations without wondering how the concrete trucks would get close enough to the ridge. The challenges of building a driveway that would have to rise as much as twenty feet very quickly led to the drainage riddles of steeply sloped land. We devised a very unappealing Plan B if the lumber company couldn't get its delivery truck to the ridgetop.

The all-business nature of our meetings was a relief. Problems had to be solved—lots of them—and listening to Jeff and Walter think through them was almost like listening to Anton play. Dark thoughts were crowded out and I was fully in the moment. The only time the fire came up was as a possible cause for subcontractor shortages. Foundations were already being framed up on McAllister Road and in nearby Tahitian Village. It was only a matter of time before we'd have to take our place on a list.

The fact that our personal circumstances were never discussed didn't mean that Jeff was insensitive to our situation. In fact, the opposite was true. Our project consumed him. He thought about it when he watched evening television and as he went to sleep. Even as he completed his other commitments, he was thinking through the problems he'd confront with a complicated design and even more complicated building site. It was fortunate for all of us that he didn't use e-mail and barely knew how to text.

For fear of jinxing the situation, I didn't dare ask Walter how he found the wherewithal to crank out the work he was producing. He promised a full set of plans by late January, and he was off to a fast start.

While our planning meetings kept my mind productively occupied, the time I spent waiting to pick Miranda up was another story. Most days, I hung out at Amelia's, sitting at her small dining room table with my laptop, trying to focus on consulting work that had piled up after three months of neglect. But looking around her living room, with the two tubular skylights and hand-hewn red stone fireplace and Walter's bookshelves, I couldn't stop thinking about what might have been and what actually was. By the time I pulled up to the Bastrop Works parking lot—where an always-smiling Miranda waited, usually laughing it up with her best friend, Molly—I was rarely in a good mood.

More than anything else, our Cottletown property weighed me down. As long as we owned it, I was in danger of tending to it and slamming my therapy gains into reverse with each visit. One afternoon in mid-December, as I headed westbound over the Colorado River Bridge in Bastrop, I was suddenly seized by the conviction that we had to sell it, no matter what, and right away. Holding on to it would eventually kill me, in spirit if not in body.

I made a northward turn off Highway 71 and pulled up to a real estate company owned by a woman I had known since my days as county judge. I was escorted into her spacious office. Her desk was piled high with papers and small, framed photos.

An elegant and well-spoken woman who once chaired the Bastrop School Board, she skillfully balanced the professional with the personal. Taking my lead from the sensitively posed "where are you living and how are you doing" inquiries, I explained to Kay why I was there and why we had to sell our land.

"I have just the right man to help you," she said.

"You're not going to do it?"

"The person I have in mind will do a better job for you."

"But I want you to represent us."

"I understand. But Tim lost his home as well. He knows better than I ever could what you're going through and why you're selling. I also think you'll enjoy getting to know him. You have a lot in common." It was a remark so freighted with possible meaning that I didn't dare ask her to elaborate.

I followed her down a narrow hallway to Tim's office. It was barely big enough for him and a couple of clients. She introduced me, briefly explained why I was there, and left. After shaking hands, I took a seat just inside the door and faced him across his cluttered desk.

Tim looked to be about ten years younger than me. He had a well-trimmed beard, thinning hair, and a welcoming smile tinged with sadness. I immediately liked him.

I told him where our property was, its size and topography, and its current condition.

"But I can't tell you what it looks like now," I said. "FEMA just tore out a bunch of dead trees, and I haven't been back."

"That'll probably make it more appealing to prospective buyers. You know what it looked like before the fire, but they won't. Better for them to see a cleared-out property than one with dead trees everywhere."

"I see your point. Still, I can't believe anyone will want to buy it."

"You'd be surprised," he said. "After the fire, stuff that had been on the market for months was snapped up, just like that. Things have slowed down since then, but unexpected sales keep coming. It's what happens when a family finally decides they have to move on."

"Just like us."

"And maybe us as well," he said. "We go back and forth, over and over. Right after the fire, I thought we'd stay. Then we changed our mind. We had to get out of here for good. Too much pain, too many memories."

"So what happened?"

"I suddenly had a lot of business. By the time things settled down, we decided to stay a little longer. We're still here."

With a mixture of sadness and fond remembrance that felt very familiar, he described his destroyed house. Like me, he had built it himself with the help of some subcontractors. He designed it specifically for his personal and professional needs, with some one-of-a-kind features. It sat on an expansive and pine-filled corner lot a mile or two from our new place, as the crow flies. It was to be his final domicile.

Even though I had seen this movie before, the pain felt fresh, as did my guilt. I had a future, and he was still looking for one. I had an idea of what our life would look like in a year, and he didn't. As bad as I felt when I came into his office, I wouldn't trade places with him.

"I wish I had some advice for you," I said. "But I think we both know that I can't say anything that will help."

"I know."

"Except maybe for this. If you've been wondering whether you're alone in how you feel, and what you've gone through, you're not. Trust me."

He nodded and smiled weakly.

"We could probably sit here for two more hours and not run out of things to say," I said. "But I have to get my daughter from school in a little bit."

He gave me some forms and I stood up. I had known him for less than fifteen minutes, but I wanted to show how I felt about his situation with a hug. I shook his hand instead.

"You did what?" said Holly when I called her with the news.

"You heard me right."

"You just decided to do this on your own, without even asking for my opinion?"

"We haven't signed any papers. If you're against it, we'll pull the plug."

"And who is this guy exactly?"

I told her about our conversation. "I like him. He'll do a good job for us."

"This is a lot to take in."

"We have to do it eventually. Why not get it over with?"

After a difficult conversation with Holly that evening, we signed the broker agreement and hunkered down for a long wait. A few days later, our real estate agent delivered the goods. A couple made an offer, we countered with a split-the-difference price, and they accepted. We would swap neighborhoods. They would abandon their burned-out McAllister Road property for ours, which we gave up for land two blocks from McAllister.

December 18, 2011, 11 a.m. For the many years I accompanied the Calvary Episcopal Church choir, one of the annual highlights was the Advent Lessons and Carols service, an alternating combination of scripture readings and seasonal music. As the service progressed, I reflected back on a year almost gone.

There was never any question of my attending this service at St. David's. Holly and Miranda preferred the informal service with guitar music, so I took a solitary aisle seat in the third row of the historic sanctuary, a long rectangular room with a vaulted ceiling and an ornate, Anglican-style white altar. As I settled in, I gratefully remembered what had happened in this space when the St. David's choir sang a sublime and moving Fauré Requiem on November 1: All Saint's Day.

I sat between Anton and Miranda that evening near the back of the sanctuary and held my breath as I looked through the program for a sign that the rector had heard the plea I e-mailed to him several days after I tore into him the morning we first met:

I am the person you met at the 11:15 service who lost his Bastrop County home in the fire. I apologize for the somewhat snarky way I responded to your offer of help. Upon further reflection, there is something perhaps you can do. I am planning on attending the Fauré Requiem as I love this piece and I am going to be thinking of my now-dead trees as I listen. Most of us who lived out here are grieving the most over the loss of the forest. This is a death in a very real sense. Is it possible to tie the Requiem in some way to the loss of 1.5 million trees in the Bastrop wildfire?

On the third page of the program, I saw that he had heard my plea by writing a simple prayer about the catastrophic taking of life:

Lord Jesus Christ, we ask your blessing and grace on those who have suffered loss of any type—loss of loved ones, loss of property, loss of livelihood. And we pray for all living beings that have been harmed by fire, drought, earthquakes, hurricanes, and other natural disasters. With all creation, we grieve the loss of tree and forest, of creature and plant, all of which are precious to our God.

Reading it had an instantaneous effect on me. For the ten minutes before the Requiem Mass began, I audibly sobbed from gratitude at this simple yet profound gesture of pastoral love and the prayer's meaning. Anton put his arm on my shoulder and Miranda stroked my hand. Those who were seated near us resisted the urge to see what the commotion was about. I was enveloped by the kind of love that is often spoken of in church but rarely felt, at least in the moment. As the ethereal music of Gabriel Fauré quietly began, I finally received the catharsis my leaky tear ducts had been trying to deliver over two months of hard labor.

Seven weeks later, no longer craving catharsis, I scanned the Lessons and Carols program and my heart sank. The problem wasn't the music. It was the list of performers.

Instead of the extraordinarily capable adult choir, several children's choirs would perform most of the special music. Apparently this was the St. David's proxy for a Christmas pageant, with parents and relatives forgiving all musical sins and innocent bystanders fighting the urge to plug their ears and bolt for the exits.

I briefly closed my eyes. With a mild din of chatter and laughter, St. David's on this Sunday morning sounded like a school auditorium before a talent show. I said to myself: "This too shall pass."

The service began and the children—mainly girls—started filing in from the side door and toward the back of the church, two by two, clad in white choir robes, with the youngest ones followed by the tweens and young teens.

As they made a U-turn at the back and began processing down the center aisle toward the altar, cameras clicked, grandparents beamed and waved, and an occasional parent on the aisle instinctively reached toward a child. The children were gorgeous and radiant. My eyes would be favored even if my ears were assaulted.

And then the music began. Defying my expectations, every piece was performed with sensitivity and loveliness. In the most overused of clichés, the children sounded angelic.

How could a group of children sound like that, no matter how long and hard they practiced? I was in a God-drenched place. Through their radiance and music, the children asked me to forget about myself for a moment and heed their messages, which were:

We come to you, in a holy place, to deliver a divine gift.
    Remember when your three daughters were like us—golden-haired and beautiful, a daily blessing to you.
    Remember the houses in which you raised them. Don't dwell on the messes the houses became or the deathless voids they are now.
    Remember what happened in them at a time in your life when your children could not have been more precious to you.
    Those memories can never be taken from you.

December 31, 2011, 11:30 p.m. The entire Fritz clan gathered at the Travis Heights rental house on New Year's Eve. The motto of the evening was "Good riddance, 2011. May we never see the likes of you again!"

Holly prepared a delicious dinner, I poured a high-end Cabernet from my revitalized wine collection, Ben chased the dogs after he finished off his mac and cheese, and good feelings flowed in abundance. Later that evening, after we clicked our toasts and kissed our good-byes, I took an outside seat on the lower deck. I wasn't interested in the view from upstairs. I wanted a quiet moment to reflect without the visual distraction.

The next day Holly, Miranda, and I would share a New Year's champagne lunch on the riverbank of our new land. For now, I wanted to think about the events that had brought us to this point. I hoped to gain some insight for the future, as in therapy, by reminding myself what I had gone through to get to this pivotal moment at year's end. I intended to race through the bad and linger on the good.

I never made it past the you-know-what.

As I mentally reconstructed the events of Miranda's birthday, I reached for my phone and the photo album containing pictures of the Cottletown house. I hadn't look at most of these for several years.

The first pic was the concrete slab's rough-in, with rectangles of rebar nestled between squarish and manicured dirt piles. I scrolled through every phase of the building project, pausing with a smile at a picture from a wet and chilly December day. Jeff was wearing a cheesy yuletide cap while his two-man crew blankly stared at the camera, hands on hips, tool belts sagging.

I zipped through the roof installation, stonework, drywall floating and taping, and landscaping. There were two ridiculous photos Holly had taken of me sitting in a rented miniature bulldozer, with a purple bandanna tied to my head and scrunched-up black shorts. With a steering mechanism that looked like giant joysticks, I moved surplus stones from the building site to a garden area.

The lumps in my throat started forming with the interior pictures: books and pots—including the Bernard Leach cup—on the bookshelves, Holly playing Scrabble with the Chagall and my piano behind her, and Ben crouched under Charlie's face, a photo Amelia snapped on the long Memorial Day weekend when my grandson stayed with me.

Even though I knew what was coming, I kept at it until I reached the first of fourteen post-fire pictures, starting with the remains of the carport: a raggedy pile of silvery metal.

The phone's glassy interface trapped me in a pictorial time-loop. Back and forth I swiped: before and after; after and before. By the time Holly caught me in the act, just as the downtown fireworks were starting, I was a lost cause.

"What in the world are you doing now?"

"You don't want to know," I croaked.

"When are you going to learn?"

"Who says I will?"

"Please put that away."

"In a minute."

"You need to give it to me."

I handed it over, exchanged a perfunctory New Year's kiss with my wife, and staggered off to bed, taking a self-prescribed double dose of medication to speed things up and lock them down. An hour into 2012, I would have probably slept through a bomb.

New Year's Day was clear and gorgeous, the best that Central Texas has to offer in the winter. We arrived at our land around noon. By this time, most of the trees were denuded. The leaves that remained had changed from red or orange to a crumbly brown.

In several grocery bags, we toted our sandwiches, potato salad, chilled Cava, and plastic champagne glasses down to the river. We spread the blankets on the edge over a pile of fallen sycamore and cedar elm leaves. The river was smooth, barely moving, glassy and clear.

We reminisced about why and how we bought it. I accepted the good-natured abuse about my initial reaction to it when we were still living at Amelia's and I was stoned by sleep deprivation. We made a few predictions about our future life there. Mainly, though, we ate in silence and reveled in the beauty around us.

"This is a blessed spot," I said.

"We're going to be happy here," said Holly.

I held my phone in front of our three faces, trying to do my best imitation of a teenager at a rock concert or party, and snapped a selfie.

When I bring up the pic on my phone or computer, I see a red-faced man wearing aviator-style sunglasses and an unhesitant smile, a squinting, narrow-faced young adult with an enigmatic smile and her blond hair pulled back, and a grinning woman with her arms around them. Behind them, the sky is as blue as a Queen Angelfish's lips.

CHAPTER 11

January 5, 2012, 11 a.m. The closing on our Cottletown property took place in a nondescript office in a nondescript strip mall on Bastrop's outskirts. Whether by accident or design, everyone arrived at almost exactly the same time, minimizing the need for chitchat. The closing officer, a pleasant and efficient woman in her late twenties, led us to our places around a conference table in a windowless room. Holly and I sat directly across from the buyers, a middle-aged couple like us: informally dressed, graying, and slightly staggered by what we were about to do.

At opposite ends of the table sat Tim, our real estate agent, and the closing officer. We were five walking wounded and an unharmed civilian.

The closing officer distributed the paperwork and mechanically explained what we were signing and initialing. When the buyers handed over a cashier's check, she excused herself to make copies.

"Do you know what you're going to do with our property?" I asked.

"We've been living in a trailer since the fire," she said. "First thing we'll do is relocate it to your slab. We have no plans after that."

"We're going to take our time," her husband said. "We're just glad to have a place we can call home."

"What about you?" she said.

"We're kind of switching places with you," Holly said. "We'll be in the Colovista area."

The small talk quickly turned serious, hot emotion sizzling just below the surface. We explained why we had to sell, they explained why they had to buy, and our real estate agent explained why he and his family remained in limbo.

"It's hard for me to understand how anyone can rebuild on their land after it's been reduced to little more than bare ground," I said.

They nodded in agreement.

"That may be where we end up too," said our agent. "But my wife and I aren't there yet, even though we came close in September. Speaking only for myself, I think someone rebuilds because they still see potential in their land, hard as that may be right now."

Then we exchanged stories of where we were during the fire, when we knew our places were gone, and what the past few months had been like. I wondered if they had the same too-personal questions about us as I did about them. Even though we just met, we had an undeniable bond, just as I immediately did with Tim.

The closing agent distributed the copies and then sat quietly and patiently. Finally, our emotional tanks emptied out and we agreed it was time to leave.

After shaking hands with the buyers and our agent, I went straight to Holly's car and took my place in the passenger's seat. She stayed back and kept talking. The conversation lasted for almost ten minutes, and then Holly and the woman embraced. They were both crying.

"What just happened?" I asked as Holly climbed into her car with a reddish nose and puffy eyes.

"They were telling me why they bought our land," Holly said. As we had during the closing, we couldn't stop referring to the Cottletown place as "ours."

"And?"

"It was my gardens. She said that when they saw all those spots of green, it gave them more hope than anything they'd seen since the fire. My flowers and plants are why they bought it. They love what I loved."

The moment was so fraught with feeling that we did the only thing possible: drive silently to the bank and deposit the check. The last time we swelled our bank account with the proceeds of a property sale, we hugged the buyers who we knew would eventually become some of our closest friends.

OUR LANDLORDS, OUR FRIENDS

When Walter and I were building Betty's house in Colovista, I had a "what-if" conversation with Holly that began like the one fourteen years earlier when we fantasized about trading our "best small house in America" for the spacious one on Long Trail that our friend Nancy was thinking of selling. While it was more speculation than real, it wasn't entirely make-believe.

"The farther along your mom's house gets, the more I wonder why we don't build one like that for ourselves. This house is too big for us with Hillary and Amelia gone, and why shouldn't we live in a house with tubular skylights and limestone exterior walls and Walter's special touches? Maybe we should think about enlisting him to design something for us."

"But how would that work?" said Holly. "We'd have to sell our house and find some place to rent. If it weren't big enough, we'd have to put some of our things in storage. What would we do with your piano?"

"Or we could do a home equity loan and use that money as a down payment on a construction loan. Which would assume we could eventually sell this place at a decent price when we move out."

The more we talked about it, the less appealing both options were. We were just about to give up on the idea when a near-miracle happened.

Steve and Linda, a couple about our age from Nevada, had hired a Bastrop real estate agent to look for land that they could buy as an investment and future building site. The agent knew Walter, and he suggested that the couple make an offer on a portion of the land that Walter and his family owned that bordered Park Road 1C. Walter wasn't in the mood to sell, but he knew we might be.

On a late spring day in 2007, they arrived at our house, skeptical but open-minded. Less than two hours later, the deal was done. They would buy our house, and the sixteen acres that went with it, but we could keep living there indefinitely. After we left, they'd rent it out until Steve's retirement, when they hoped to split their time between Texas and Nevada.

We enthusiastically signed the initial paperwork and agreed on a day late in June when they would return for the closing.

The week after the summer solstice, in a poorly lit room in one of Bastrop's oldest downtown brick-façade buildings, we sat around an old and pock-marked wooden conference table, grinning like a group of giddy teenagers. Steve and I looked like tall and reasonably fit stepbrothers in our similar khaki shorts, collared T-shirts, and small bald spots surrounded by lots of hair.

Holly and I had just begun our search for the land on which we would build our final home. Because they were acquiring a place that seemed to them too good to be true, they wanted to know how we intended to replace it.

"Since you're letting us stay put, we're going to take our time," said Holly.

"We're probably not going to limit ourselves to properties that are for sale," I said. "My plan right now is to find the right area and then put some feelers out."

"Are you staying in the woods?" asked Steve.

"Not necessarily, although we'll never move entirely out of the Lost Pines," I said.

"We've been talking about how nice it'd be to have a view and a little more open space," said Holly.

"We both want gardens," I said. "We had a big vegetable garden many years ago, before the girls were born. Now that they're grown, I'd like to do that again."

"And I'm going to grow lots of other things, none for eating," said Holly.

"Since this is the last time we're going to move, it's a big decision. Probably won't happen for a while."

"Well, this is a big decision for us too," said Linda. "In fact, Steve is so excited about it, we have something we'd like to do before we go back."

"If it's OK with you," added Steve.

"Since you're our landlords now, we're hardly in a position to say no," I said.

We all laughed. The novelty of the situation was still fresh.

"Steve wants to take back some pine seedlings," said Linda. "He's hoping to grow a few loblollies outside of our house to remind himself of what awaits us in Texas." Steve broadly grinned while Linda filled in the details. An hour later, under a hot early summer sun, we were tromping through the woods, repeatedly wiping the sweat off our faces as the wieners hyperactively barked and darted about and Charlie loudly panted, barely keeping up.

With more shade than sunlight, we followed a primitive trail on the back of our property that led to another footpath that Gordon had cleared out. Along the way, Steve carefully dug up several foot-tall pine seedlings that he transplanted into plastic containers.

"You think they'll let you take those on the plane?" I said.

"I don't see why not," said Steve. "If nothing else, I'll hold them on my lap."

"His little babies," said Linda.

The Lost Pines was nothing like the open spaces of their home in northwestern Nevada. Seeing how they responded to everything around them, it was easy to recall how Holly and I felt that late summer day in 1979 when we first knew we couldn't live anywhere else. We were simpatico with them.

We exchanged another round of hugs and said our good-byes, confident that more good times were in store for us if we bought land close to what was now our rental home.

A month after we moved into our new Cottletown house, we invited them over for dinner on our deck.

On a gorgeous April evening in 2009, sharing a bottle of wine and another culinary masterpiece from Holly that included greens from my garden, we toasted our incredible good luck in finding one another. Then we clinked our glasses in honor of a friendship we agreed would be long and durable, built on a shared love of the forest.

As Holly and I stood in line to deposit our check, I looked at the outside tables at the coffee shop next door and remembered the last time I saw Steve and Linda, a week after the fire. They had just arrived from Austin, where they spent the night in a hotel. We arranged a short meeting at the Bastrop Starbucks.

Even though they hadn't yet seen what the fire did, they already were feeding off a carcinogenic mental image built from the news reports they followed from two thousand miles away and the onsite reports they received from Roland, the fire chief. As we sat outside under the already-hot morning sun, sipping our tepid coffees and poking at our pastries, we didn't know what to say to each other. Because I knew what awaited them, there was nothing I could do to prepare them. Because they couldn't truly fathom what they were about to see, they couldn't adequately empathize with me.

What once seemed a miracle now felt almost like a curse.

January 26, 2012, 9:30 a.m. On the surface, Amelia's longtime boyfriend Luke seemed about as different from me as anyone who adored my daughter, and her bookish ways, could be. But I respected him because he could do things, and solve problems, that were beyond me. It didn't hurt that Jeff and Walter had a high opinion of his way around heavy equipment and knowledge of drainage, a topic that was as fascinating to me as it was intimidating and scary. I knew from the steep drop at our Cottletown place what uncontrolled runoff could do during a torrential rain. Without the kinds of insights Luke could bring, our river place would turn into an ankle-twisting, axle-busting landscape of ruts and impromptu ditches.

Luke grew up in the nearby town of Rockne. He was a sandy-haired, medium-sized guy who usually wore a cap, an amiable expression, and a shadow of hipster stubble. Amelia's friends gushed over his good looks, and I took their word for it. He spent his free time fishing, hunting, and hanging out at the bottom of his parents' prairie land a dozen miles southwest of the Lost Pines.

Luke had already done us a favor by connecting us to his uncle Kenny, the Austin realtor who found our Travis Heights rental. But before he rolled up to our new property pulling a trailer as long as a mobile home, I couldn't have imagined what he would do to prepare our building site. I could barely picture how he had negotiated the trailer through highway traffic, the right-hand turn off McAllister, and the left-hand turn into Colovista.

The ridiculous trailer was hooked up to his work pickup because of what was on top of it: an excavator with wide, grooved steel belts for tires, a glassed-in cabin that could spin 360 degrees, and a hydraulic boom as long, powerful, and toothy as a T. rex. Luke's job was to ply this incredible piece of machinery against the north-facing side of the ridge and dig out the hole where the garage would sit. Like many of the foundational tasks, its outcome would dictate the success of whatever else followed.

On a cloudless and chilly midwinter day—wearing his standard outfit of work boots, heavy jeans, light winter jacket, cap, and "let's get after it" expression—Luke got his marching orders from Jeff and Walter. My self-appointed job was to eavesdrop and be incredulous. The previous day, Jeff and Walter had marked the garage's corners with small wooden stakes topped with orange tape. After about ten minutes of the scantiest detail, Luke was ready to climb into the cab and get going.

"You can actually maneuver that monstrosity with enough precision to do what they're asking?" I asked.

"Sure."

"How will you know where the hole is supposed to be if you accidentally knock over one of those stakes?"

"Don't worry. I'll know."

"What'll happen if the hole is too big?" I asked Jeff.

"I think Luke has things under control," Jeff said.

Walter nodded.

"You think I should hang around?" I said.

"What for?" said Jeff.

I took the hint and went to Amelia's to get some work done. But I was too distracted and anxious to be productive, so two hours later I found myself standing thirty yards from the noisy and stinky machine, gape-mouthed and vacillating between fear and astonishment. With the boom as the extension of his arms and will, Luke was wrestling a four-ton oval-shaped red sandstone boulder out of the hillside. He had already dug out several of similarly gigantic size and piled them up near the ravine. Judging from the size of the hole, I guessed he was less than a quarter done.

The object of Luke's attention was wedged between another boulder and sandy dirt that had compressed over centuries into something almost as resilient as concrete. Moving the excavator's twin levers back and forth, Luke wedged the boom's teeth under the front of the boulder and rocked the entire machine back and forth, repeatedly lifting the edges of the steel tracks off the ground. When that didn't work, he tried knocking the boulder from the side with the boom's bucket as a battering ram. After about ten minutes of this, the score was Boulder 1, Luke 0. I walked over and he cut the engine so we could talk.

Even though it was a cold day, he had a sweat ring on his cap. Instead of worried, he seemed pissed off.

"What do you think?" I said.

"That piece of shit will come out eventually. Just gotta keep after it."

"These rocks are enormous. Would you have agreed to do this if you knew they were in there?"

"Probably not," he said. I didn't want to know if he was serious or joking.

"You think this is the worst of it?"

"Not nearly. I'm just getting started."

"At least they'll be incredible for landscaping. Lots of people around here would die for these."

"I just hope they don't kill me first."

That evening, I tried to describe the scene to Holly in a way that would impress her. But she quickly saw through my vivid description to my trepidation.

"I'm pretty sure Luke is up to this, but I guess there's only one way to find out," I said.

"You have to have faith in him."

"I do. Still, I can't help but wonder what'll happen if he hits a wall that he can't get around."

"Jeff is helping us because you're not up to managing the subs. So you can't be worrying yourself sick like this at every stage."

Her argument was logical, which meant it was useless.

"It's your turn to take Miranda to school tomorrow," I said. "How about I go with you and we can both figure out if there's anything to worry about?"

"That's fine with me if you think it will help."

"It's worth a try."

The next morning, my plan spectacularly backfired as Holly and I stood at the top of the ridge with our hearts in our mouths, nearly incapacitated by the noisy, dusty, and rollicking scene in front of us. Luke had parked the excavator at the top edge of the hole, which was now at least twenty-five feet high, and was using the boom as a lever to keep from tipping over. He was rocking another boulder loose, the pebbly dirt underneath the excavator crunching and spraying from the motion. If he inadvertently slipped the excavator into reverse, he'd plunge off the other side.

One of Luke's coworkers stood at the edge of the drop-off, and they were communicating with hand signals. I motioned to Luke to stop but he ignored me. Barely able to speak, I walked over to the other man and asked, "How long has he been perched on the edge like that?"

"For a while. It's just one big rock after another."

"And your job is to keep him from going over the other side?"

"Are you serious?" he said. When I didn't reply, he knew I was. "We're talking about Luke here. I don't have to tell you he doesn't need or want any help from me. He's having the time of his life, giving those big-ass stones the hell they deserve."

"If you're not helping him, then what you are doing?"

"Enjoying the show. He texted me what he was up to, and I had to come over and see it for myself."

Holly and I looked at each other, and we both looked at him, and he finally realized we were about to have twin strokes.

"I can see you're worried, but you shouldn't be. He does this kind of thing all the time. In fact, he's been in a lot worse fixes than this."

"That's supposed to make us feel good?" I said.

"I'm only saying this is no big deal for Luke. He's a big boy."

Holly and I turned away, walked back to her car, and drove to Amelia's without saying anything of consequence. That night, as we ate our take-out dinner with Miranda around the breakfast nook table, my smartphone dinged. Luke had texted a pic of the finished hole. It was picked clean of boulders, smooth on the bottom, and gently curved upward on the side just as Jeff had ordered up. Assuming it was correctly placed, it was as perfect as that kind of work could be.

Luke had skills that I couldn't aspire to even in my most delusional moments. But now I realized he also had a lot in common with the pre-fire me: his self-confidence bordered on bravado, he wasn't easily intimidated, he didn't cotton to critics or naysayers, and he didn't ask for help. Our garage had a place to go, and it was mainly because the man my daughter loved had some of the attributes that I most valued in myself before the fire swapped out my cranial motherboard.

But just when I thought I had him sized up, he toppled my assumptions the evening that we all gathered at Hillary's house for Amelia's twenty-fourth birthday party. In an improbable and shamelessly romantic gesture staged just before Valentine's Day, he proposed to my middle daughter in front of her astounded parents, sisters, brother-in-law, and nephew. On one knee, Luke held out the opened ring-box, and Amelia's affirmative shriek proved that I did the right thing by clutching the two bottles of red Burgundy against my chest as I shut the front door of our doomed house for the last time.

April 3, 2012, 4 p.m. Six months into therapy, I was sleeping better and thinking more clearly. Through the self-knowledge I gained by saying things out loud in the safety and privacy of my therapist's office, sometimes repeatedly, I had survived the anger stage of grief, skipped over the bargaining one, and was teetering on the last transition, from depression to acceptance. While it was too soon to send out a self-congratulatory announcement, it felt like my PTSD would be defeated.

On a warm and sunny spring afternoon, as I settled into the light brown stuffed chair opposite the door and waited for my therapist to bring a paper cup of chilled water from the refrigerator, I thought back to the morning at Amelia's house when I stood on her front stoop and debated with myself whether to call the woman who was coordinating mental health services on behalf of the therapists who wanted to help families wiped out by the fire. It wasn't dumb luck that had brought me to this physically slight woman who had played a more significant role in my recovery than anyone else. Something beneficent had led me to this healing place and compassionate woman. A surge of gratitude poured through me that was so palpable it bordered on the physical.

As the therapy session began, I described an experience from 2005. Although it took place in an environment that was the opposite of flame and heat, it seemed to perfectly describe why the acceptance stage felt within reach.

I was on a dive off the northeastern coast of Tobago, a densely green island that is a speedboat ride from Venezuela. I was there to see some of the largest brain coral in the world, wondrous and sinuous half-globes that look like the inside of a giant's head. Along with the others on my dive, I lazily rode the current over the coral formations, knowing that the chase boat at the surface would track the progress of our bubbles and be waiting for us wherever we surfaced.

Suddenly the underwater stream turned into a torrent, and I was propelled forward at a speed I could not control. My initial impulse was to fight to stabilize my body and gain my equilibrium, but I quickly realized that would probably lead to a speedy and unpleasant death. I relaxed as best I could and willingly went where the current took me, eventually surfacing almost a mile from the chase boat and hundreds of feet from my nearest diving companions, all of whom had been distributed at random locations by a force as implacable as it was powerful.

We inflated our diving vests and swam toward a central location. Then we bobbed and fretted about how long it would be before we were spotted and picked up. Although we had air horns and inflatable markers, we knew it could be an hour or more before help arrived.

By the time we climbed into the boat—the sun melting into the sea and twilight's murk spreading, our hands wrinkled from the water and faces leathery from the wind and sun—our gratitude at being rescued overpowered any other feelings we had.

I spelled out the story's punch line to my therapist, more for my benefit than hers. After the fire swept away the things I valued most in this world, the grief and shock would have inundated me if I had refused to let go of them as surely as my lungs would have filled with seawater if I had resisted the invisible torpedo of water whipping around the tip of Tobago.

By allowing myself to go where the fire took me, I finally came to understand an essential paradox of a natural or personal disaster. While the wildfire seemed unbelievable, the more unbelievable thing was the general absence of catastrophe in my life despite what surrounds me every minute of every day.

A wildfire cannot be prevented in a forest. It is an essential part of the natural order, and it will happen when conditions are sufficiently dry and windy. As long as I live in Bastrop County, I should be thankful for every day that a wildfire doesn't happen.

But that was just the beginning. I told my therapist about my faithful spouse, and drives that don't end in a head-on collision, and the likelihood that I would outlive my elderly parents, and the fact that my now-grown children hadn't given into their natural teenage impulses at every opportunity. Most of all, I reminded her about the wrong turn that Amelia took out of Colovista that turned out to be the right one, and Gordon's locking of the red swinging gate.

Every day, I realized, I'm surrounded by calamities that could have happened but didn't. If I took note of them, I'd be unable to lift the weight of my head off my pillow in the morning.

In the weeks after Miranda's twenty-first birthday, I believed the universe is arbitrary and indifferent at best and evil-minded at worst. But later, with the help of my therapist and a family that supported me when it wasn't easy to do so, I became convinced that the reverse is true.

May 31, 2012, 11 a.m. Almost exactly four months from Luke's wrestling match with the boulders, the house was ready for its brown standing-seam metal roof. We chose this more muted color, instead of the silver that dazzled on our Cottletown house, because we wanted our new home to blend in with the forest rather than stand out like a shiny dime dropped on an asphalt parking lot. The roof arrived on a long flatbed truck in the form of flat, interlocking panels custom-cut for each of the roof's individual sections. I was there to sign for the delivery.

The house was ready for its steel topper no thanks to me. My urge to hang around the job site and kibitz with the subcontractors or pepper Jeff and Walter with questions was finally broken on a cloudy and cool day early in March.

Walter's foundation plan for the main part of the house envisioned a ridge-top concrete slab held up on the split-level side by a retaining wall that also kept Luke's hole from falling in on itself.

The structural importance of this wall was beat into me practically from the day Jeff turned us into split-level converts, so of course I had to be there when it was poured. By the time I arrived after dropping Miranda off at school, a group of twenty-something jean-clad guys had gathered on the garage floor, wearing caps and do-rags, chatting in Spanish and laughing. Marcus, their slightly older boss, was the only one with a collared shirt and clean shoes.

The white, rectangular pumper truck arrived, and Marcus waved it into position. With Marcus again acting as traffic cop, the first of several concrete trucks backed up to the pumper truck, parked ass-end to ass-end, and began pouring the coarse, pebbly mixture into the pumper truck's trough.

A few minutes later, a thick gray soup gurgled and sputtered out of a very wide black hose. Walking on a thin wooden plank precariously nailed to the top of the wall frame, one young guy slowly moved the hose between the forms, manuevering it like he was icing a giant cake. Following several feet behind, a two-man team jiggled out the air bubbles with a vibrating wandlike device. The last group smoothed out the top of the wall with small tools resembling spatulas and inserted long pieces of rebar at regular intervals for tying into the main slab. Not once did I see any of the men look at their feet to see where they were going.

As I watched from the top of the ridge, spellbound and anxious, Jeff walked up and said, "It's a tricky thing, what they're doing. Kind of a not-too-hot, not-too-cold operation."

"What exactly do you mean? Or do I want to know?"

"Now that you mention it, you probably don't want to know."

I slapped myself on the forehead. "It's a little late for that now, wouldn't you say?"

As the men moved slowly down the wall in unison, they exchanged brief comments in Spanish, barely looking at each other. From below, Marcus pointed and hollered out an order.

"What are they saying?" I asked. "And what's he pointing to?"

"How should I know?"

"OK, you opened this can of worms. What's the worst-case scenario here?"

"The forms split apart and the concrete goes flying everywhere. I'm not sure how we'd clean up that mess. Or start over again."

"You can't be serious."

"I am. It doesn't happen often, mind you, but I've seen the results and they ain't pretty. Those guys have to pack that concrete in tight or the wall won't be strong. That's why they're vibrating the air out. But if they do for too long, it will become so compacted the plywood won't be able to hold it in."

"How will they know if they've got it just right?"

"If nothing bad happens. Now or later."

"Why did you think this is something I should know?"

"You're right. Guess I should have kept my mouth shut."

The wall turned out perfect: dense, smooth, and plumb. Having learned my lesson, going forward I let Jeff handle things without my hovering presence and nattering curiosity. I cut back my visits, and the updates Jeff delivered to me by phone were brief and to the point. The midcourse corrections that had to be made to Walter's design, as his ideas morphed from computer printouts to a complicated skeleton of framing lumber, trusses, nails, and screws, were worked out without any assistance or input from me.

On paper, the setup for our building project was dodgy, at best. The owner was depressed, the architect was scatterbrained, and the general contractor was a guy who normally spent his days building things with his hands rather than indulging in that most disrespected of human art forms: management. Rounding out the picture were a rising and falling piece of land that was only nominally a house site, and several inopportune rains that temporarily turned the job site into mush.

But rather than driving each other crazy, Walter and Jeff formed a bond that grew even stronger from their mutual enjoyment of Holly's and my gratified reactions to what they were bringing into our lives. There were no cussings-out, stompings-off, withering looks, sarcastic remarks, or unreturned voice mails. And Jeff's reputation and obvious skill meant that the subs listened to him and showed up when they were needed.

In explaining to my therapist how this potentially toxic brew turned into something productive and soul nourishing, I could only say that grace was at work. No other explanation sufficed.

Early on, I wondered whether Jeff regretted the decision he made that October Sunday afternoon, with no hesitation, to be my eyes and ears, the project's ramrod and quality-control specialist. The one time I let the question slip out—on a day when I was nearly overcome with emotion over the trust I had put in him to lead us into a positive future—he said, with a merciless stare, "Are you asking if I knew what I was doing?"

The subject never came up again. But every day he answered the unasked question with his total commitment and a genial, can-do demeanor. He had our backs, each and every day.

One very warm morning in early May, he rang me up while I was working at Amelia's house and asked me to come over. Details were not forthcoming. All he said was "There's something here you gotta see."

Because this was not normal, I feared the worst. "How bad is it?" I shouted to him as I practically ran from my car at the end of the cul-de-sac.

The framing of the second story had just begun with the installation of the roughed-in floor. Jeff and his three helpers were taking a break, hands on their hips, and gazing from the family room north toward Miranda's room.

"What do you mean, bad?" said Jeff.

"I assume something's gone haywire. Why else would you need me to come right over?"

"Calm down," he said. "There's nothing to worry about. If there was, you'd be the last person I'd tell."

Jeff's three-man crew laughed at his affectionate disrespect.

"So what's the deal?" I said from below.

"Come up here and see for yourself," said one of the guys.

I bounded up the temporary staircase and stopped dead in my tracks at the top.

For the first time, I saw what the extra twelve feet of vertical space meant. Our view of the river in both directions was greatly expanded, making the entire southeastern bend visible. But that wasn't why Jeff summoned me. I turned my back to the river and followed him into the space that would be Miranda's room. Behind the healthy and green oaks and elms that bordered our property line's ravine stood another ridgetop at almost the same level as ours. It was invisible from the ground. Dozens of dead trees, some limbless and others like stick figures with only a couple of skinny arms, spread across the fire-decimated plateau.

The fire had raced in from the northwest and swept across the exposed ridgetop with the same ferocity as it brought to the land Les owned. But when it came upon our ravine, it crossed as a whimper rather than a blistering roar.

Until some unknown time in the future, when the last dead trees had fallen and the forest's regeneration was firmly in control, Miranda's room would remind us of what the fire took just as the upstairs deck would remind us of what it gave. Jeff knew what these opposing views would mean to me.

Three weeks later, I helped the forty-something truck driver turn his rig around on the cul-de-sac so he could back it up to the relatively flat area that had been cleared out for unloading and stacking the roof panels. Wearing a slightly grizzled gray-inflected beard and a dirty cap, he got out of the truck, wiped his face with a rag, and held out his rough, calloused hand. I shook it as he said, "Nice place you got here. Real nice."

We both looked up at the fully formed house clad in a white, paperlike waterproof skin printed with the name of its manufacturer.

"That took some doing, sticking a house up there like that," he said.

"No joke."

"I'm guessing you're the builder."

"Nope. The owner."

"No kidding. You rebuilding, then?"

I gave him the two-minute version of where-we-used-to-live and why-we're-building-here-now.

He adjusted the chewing tobacco under his lip and spat. "Good for you. Nice to see some fire victims landing on their feet. I'm looking forward to the day when that group includes me."

"It got you too?"

"It's coming up on a year, and I still have a hard time believing it myself some days."

"Where you staying?"

"On what's left of my land, in a trailer. I've been there for a while now, and I don't expect that to change anytime soon."

"Where at?"

"Up where it started. I was one of the first to get it."

With almost nine months of experience, I knew what questions to avoid and what comments to suppress. But I still hadn't learned how to hold back the brief wave of wooziness that announced my survivor's guilt.

"Man, I don't know what to say, other than I'm sorry. I'm not going to insult your intelligence by saying it'll get better anytime soon." Pointing around, I added: "Even with all this, I still have my bad days."

"I hear you," he said. "I just gotta keep hanging in there, I guess."

I thought about mentioning therapy. But he didn't look like the type, which said more about me than it did about him.

We stood for a moment, facing each other, and he correctly guessed what I was thinking, while I couldn't have been more wrong about him.

"No, I'm not jealous of you, if that's what you're wondering." It was, but I wasn't going to admit it.

"I'm happy for anyone who's doing OK," he said. "The way I look at it, if enough people like you are getting on, then it's just a matter of time before my turn comes, too. Now, if you'll 'scuse me, I got some unloading to do."

August 28, 2012, 4 p.m. I arrived at my therapy session with my just-ended visit to Wisconsin still burning in me.

The setup for this session began four months earlier, when my parents came to Austin to see Amelia receive her master's degree from the UT School of Social Work. On a bright late spring morning, I took them to see the ravaged Lost Pines and our new property.

They had already been in Texas for a few days. During that time, the fire came up only in an indirect way, as Holly, Miranda, and I recounted some of the details of our temporary stay in Austin. I assumed their Bastrop County visit would be the right time for me to tell them what I had gone through and how it had changed me. But when the time came, I couldn't do it.

We passed Bastrop State Park without anyone saying much. They asked a few questions about the new houses being framed on McAllister Road and the lots where dead trees were being cut down and hauled off. I told them a little about how we found our property and what they'd see from the building site as they looked south across the river.

I introduced them to Jeff and the rest of the crew, walked them perfunctorily through the dried-in house, and then spent the rest of the time frustrated by a problem that had suddenly arisen with a newly delivered door. They looked out the windows and talked quietly to one another while I fretted and fumed.

On the drive back, they said very little about what they had seen, and I said almost nothing about what it all meant to me, both good and bad.

I could have started with what I saw that hot and windy afternoon at the crest of Cottletown Road: the houses in the Colovista area sequentially exploding inside the greasy, serpentine smoke cloud. Then I could have described the choice I faced when I reached the red gate Gordon had just closed. Or how my mouth and stomach felt as I stared at the collapsed roof and crumbled limestone. Or the embittered indifference I had toward the river land the first time I saw it and the exaltation and relief I felt the second time.

But I didn't know how to tell them any of that in a way that wouldn't sound insufferably self-pitying. Because my fear and pride paralyzed me, and because they didn't know what questions to ask, they left Austin without realizing that their sometimes sarcastic and frequently flippant son had just gone through the most transformative nine months of his life.

Because my therapist already knew all of this, I didn't have to provide the context for what had just happened in Door County, Wisconsin, where my parents used to take my sister and me for summer vacations when we were growing up.

"We decided to go there with Miranda," I said, "because Anton was performing at a summer music festival in this little town called Fish Creek. On the way there, we took a detour to see what had become of this little red cottage on the banks of Sturgeon Bay where we used to go every summer when I was a kid."

"And how did it look?"

"The cottage was gone, and the green spaces where my sister and I used to run around were all built out with trailers and little houses. I didn't expect it to be the same almost fifty years later. But it still made me kind of sad."

I told her how my interest in the natural world had been irreversibly kindled in Door County the month before I started junior high when a summer school project sent us in search of leaves, butterflies, moths, and beetles I later rendered in meticulous exhibits my parents helped me create.

"I'm guessing you're wondering why I'm telling you all this," I said.

"I'm listening."

"My parents knew I was writing a book about the fire because I worked on it for the first few days after Miranda and I got to Wisconsin. But just like when they visited in May, I was too tongue-tied to talk about it. And they were respectful enough not to press me for details. But after we got to Fish Creek, we took a brief drive along the edge of Peninsula State Park, this gorgeous old-growth forest of birch and maple and evergreens. That forest reminded me of another one I'd loved, and I knew I couldn't keep hiding from them how my heart broke after our home burned and our loblollies died."

I explained that the morning after Anton's first concert, I offered to let them read my book-in-progress. I wanted them to have privacy, so Miranda and I took a two-hour walk along a park trail that wove between the trees and sun-splashed views of Lake Michigan incarnated as Green Bay.

"The forest was densely green and thick with musky, wonderful smells. But it was hard to enjoy it. I was too worried about how they'd react."

"You were afraid they wouldn't like it?"

"So much was at stake. My book seemed like the only way I could tell them what happened. But I was a fool to have been worried."

I took a moment to gather myself. How could I accurately describe, even to my therapist, how I felt as Miranda and I returned to our hotel room from our walk and saw my parents staring at my computer, crimson-faced, eyes swollen, and so choked up they could barely acknowledge Miranda's chirpy "Hi, Granny" greeting?

"We had no idea," said my mom as my dad quietly sobbed, hunched over and dabbing his eyes with his fingers.

While Miranda and I were hiking, my mom had slowly read almost twenty pages to my dad out loud, stopping when her eyes were too bleary and her voice too cracked. My account of the fire's outbreak and my last trip back to the house had undone them, and their reaction undid me. Miranda quietly and intensely observed, as she had done in therapy.

Later that afternoon, while I pretended to read an e-book and my father napped, I visually eavesdropped on my mother as she read about my visit to our lost family ecosystem on the day that Reverend Williams told me his R-rated joke while the young men from his church filled a trailer with the junked-up remains of his house. Several times she audibly gasped, and more than once she had to stop. When she was finished, she unsteadily walked to where I was sitting, threw her arms around my neck, and told me how much it hurt her to know how I'd suffered.

"I know this sounds weird," I told my therapist in a choked-up voice, "but her being so sad made me really, really happy. It was like the more she cried, the happier I got. Maybe 'happy' isn't the right word."

"Maybe not," said my therapist. "But I know what you mean."

"When we got back to Sheboygan, a similar thing happened with my sister and brother-in-law. Then, before I went back to Texas, my parents did something truly lovely. They escorted me through the living room, dining room, and kitchen of their little brick house, the one where my mom grew up. And they asked me to pick out the pots that I wanted back."

Just as Mother Lisa did with the Ash Wednesday urn, and several of my other friends did with pots I had previously given them, my parents bequeathed back to me a wood-fired jar, several wood-fired bowls, a large urn, and a set of white porcelain bowls with drippy manganese rims in the style of Lucie Rie.

I looked at the oversized digital clock. My hour was almost up. There's a good reason physical contact with a therapist is generally off-limits: if it wasn't, every meaningful session would necessitate an emotional hug, and that might turn into trouble over time. But without a valedictory hug, how could I communicate to my therapist what she had done for me?

We had agreed that our sessions would stop when I returned to Bastrop, although the door would never be closed. Our work together had weakened my natural-born gift for irony and the gravelly cynicism I reflexively acquired during my time in the jaggedy and often inhospitable world of politics and government. My softened-up soul had more room for introspection and gratitude. The worst effects of my PTSD had waned, although—like a self-aware alcoholic—I suspected that I would always be in recovery, never completely cured.

I had taken a chance on therapy because I saw no other way to regain my equilibrium. But in that first month, I almost faltered because I thought a real man should be able to rise above the loss of physical objects, especially when I didn't lack for food, a place to sleep, and a shower.

Now, as I left her office for perhaps the last time, I knew I had to finish my book so that other people would know, through my example, that grief and loss and regret and anger and guilt cannot be washed away through force of will or stoical silence. To keep them from becoming malignant, those emotions must be talked about, ideally in a safe place with someone who is trained to care in the right ways.

While I hoped my book would find a wide audience, its special target would be men who are like what I used to be: emotionally sturdy, skeptical of anything as amorphous as therapy, and brimming with confidence bordering on hubris.

Through my book, I had an obligation to tell self-satisfied men unhinged by a horrible event what I needed someone to tell me in the weeks after the fire: you're not alone in how you feel, and you shouldn't feel ashamed to talk about it.

And this: show your strength by accepting emotional help as naturally and unselfconsciously as you would a cast for a broken leg.

September 13, 2012, 1 p.m. An entrancing light rain fell as we loaded the dogs into Holly's SUV without their leashes for the first time in over a year. While they couldn't have known what awaited them, the dachshunds' restlessness and Charlie's wheezy pants showed that they knew something momentous was afoot.

The midday shower followed us from Austin to Bastrop, and it kept up while we waited for the two-man moving crew, a misty veil pleasantly obscuring our view across the river. Suddenly free of human supervision, the wieners were beside themselves with excitement and relief as they immediately slipped back into their old habits of chasing rabbits and rodents, yipping at birds, and darting around pointlessly and joyously. Their business was too urgent to be sidelined by a little precipitation. For his part, Charlie sat magisterially on the front stoop, the apparent guardian of the realm and master of his new world.

"You left in fire and you're returning in rain," said Amelia as she met us at the front door with hugs and smiles.

As if by magic, the rain stopped as the movers started lugging in our new furniture, dishes, and appliances. The house had paint and wood smells that we instinctively associated with our move into the Cottletown house. I ran my hands over the immaculately clean and smooth living room wall. The house would never be this unblemished again, and I wondered when it would have the slightly gritty but blessed feel of being very lived-in.

As the empty house slowly filled up, I tried to imagine birthdays and Christmases and coffee in the morning and afternoon naps on the sofa and sunset on the deck. How long would it take for this beautiful thing Walter conceived and Jeff created to feel like home? And how many months would pass before it stopped feeling strange to have Bastrop rather than Smithville as our mailing address, to turn south from the highway rather than north to get home, and to drive through a neighborhood of tidy brick and stone homes rather than the motley group of dwellings we knew so well from our many years on Long Trail and Cottletown Road?

For the second time, Holly and I were moving into a house where we could happily live out the remainder of our lives. But this time it was a hope rather than a given, an aspiration rather than a conviction.

Holly and I don't know how long Miranda will live with us, or what her life and ours will be like if she pursues independence from her parents. Similarly, we have lost the impulse to predict the contours and content of our futures or the presumption that we can control them. We've had mindfulness and acceptance forced upon us and we're not upset about it.

A week after we moved back to Bastrop County, we were reminded of what we missed while we were in Austin and why we eventually had to return. Instead of streetlights or the glittering downtown skyline, we were surrounded by a palely lit forest overflowing with unseen creatures. Rather than traffic noise or an occasional siren, we heard the soprano buzz of insects and the rhythm section of amphibians on the riverbank. From high in the sky, the waxing gibbous moon reflected off the river like a silver talisman quivering on a strip of pewter.

CHAPTER 12

March 5, 2013, 10 a.m. Since the day I counted out the numbers that the FEMA contractor had spray-painted on our trees, I had avoided going north of Highway 71, where the fire did its most malevolent work. This meant no drives through Bastrop State Park or along Park Road 1C, no checking out our old neighborhood, and no investigation of the area along Highway 21 where the conflagration began, and where Richard Linklater filmed the East Texas scenes in his movie *Boyhood*. The view from the highway was my only source of information about what was happening in the former forest as life tried to reestablish itself.

But several months after our Austin exile ended, I added an item to my calendar: a visit to Bastrop State Park on the fire's one-and-a-half-year anniversary. This would be the milestone date when I would force myself to enter the epicenter of the park's annihilation.

My reasons for doing so weren't the kind that could be articulated in a list. I didn't have tasks to accomplish or even a coherent rationale for picking that date. I resisted the impulse to analyze or dissect my intention for what increasingly felt like a sacred duty.

As I prepared to leave on a crisp late winter morning, the only way I could answer Holly's "Why are you doing this?" was "Because I have to."

I had to first stop at the park headquarters to get a daily pass.

"Are you here from out of town?" said the friendly and youngish park employee in a crisp uniform as she wrote down my vanity license plate number: LBJ FAN.

"No. I've lived around here for a long time. I've been to the pool with my daughters about a million times." She didn't need to know about the one-year exception.

"So you know the ropes, then."

"Pretty much. Although this is the first time I've been back since the fire."

"Well, in that case, be prepared for a lot of changes," she said. "As you can imagine."

"I'm not sure that I can. That's why I'm here. To see it for myself."

"In that case, is there anything else I can do for you?"

"Actually, there is, if there's a ranger close by."

Five minutes later, I faced a burly thirty-something man in a beige uniform with a medium haircut and a no-nonsense attitude.

"What's y'all's plan for the dead trees?" I asked.

"If you mean the ones on the side of the road, they're coming out. We're doing it as fast as we can."

"I'm not talking about those. I mean the ones in the park's interior that I can see from the highway."

"Nothing. They'll eventually fall over and then rot."

I cocked my head, too flabbergasted to reply.

"I probably know what you're thinking," he said. "Believe me, we've talked through all the options. And this seems to be the best one, though I'd be the first to admit no one will enjoy looking at it."

"So we'll just have to be reminded of all these massacred trees for as long as their awful-looking trunks stay upright?"

"If we go through there with heavy equipment, we're going to compress the soil and do a lot of damage to whatever life is trying to come back. It might be better looking in the short run, but it would be terrible for the land in the long run."

Three simple sentences and I had the whole picture.

"So ugliness now turns into beauty later?"

"I couldn't have put it better myself."

"Only problem is, I might not be around long enough to see it." I shook his hand and turned toward the door. Then I stopped, surprised that I had almost forgotten the most important question: "What about the toads? Any evidence they're still around?"

"Actually, yes."

"Really?"

"Nobody heard any the winter after the fire. But a couple of weeks ago, one of our biologists heard them on two separate occasions. So at least a couple are still here."

"Thank God."

"All of us feel the same way," he said, as the two other park employees smiled and nodded their heads. "It gives us cause for hope." Buoyed by that optimistic news, I set off for the deserted overlook parking lot.

My feel-good moment would be short-lived.

LATE WINTER NIGHTS

The coloratura trills of male Houston toads greeted five-year-old Miranda, eight-year-old Amelia, and me as we stumbled out of the car on an inky and damp night in late February, the scent of that day's rain still in the air. After I turned off my headlights, we couldn't even see an outline of the overlook pavilion thirty feet away.

"Hear that?" I said. "I think we're in luck tonight."

I turned on my dive light, a megalamp that was weightless underwater and a three-pound lunker on dry ground. "Just follow close behind me," I told them. "Don't get off the path."

My two youngest girls trudged behind me on the slightly muddy downhill trail. We fought to keep our bodies upright as our sometimes-slipping feet angled downward. "Watch yourselves. It'll be easy to fall."

I didn't have to wait long for their grumbling to start. "Just remember, it'll be worth it once we're there," I said.

Miranda asked a question she would repeat four more times: "How much longer?"

"Not much."

"But how much?"

"Not much."

"OK."

At unpredictable intervals, the trills briefly started up, a single call that almost immediately turned into a men's glee club. Twenty or thirty seconds later, the silence was broken only by an occasional insect chirp or the call of an owl. If any coyotes were nearby, they weren't letting on.

The night was cloudy and moonless, so it was impossible to see anything outside the light's cone except the indistinct outline of a landscape clotted with branching limbs. If I shone the light upward, we could see the glint of raindrops on the nearest pine needles and leaves.

I followed the tiny tin rectangles nailed to the trees that marked the trail while also keeping an eye out for snakes and spiderwebs. We had to stop more than once for one of us to pull a sticky and icky remnant from our face and hair and swipe away the temporarily homeless arachnid.

Every time we took this nocturnal hike, I wondered about the multitude of creatures close at hand that were invisible to me as a biped uniquely out of its element. Except for humans, was there any other species so adept at going where it didn't belong?

About thirty minutes after we started, with our shoes muddy, we arrived at the park's most prolific toad pond. As usual, we were the only human intruders.

"Remember, we have to keep quiet while we wait for the singing to start," I whispered as we sat on our haunches near the edge of the water.

"How long before they start?" said Miranda.

"What does he always say when you ask him that?" said Amelia.

"There's no way to know," I said to Miranda. And to Amelia: "Please be nice to your sister."

"I wasn't being mean."

I shushed them up and we all waited. It was quiet enough that I could hear their breathing, staccato inhalations that bespoke excitement and anticipation. No matter how many times we did this, seeing the first toads was always a thrill.

We didn't have to wait long. I turned on my light in the direction of the closest sound, and there they were: three diminutive amphibians, one on the muddy bank and two squatting on dirt outcroppings near the pond's edge. Their drab bodies were a stark contrast to the red semi-balloons they had inflated just underneath their mouths. They all seemed to be very pleased with themselves to be making such a racket from such a small flap of flamboyant flesh.

I felt a little bad about shining my heavy-duty light into their eyes at such a carnal moment. But the comparative mental image of an intruder training a floodlamp on our bed as my wife and I started to cozy up to one another didn't generate sufficient toad empathy for me to turn the light off. The sight was simply too wonderful. Out of the corner of my eye, I could see the delighted smiles that went with my daughters' barely audible gasps.

On the way back, as my girls' missed bedtimes started to manifest themselves in uncooperative legs and feet, I had to walk more slowly and deliberately. I had to repeatedly remind Miranda why I couldn't carry her on my back. But the forty-five-minute walk had one advantage: it gave me a little more time to contemplate the vast amount of life that surrounded us in the Lost Pines and be grateful for the gorgeous and teeming ecosystem in which Holly and I were privileged to raise our towheaded daughters.

March 5, 2013, 10:15 a.m. As I began my hike, I wondered what I would do if the trail were no longer marked. But I quickly realized that either the tin rectangles were still there or new, shiny ones had been added as replacements.

On the trail's downhill sections, there were slashes in the soil where torrents of rain had eaten out the sandy gravel and deposited it in mounds near the bottom. This was what often happens after a killer drought. Too much rain—a ludicrous concept during the drought—victimizes landscapes that have lost their protective cover of grasses and small plants. That's what happened in

Bastrop County in January 2012, and the proof of it was still visible over a year later.

A halfhearted breeze blew, the only sound in an otherwise menacingly quiet landscape. There were no insects humming or chirping, no birds warbling, no tiny mammals scurrying nearby, and no heart-stopping swish of a snake on the move through the underbrush.

I needed to know what kind of life was fighting back in a denuded landscape after the passage of twenty lunar cycles. Up close, the trees looked worse than I would have guessed from my fleeting glances along the highway. The only green was on stubby shrubs and bushes, mainly invasive species that I had spent many sweaty hours trying to get rid of on our Cottletown property.

The trees without bark had a spectral color that showed no sign of insect infestation. Some had fallen into one another, trapped in a vertical limbo that would probably persist until the supporting trunk gave way. I kicked at the bottom of several trunks and was surprised when they didn't crumble.

Where were the tiny critters that feasted on this type of organic matter? Why didn't I see any insects or smell the visible by-product of their larval appetites: decomposing and musky organic matter inching its way back to its primordial state?

In a place where insects are scarce, or practically nonexistent, could there be birds? With little hope, I scanned the horizon while hoping for a melodious interruption of the deathly silence. No birds anywhere.

I wasn't in the park as a biologist applying the scientific method. My observations were haphazard and on the fly. But in a place where I used to have to consciously avoid stepping on creatures or walking into them, and where every downed tree trunk was a city of wriggling life that only a four-year-old boy would want to touch, the fact that I didn't see or hear anything moving spoke for itself.

The absence of life was like a reverse shock wave. As each link of the food chain went missing, presumably starting with the pollinators, the one above it had no chance. Even though it was wide open, the whole environment felt claustrophobic and pulled in.

In the daylight, the inert landscape and its accompanying silence were oppressive. But what would it be like to make this walk in the dark, knowing that nothing was peering at me with night-vision eyes or slithering alongside my sneakers or alighting on my clothing or swooping through the air? The absence of creaturely hazards would be the opposite of comforting.

I reached the toad pond with the park ranger's optimistic report flattened by my empirical verdict: Bastrop State Park is sputtering back to life, but not in abundance and not with the species that used to thrive there. Did it make sense any longer to speak of the Lost Pines when the name was an utter misnomer for the land between Bastrop's eastern edge and the midpoint to Smithville?

The toad pond had gone dry during the worst of the 2011 drought. Now it was filled with brown water almost to its natural level, with moldering chunks of vegetation on the surface. I sat down on the previously grassy slope leading down to the pond, now just sand mixed with clay. My short walk had turned out far worse than I could have imagined. Staring at the pond and the lifeless hulks behind it, my thoughts turned global and apocalyptic.

Unlike its prior invitation to mindfulness and peaceful contemplation, what was the new meaning of Bastrop State Park? Perhaps it was as a symbol of man's impact on a planet whose exquisitely delicate balance is always at risk of tipping toward one type of ecological overreaction or another.

Fire in a pine forest is usually beneficial. When it turns deadly on a massive scale, humankind usually has a hand in it.

A massive wildfire is what happens at the end of a mind-bending heat wave and drought when too many people choose to live in or near a forest. Besides our adoration of trees and nature, we humans bring to the environmental table houses and carports and barns and propane tanks and electrical lines and an aversion to know-it-all bureaucrats coming on our land and telling us how to be better stewards of it. We share a fear of controlled burns in our neighborhoods. We loathe limits on development even when we live among species facing extinction. With our tools and arrogance, we have earned the right to be masters of our environment.

For most of us, including me, the safety and comfort and security of our families trump any abstract notion of environmental stewardship or communal sacrifice. But if that's the way humans have evolved to think, then we have to accept the bad with the good.

The more I thought about it, the less I could see how the assault on Bastrop State Park could have been prevented. Almost nobody wants to go back to a preindustrial time of no electricity and no fossil fuel–burning personal transportation. Very few are willing to sacrifice the comfort of central heat and air-conditioning on the altar of a higher good. I couldn't do that.

Humans in the twenty-first century have reached a point in their technological, sociological, and political development where we have definitively weighed in on earth's ecological tipping points. We have already made the choice between the blue marble on which we live and our contraptions and personal freedoms and comfort. Anyone who thinks that choice can be undone is probably delusional.

Is life on earth facing a long-term cataclysm due to man-made activities and inventions? Would the 2011 drought in Texas have happened anyway, as part of the planet's inevitable veering between periods of benevolent and vicious weather? Is the precipitous global decline in frogs, toads, and salamanders a natural diminution of species no longer adapted to a changing world, or is it the result of forces that people control or influence?

Nobody knows the answer to these questions for certain because there is no set of alternate universes in which proponents of each theory can test their hypotheses or validate their convictions or justify their ideologies. But as I began retracing my steps back to my car, it occurred to me that maybe it was time to retire the old "canary in a coal mine" cliché as the shorthand way of describing signs of looming catastrophe.

Very few people today have been in a coal mine or even know that coal miners used to detect the presence of toxic gases with little birds that would drop dead before they did. But almost everyone knows that the climate is changing or, at the very least, appears to be. Perhaps the new metaphor for our present condition should be "amphibian in a drought."

Spring 2013. In Central Texas, the balmiest and most blessed month of the year is March. Unlike the Northeast's muddy season, or the slushy and sloppy onslaught in the upper Midwest, or the final round of storms slamming into the West Coast from the Pacific, there is almost nothing to complain about in Bastrop County during the month of the spring equinox except the yellow film of pine pollen on furniture and clothes left near an open window.

Prior to the fire—as the breezes turned warm, my sweet peas bloomed, and I transplanted tomato and pepper seedlings into my garden's beckoning soil—Holly and I would know that spring was definitively upon us by running our fingers along any surface exposed to outside air. During the worst of it, we could write our names in yellow the same way my teenage buddies and I used to scrawl "wash me" on the sides of filthy cars and vans.

But during our first spring back in Bastrop County, there was no yellow pollen. It was like a winter without having to shovel snow: the absence of this unpleasant cleanup job bespoke something potentially ominous.

There were still pine trees in our new neighborhood, although far fewer than before the fire. We had four large ones, including the loblolly we saw each time we looked out from our deck across the river. Why weren't they pollinating?

As the month progressed, there was more to fear. The oak and cedar elm and cypress trees still had not leafed out by the time Holy Week began. Like I did during the final month of the drought, I started each day by inspecting the largest trees, my left hand over my eyes to block out the morning sun slanting toward me from the northeast.

I didn't know whether the trees were still dormant or dying or already dead. While I feared the most for the trees whose trunks had partially burned, I wasn't relaxed about any of them and wouldn't be until I saw new buds.

I took my anxieties to the traditional noon Good Friday service at Calvary Episcopal Church on March 29. Mother Lisa's meditation reminded me that I couldn't expect the leafing out of our trees to be any different from the other lessons I'd learned since the fire. This is some of what she said:

> *My God, my God, why have you forsaken me?*
> *On Good Friday, these words rend our hearts, not because they are on Jesus's lips, but because they are on our lips. In those times when we are in the midst of suffering and can see no sign of deliverance, we cry out to God like a child abandoned by the mother who loves her. When we are helpless to stop the suffering of the people we love, we accuse God of forgetting us.*

I thought: She forgot to mention ravaged ecosystems that don't come back to life as they were or trees refusing to bud.

> *They are honest words that acknowledge the depth of human misery in the world. But they are also words of faith that insist both that God is and that He cares about his human creatures. The words may be naive. They may misunderstand the nature of God, who does not so much rescue us from suffering as show us the way through suffering to Him. But they are faithful, even hopeful that the God who seems absent nevertheless hears us when we cry.*

Maybe. You'll need to keep talking before you persuade me, Mother Lisa. But at least, as is your custom, you're not dishing up baloney on the most solemn and conflicted day of the liturgical calendar.

> *There is an old story about rabbis who gathered to prove that God does not exist. Fed up by long and painful experiences of divine neglect, they at last reached the conclusion that humanity is completely alone in the universe. Just then, one of them interrupted the others to say, "We will have to finish this conversation later. It is time for our prayers."*

It would be wrong to say that I left church feeling better. But I did feel wiser. Mother Lisa's poetic thoughts reinforced what I was slowly, and sometimes grudgingly, coming to accept after a year in therapy: easy answers are lies, and the truth bobs on a sea of ambiguity. We often don't notice it or can't see it. But when we do, it's because of what it is floating on: a kind gesture spontaneously given, a harsh word that isn't reciprocated, beautiful music, soul-stirring art, a metaphor that crushes a preconception. In our best moments, it's a quiet spirit that expects nothing but is open to everything.

Two weeks after Easter, all of our trees had either leafed out or were beginning to.

April 6, 2013, 7 p.m. Several weeks after Luke proposed to Amelia, I called the Bastrop County Clerk's office and confirmed that I still could preside over weddings as a retired county judge. At my daughter's request, and with Luke's concurrence, I joyously agreed to walk her down the aisle and then take my place in front of them as the officiant.

Two evenings before the wedding, Luke, Amelia, Holly, and I took our seats around the small dining room table in Amelia's house. Joining us was Laura, who had flown from Paris for the wedding. Miranda wasn't there because she had returned to her teetotaler ways after our 2010 flight from Europe landed in Houston. I held my breath as I twisted a corkscrew into one of the Gevrey-Chambertin 2008 Premier Cru bottles. I carefully pulled it upward and exhaled with relief when it popped loose.

After I poured most of the bottle into our five bulbous glasses, we jointly swirled, sniffed, and tasted the wine—it was as deliciously funky as Amelia and I remembered—and made appreciative comments about its subtle ruby hue. The first sip filled our mouths wonderfully, and it got even better with the cheese and bread that Amelia and Holly had set out with the wine in mind. It wasn't like the Pinot Noir we normally drank, and we didn't feel compelled to say precisely why that was. Nobody caused offense with one of those lame-brained fruit analogies that plague wine tastings or magazine write-ups.

The wine's journey from the Côte d'Or to our prewedding celebration needed no elaboration or commentary from the group. But rather than thinking about the bucolic August morning in Burgundy when I bought the wine specifically for this occasion, each sip silently summoned memories of my thoughts and feelings as the sun blasted through the kitchen skylight and the wind screamed outside.

So much had happened since that noontime moment. But I had thought about my decision to save the wine enough times that I still trusted my recollection.

I had made my final walk through the family room and past Miranda's bedroom. I was heading toward the front door through the kitchen. I wasn't going to leave the house with empty hands, so my plan was to grab the ochre-colored urn on the small wooden stand that Holly placed just to the right of the front door on one of her father's oriental rugs.

But the pantry door was open, and I couldn't help but glance at my wine rack. My eyes instinctively went to the Gevrey-Chambertin. Weirdly, they reminded me of one of Amelia's pet phrases from the nightly moment when she was about to fall asleep in the Long Trail house, with her preadolescent body wedged next to mine and Miranda's music drifting over us. She would whisper, "Zuzu's petals," and we both would quietly giggle at the image—from the movie *It's a Wonderful Life*—of George Bailey reaching into his pockets on the snowy bridge and finding the remnants of a flower that his youngest daughter had brought home from school on what was turning out to be the worst day of his life.

The astounded and goofy look that Jimmy Stewart conjures up as he pulls out the petals seems to say: "OK, I've been a dumb-ass, but I get it now. In fact, I get all of it." I loved the phrase because of its universal symbolism, but I suspected that my middle daughter adored it mainly because it was fun to say.

I stared at the bottles several inches above the tile floor. What would it mean if I took them instead of the ochre urn? What would that—choosing something ephemeral rather than something permanent—say about my priorities?

It was a debate I couldn't afford to engage in. I took them because they were like Zuzu's petals: a tangible thing that spoke of far more than I had the time or emotional clarity to articulate.

Amelia emerged from her girl-cave a minute before it was time to lock arms with me just outside the room in the Lady Bird Johnson Wildflower Center where she would exchange her vows with Luke. With a garland of fresh greens and delicate pink flowers topping off her flowing shoulder-length blond hair and setting off her blue eyes, she made me think of the Fairy Queen in *A Midsummer Night's Dream*.

Like her older sister had done when she got married, Amelia asked Miranda to do one of the readings. In a knee-length and V-necked gray dress, and with her straight blond hair dusting the tops of her shoulders, my youngest daughter—who at one time could only conversationally string together a few monosyllables—read the e e cummings poem "i carry your heart with me."

After another reading by Luke's uncle Kenny, I began my brief remarks. After thanking the bride and groom for giving me the great honor of presiding over their marriage, I said:

Seventy-five years ago, Thornton Wilder's play Our Town *had its first performance. Since then, millions of Americans have watched their children, friends, and neighbors take on the personas of Emily, George, Mr. and Mrs. Webb, Mr. and Mrs. Gibbs, and the Stage Manager in countless school, community, or semi-professional productions. Every so often, it even shows up on Broadway.*

Our Town *has a wedding in the middle of it, and it was the first wedding over which I presided when I played the role of Stage Manager in a college production in 1976. If that hadn't happened, we wouldn't be here today because I began dating my wife, Holly, during that production. She was Mrs. Webb, the mother of the bride. And if I hadn't dated Holly, I wouldn't have married her. And that would mean, of course, no Amelia and no wedding today.*

So you might say that me standing up here is the Fritz family coming full circle with a work of literature that has a lot to say about weddings, families, communities, and what's important in life above all else. And those things are what I want to leave with Luke and Amelia as they marry one another.

The real meat of Our Town *comes in the third act. Nobody who has ever seen the play can forget Emily's "Good-bye World" speech when she realizes, probably for the first time, how valuable and wonderful everyday life is when we're surrounded by those we love and who love us in return.*

As Emily looks around at her home, parents, brother, and the town she has left behind in death, she says with a combination of wonderment and regret: "I didn't realize. So all that was going on and we never noticed."

I am going to take the liberty now of turning Emily's speech around for Luke and Amelia. Rather than "Good-bye World," it's "Hello Married Life."

Hello to Pinot Noir, a grilled steak, and evening conversation.

Hello to sleeping in and waking up with the sound of rain outside your window or a mockingbird singing in the back yard.

Hello to backrubs and affectionate kisses and cuddling on the sofa.

Hello to swims in the river and fishing and napping on a white-sand beach licked by turquoise water.

Hello to winks and smiles that nobody else understands.

Hello to turning off your phones so you can share an hour or two that nobody but you will ever know about.

And maybe, just maybe: hello to a baby bump that is destined to turn into someone who is gorgeous and beloved and doted on.

We know what had to happen to Emily before she had her moment of blinding insight and searing regret. But, thankfully for all of us living folks, we can say "Hello World" anytime we let our eyes see what is in front of us every day.

My hope for you, Luke and Amelia, is that you keep your eyes open and "Hello World" on the tip of your tongues. I'm not saying every day and all the time, because nobody can do that, not even the saints and poets the Stage Manager mentions at the end of the play.

Just do it often enough to make the good times even better and the bad times a little less bad.

And now, my last quote from the play: "Well, that's all my sermon. It wasn't very long anyway."

CHAPTER 13

September 6, 2013. I will always know how many years have passed since the fire by subtracting twenty-one from Miranda's age. Yesterday was her twenty-third birthday.

When Hillary called with birthday wishes for her little sister late in the day, she asked me in a whispery voice, "How are you doing?"

"In what respect?"

"The second anniversary."

"I'm OK."

"And Mom or Mir?"

"The same."

"You haven't talked about it?"

"It hasn't come up and I doubt it will."

My answer to Hillary bordered on a lie, given the depth of its understatement. Except for Amelia's wedding and the birth of my second grandson, Wyatt, I feel better than anytime since the Lost Pines burned.

Summer 2013. Three months earlier, my recovery began unraveling after the sickening removal of a tall and elegant cedar elm with a scorched bottom that Holly and I loved. It went from green to brown to dead in less than a week.

With most of the fuel gone, I didn't fear another fire as Bastrop County once again baked and browned. But everything else felt like a reprise of the 2011 summer, with the sun directing and producing a bitter environmental encore.

It was as if I were nearing the end of a marathon, only to take a wrong turn in the direction of the start. I was going backwards, my stamina weakening and my resolve slipping.

The upstream reservoirs of the Colorado River flirted with the lowest elevation and flow levels since the dams were built. With the river stagnant and overheated, vegetation took hold. By August, it looked like I could get out of my kayak and walk across the river on a green carpet flecked with yellow.

Holly and I planted, mulched, and faithfully watered several dozen lob-lolly pine seedlings in the spring only to watch them shrivel into lifeless, brittle miniatures from the drought-driven heat. Cutter ant armies on reconnaissance for anything green denuded our flowers, vegetables, and ornamental bushes in ravening overnight raids. The grass on our river bluff that had come back to life the previous spring was now stunted and lifeless.

Low-pressure cells occasionally popped up on the weather radar but almost always disappeared as they entered the Central Texas no-rain zone. Pines and oaks that had escaped the grim reaper's attention in 2011 ran out of luck.

The living things I loved about our new life were in danger, and I took it personally.

Then, as the Fourth of July holiday came and went, my situation evolved into something worse. On more than one occasion, as I waited to cross Highway 71 into the westbound lane, I wondered if my attention and judgment might falter. I could think of worse things than an instantaneous highway death.

I wasn't suicidal or thinking about intentionally hurting myself. But the concept of permanent deliverance was not wholly unattractive.

These contemplations were unprecedented for me—even at the lowest point in the month after the fire, I never fantasized about the possibility of imminent mortality except for that one afternoon with the slab engineer. I was sufficiently self-aware to schedule several therapy sessions after a nearly year-long hiatus. As I took my seat in her office on a scorching midsummer afternoon, my therapist looked at me piercingly and with compassion. My eyes and body language gave me away. I was back in the depression stage.

She said I was unconsciously associating the drought's newest phase with our great loss. The mystery of how the brain processes a momentous event over time was also at work. For almost a year, I tried to make peace with the fire's ruins and give thanks for its gifts, with the expectation that doing so would make my PTSD scab over and heal, like a deep cut that only leaves a faint scar. Now I was numb and discouraged at the thought of my mental illness turning chronic despite all my effort.

As my therapist suggested, I paid Robb another visit, and he added an antidepressant to my pharmaceutical regimen. Holly gave me some homeo-pathic remedies. These compounds inhibited my dark musings and cooled my anger and resentment toward the environment. But I was still anxious, and sleep became dodgy again. I had a persistent, low-grade stomachache that I knew had nothing to do with digestion. Nobody could accuse me of being happy.

Less than three weeks before the fire's second anniversary, I took an early morning kayak ride, slipping my skinny yellow boat past a blotch of curled aquatic leaves and tiny lemon-colored spores. I paddled upstream, past a creek bed on the right where I sometimes saw a heron poking in the shallows or a roosting barred owl. The rising sun brushed a yellow streak over the tops of the trees on the south bank. A family of feral hogs rustled and grunted, and a large fish—probably a gar—flopped on its side.

The river momentarily wiped my mind clear of negative thoughts, as it usually did. On the way back, I pulled into a shady spot beneath some syca-mores, and propped up elbows with my knees and my face with my hands. It was time to take stock of things.

My friendship with my former artistic partner was over—irredeemably and with prejudice—because of the countless trees it killed. I couldn't forgive the gutting of Bastrop State Park and our old neighborhoods, the destruction of my pottery and Holly's grandfather's art, and the ongoing struggles of families who remained in limbo or had settled into far worse circumstances than before the fire.

But I couldn't declare it my enemy either. The fire gave us a home and land that are lovelier than anything we had before. I received a centenarian piano with a shimmering soul from a mother-in-law who saw my desperate need and met it. Our losses showed me the true meaning of friendship and trust as brought to life by Jeff, Walter, and Anton. By driving us from our old neigh-borhood, the fire gave me a water-filled haven of solitude where I take plea-sure in the subtle changing of the Texas seasons and the never-commonplace rotation of migrating and nesting birds. The vegetables we eat from my garden nine months out of the year sip water and nibble nutrients from river-bottom soil as palatable as anything else in Central Texas.

The fire turned my linear mind into one that accepted this irreconcilable reality, a riddle without a solution. My old self would have found it hard to suppress the question that many undoubtedly thought but only a few dared speak: "Didn't the fire leave you better off?" My new self knew enough to set it aside as specious and irrelevant.

Thinking through all of this gave me clarity but not peace.

"How was your ride?" Holly asked as we drank our morning coffee.

"I feel better. But that doesn't mean I feel good."

I remained anxious as my diving excursion to Cocos Island approached. My original Cocos trip was supposed to begin three days after we lost our home. I rebooked the trip, even though the name "Cocos" had regrettable associations. Now I wished I hadn't.

"I should be excited as all get-out," I told Holly and Amelia the day before my flight to San José, Costa Rica. "That's the way I always am when I'm packing up my gear. Not this time. I'm nervous and worried."

Nobody seriously suggested canceling the trip and forfeiting what I paid for it. But as I drove to Houston, my anxiety grew, and I almost turned around. What kept me going was something Holly said to me as I was heading out the door: "This trip will be good for you. You will come back refreshed and renewed."

It was, perhaps, the understatement of her life.

My destination was a UNESCO World Heritage site 350 miles from civilization on Costa Rica's southwestern Pacific side, accessible only by a thirty-five-hour boat ride or helicopter evacuation. In the water I would contend with strong currents and startling thermoclines as hundreds of sharks gathered and cruised nearby. The point of the trip was seeing the sharks, but I was thinking of the things that might go wrong underwater.

The crossing wasn't easy. For more than a day, the boat pounded through uncooperative surf, lurching and rocking. Some of the divers retreated to their bunks, assumed the fetal position, and counted down the hours until they stopped wishing they were dead. I fought off the worst effects with pills and my natural resistance to motion sickness. But meals were unappealing and sleep was hard work. By the time we arrived, just after dawn, I would have traded my drought-stricken, malaise-filled life in Bastrop County for what had just passed and what might lie immediately ahead.

And then I saw the island.

Steep basalt walls shot out of the ocean, the product of a long-ago volcanic upheaval. A monochromatic tapestry of ivy and vines and moss hung from them with a color that was the definition of tropical green. Misty waterfalls—as tall and skinny as the limb of a Giacometti sculpture—poured the island's prodigious rainfall into the sea. Defying gravity and my assumptions about how trees proliferate, coconut palms and purple coral trees grew out of the sheer walls. Billowing and dense cumulonimbus clouds hung over the island, waiting for their afternoon cue.

Cocos Island is primordial and pristine, untouched by humans except for a tiny ranger station on a spit of sand. It is the opposite of what I mourned and regretted in Bastrop County. But instead of making me wish I never had to go back, I received a different message from the island's avalanche of life: nature is resilient and powerful and, over time, unstoppable.

If this much life could grow on inhospitable surfaces splashed with ocean water, how could I believe that the Lost Pines would not come back, or the Colorado River would stop flowing, or the trees that had died on our land in the past year would not be replaced by their heirs? I would have to wait years for most of this to happen, and some of it might happen after I was gone. But just as volcanic rock squeezed out of the sea had turned into a tropical rainforest of indescribable density and vigor, the Bastrop County ecosystem would reassert itself as long as my species didn't get in its way too much.

With patience and a spirit of stewardship, my community would be beautiful again. Taking the long view would be hard for me, and I would undoubtedly falter on a regular basis. But now I had a living icon to remind myself of what was possible, and perhaps even inevitable.

If this was a healing epiphany that I could take back with me to our home on the river, then my trip was already worth it. But Cocos Island had other lessons, and I was in a receptive mood.

The divers split into two groups, each assigned to an inflatable dinghy equipped with an outboard motor and a rack to prop up the dive vests, regulators, and tanks. My group included two couples and six other divers who paired up with one another. While I enjoyed diving, most of my companions were fanatical. With over four hundred dives, I was one of the least experienced and traveled. My dive buddy was a forty-something farmer from Indiana with a warm smile, a quick laugh, and a bald spot that made him easy to find among the other divers as we drifted with the current or clung to undersea boulders, waiting for hammerhead sharks to swim past us, sometimes over us.

We entered the sea with a backwards tumble and weightlessly floated down to rocky bottoms or pulled ourselves down rope-lines when strong currents were possible. We encountered dozens of sharks on some dives, hundreds on others. Shy around humans, they were the antithesis of Hollywood's man-eating terrors. The only way we could get close was by making ourselves small and staying still.

After two days, I had seen schooling hammerheads with powerful silvery bodies and pancake faces with eyes glued to their sides, and sleek silky sharks stalking the blue water, the stuck-up loners of Cocos Island. I crouched near a small conclave of Galapagos sharks with he-man bodies and vacant stares. And I swam within thirty feet of a whale shark, the largest fish in the world, which doesn't look like a shark or a whale. I barely paid attention to the enormous, swirling and corkscrewing schools of silvery, yellow, and reddish fish.

From the first dive, I felt comfortable and safe. Coming up with a new batch of superlatives after each dive quickly became tedious because everything I saw was like nothing I had ever experienced before. During our communal meals, even the hardest-core divers on our boat talked about the life around Cocos Island like it was a singular and matchless world.

On the third day, an hour after nightfall, I came to the surface, inflated my vest, and waited my turn as my fellow divers took their time climbing into the dinghy. I was coming to the end of the greatest diving day of my life. On the morning's first outing, I saw a silhouetted city of hammerheads congregate and slowly swim fifty feet above me, a promiscuous display of prehistoric life oblivious to my presence. In the afternoon, I had my second up-close-and-personal with a whale shark. I had just finished hovering over a horde of silvertip sharks as they hunted in nocturnal packs for prey trapped between the rocks. Our lights attracted the prey, and the hapless little fish drew in the snub-nosed sharks that wrestled with each other to eat them.

Everything I encountered underwater that day embellished and expanded the first day's lesson. Life on earth was not only inexorable and irreversible; it was humbling and beautiful beyond any means of human expression, and it had been that way for eons. What I experienced that day was just a couple of hours in the ocean's endless march of time, completely unexceptional in one respect and utterly exceptional in another.

Then I beheld the night sky as I floated on my back. If the sharks of Cocos Island said one thing about my place among living things, the darkest sky of my life said another. With the nearest light pollution hundreds of miles away, and the moon absent like an unwelcome relative who knows better than to crash the party, the Milky Way took the shape of a large ethereal cloud surrounded by other smaller clouds, our home star's galactic environment the most prominent among many.

At my dive buddy's suggestion I turned over, put my mask below the surface, and stirred the water. Like an inverted night sky, the sea lit up with innumerable sparkles of light, the bioluminescent creatures of the sea paying homage to the stars above me.

After dinner, it was bedtime for most of my companions. But I still had work to do before I could sleep. I went to the top deck of the boat and climbed into the green, woven hammock that was keeping time with the boat's water-induced rhythm. I needed to sort out the cacophony of feelings that were threatening to overwhelm me.

The infinite sky, the life-gorged sea, and the timeless island that stood between them could have made me feel insignificant beyond anything I could express or give form to. But on that night, after those experiences, I came to a far different conclusion, one that had much more to do with the fire's unwillingness to take Amelia's life or mine.

My conclusion that night in the hammock under the black sky speckled and smeared with light just now reaching me from millions of years ago: I am healthy, I live with people who love me, and I them, and I live on a planet, and a community within that planet, that gives me everything my soul requires, even if I sometimes lack the faith or spirit to perceive it. The fire changed none of this, nor could it unless I gave it permission.

September 6, 2013. The lone pine that stood among the deciduous trees on our riverbank began to turn brown in August. From the early November day in 2011 when Walter and I first stood together on the ridge and discussed its prospects, I had adopted this tree as an emblem of our fire experience: burned but not destroyed, endangered but still standing. During our first year in the new house, its survival was more than symbolic: it was the only loblolly pine among the trees we reveled in from our kitchen, living room, and decks.

On the day after Miranda's birthday, I remain hopeful it will live, although I know it probably won't. When it dies and is left on the ground to rot, the no-longer-there pine will be an emblem of the passing of one phase of our life into the next. We no longer live among the trees that drew us to Bastrop County three years before Hillary was born. Instead of the pine forest where our daughters grew into adults, we now live among cypress, hickory, elm, sycamore, willows, and two large loblollies that stared down the fire, their improbable resistance documented by a band of charred bark at the bottom of their trunks. We share our lives with bluebirds, hummingbirds, owls, woodpeckers, cardinals, warblers, and the other birds that use the river as a migratory map.

When it begins raining again, the meadow across the river will bloom with wildflowers and the grass will wake up.

MY POST-FIRE LIFE

My youngest daughter's birthday and the fire's anniversary share more than a common date. Each represents an ongoing lesson for me about the intersection of what humans increasingly understand scientifically—how the electrical impulses and nerves and synapses in our brains create emotion and language and consciousness—and what we cannot deny but will never truly know: the thing we call our soul or spirit or metaphorical heart.

With every new discovery, modern neuroscience gives hard-core empiricists—people for whom there is no reality but the observable, measurable one—another reason to dig in. More and more, experiences that have baffled or thrilled humans for millennia—near-death visions of a life beyond this one, telepathic communications between loved ones across great distances, prescient intuitions—are deconstructed as unusual but entirely explainable consequences of our cerebral biology and natural selection's relentless refinement.

Some good can come of this. Describing mental illness objectively and clinically can shift it from something shameful and ostracizing to a condition that is as common and treatable as diabetes or arthritis. Rather than a path to self-destruction, it can be viewed as a means of family healing and acceptance, sometimes with the help of therapy and the kind of pharmaceuticals that helped me sleep and fight off depression.

But there is something about being human that brain scans and biochemistry and all the sophisticated machinery that twenty-first-century humans devise can't explain. It's the thing about us that makes us create and crave music and storytelling and poetry and beauty in all its other forms. It's why most people are religious and don't easily dismiss the possibility of life independent of a physical body. It's why we have words like "mystical" and "peace" and "reverence" and "grace."

If an externality could alter Miranda's mind so profoundly, giving her the serenity and patience that usually only comes with old age, I shouldn't be surprised that the fire changed me. But I refuse to believe that the fire's effect on me can be explained purely with diagnoses and data.

I was a fifty-six-year-old adolescent when the fire happened. I enjoyed giving authority figures fits, was happy to solve problems without the advice or involvement of others, instinctively took the opposite side of most arguments, and had the self-confidence of a politician, which I briefly was. When people referred to me as "a man," I couldn't help relishing how I had them fooled.

I don't regret having been like that. It was right for that time of my life and what I wanted to accomplish. It was never boring and was often fun.

But since the fire, maybe for the first time in my life, I consider myself a grown-up. Instead of strong opinions and a need to defend them, now I have one sole unshakable conviction: the futility of dogmatic belief. What could be worse than certitude for a self-aware being in a universe of endless ambiguity and countless contradictions?

I am reminded of this each time I drive from Bastrop or Austin to our river home.

With each passing month, the boundary of Bastrop State Park that ends at Highway 71 looks more forlorn and suffused with decay. The pine trees whose carcasses could no longer hold up against the wind lie on the ground in the form of an attenuated L resting on its two tips. As long as these limbless tree trunks remain trapped in midair between their not-quite-perpendicular joints and what used to be their tops, it will be hard for them to return to the ashy soil as humus, beneficially eaten through by insects and bacteria. In the meantime, they are a visual blight.

Many of the dead trees that remain standing are ghostly, having lost most or all of their bark. Those that still have limbs inevitably lose fragments of them when a storm whips up the wind. Nature's unstoppable regenerative forces remain undetectable while I drive by the park at 70 mph, although I know they can't stay invisible forever.

I almost never see this without feeling a bit sick to my stomach, and I hope I never reach the point where it fails to move and grieve me.

The man-made parts of McAllister Road have largely recovered. With a few exceptions, all of the debris has been hauled off, the dead trees cut down, the stumps removed, and new houses have replaced most of the ones that were destroyed. But the undeveloped lots look no better than Bastrop State Park, and the highest ones open up to a stark and depressing panorama.

Just before I turn onto my driveway, I pass the nearly two acres of our land that burned. But as I approach the garage, life spreads out in every direction from the gorgeous house Walter designed and Jeff built, and the river beckons just beyond it. Between April and November, our land is a multihued cloak of green offset with the perennial wildflowers Holly planted during our first fall. In December, amber and brown briefly prevail, with a few flecks of red. In winter, the naked trees expose the multitudinous birds that are otherwise visible only as they flit from branch to branch or take a quick bite of seed at one of our feeders.

I rarely see this without feeling grateful for what we have and a little astounded at how we arrived here, and I hope I never become complacent or jaded about any of it.

In summer, when I take Miranda to the park pool for a late-afternoon week-end swim, the staggering loss that Bastrop County has suffered is depicted in an unintentional "before and after" tableau. Because of the courageous, round-the-clock efforts of state and local firefighters during the 2011 Labor Day weekend, the park's Depression-era buildings and pool remained intact while almost everything around them burned. When I sit in one of the plastic chairs around the pool or float on my back and look up, I am blessed by more than a dozen mature loblollies. They are among the final remnant of the park's formerly extravagant beauty. But as Miranda and I leave the pool grounds through the brown, two-inch-thick old-fashioned wooden doorway, we see two- and three-story stalks with the pallor of death and broken-off pines stuck in their L-shaped limbo.

The ruined side exaggerates the beauty of the other; the poolside magnifies the other's desolation.

The lines and stanzas of a dozen Pulitzer Prize–winning poets could never convey what that 360-degree real-life diorama whispers to anyone who loved, or still loves, the Lost Pines.

AFTERWORD

I wrote this book to reassure anyone who loses much through a natural disaster, or some other life-changing upheaval, that pain and grief and anger and deep-down sadness are normal and nothing to be ashamed of or embarrassed about. There's also nothing strange or unusual in not talking about it or pushing away those whose arms are open.

Just as it's possible to tumble deeper into misery, with personal relationships unraveling, it's also possible to emerge wiser and stronger, with a deeper appreciation for family and friends and a greater openness to an inscrutable universe that is at once merciless and merciful. I have tried to convey all of this with descriptions and dialogue and metaphor.

But I know that while everyone enjoys a good story, most people also appreciate simple suggestions straightforwardly delivered. That is why I end my book with the information I wish someone credible and experienced had given me in the days leading up to the fire, as the drought's dangers were nearing the flashpoint of inevitability.

I do this not just as the survivor of a historic natural disaster but also as someone who has a deep-down aversion to simplistic solutions to complicated problems. I know better than to claim superior understanding. I offer these not as must-dos but as please-think-abouts. I do so humbly but also with confidence.

First, there's the easy stuff. If you live in an area that is prone to natural disaster—hurricane, tornado, wildfire, flood, or earthquake—there are some things you can do right now that will make your life much easier if the unthinkable happens.

- Store all of your irreplaceable digital belongings in the cloud or on an external hard drive that you periodically update and securely store away from your home.
- Take digital photos of your furniture and any other possessions that might be disputed by your insurance company and keep copies on your smartphones and in the cloud, including art, musical instruments, tools, jewelry, or rare items like old books.
- Make sure you have enough homeowners insurance—many people don't have enough to rebuild and replace everything—and find out whether you also need flood insurance. If you have unusually rare or expensive objects, look into additional insurance to cover them because many policies have set limits on art, jewelry, and the like.
- Create a family plan for evacuation—where you will go, how you will get

out, what you will take—and put this list on your smartphone and keep a hard copy where it can quickly be found.

If disaster strikes:

- Don't second-guess evacuation orders or recommendations.
- Be prepared to *not* know what is happening in your neighborhood, and be skeptical of rumors and anecdotes on social media.
- In the absence of meaningful information, resist the natural impulse to find out what is happening by avoiding roadblocks and barricades (i.e., do as I say, not as I did).
- Take advantage of the temporary help available from nonprofit organizations for short-term housing, food, and basic necessities.
- Be courteous with your insurance claim adjusters but also firm, resolute, and clear-cut about what you expect to receive and why (ideally backed up by your digital photos). If you run into problems, contact a consumer advocate at your state's Insurance Department.
- Get your claim going quickly, because they're usually processed in the order they're received.
- Don't make long-term decisions in the heat of the moment.

If you decide to rebuild:

- Hire contractors or crews that you know are reputable and qualified or that come recommended by someone you trust—unfortunately, fly-by-night operators are irresistibly drawn to disaster areas.
- Put together a comprehensive budget that will help you rebuild and furnish your new house without pushing the limits of your insurance coverage or personal finances.
- Find out what kind of governmental help is available for neighborhood or individual property cleanup and debris removal.

These are all practical things that have to do with money and property and physical possessions. As my story shows, the hard stuff shows up with sleepless nights and anxious days and fraying relationships and darkening moods. If you feel this way, I encourage you to seek help through therapy if you have the means to do so. You will almost certainly find greater self-knowledge and help by talking to someone who isn't your spouse, parent, child, friend, or someone from your church, temple, synagogue, or mosque.

The objectivity and safety that comes from talking to a trained professional who carries no weight from a prior relationship is an important part of the healing process. While I don't mean to downplay the important role clerics can play in a believer's life, most of us would not seek one out for an illness or injury, so why do that for a condition of the mind?

If you decide to go into therapy, please think about the kind of professional you could best work with. Some of the basic things to consider are gender, age, and professional credentials (type of degree and ability to prescribe drugs). While I don't believe that a common set of religious beliefs (including atheism) is necessary, I was fortunate that my therapist and I coincidentally came out of the same Christian tradition. That was a positive thing for me, and it might be for you as well, depending on your spiritual practice and commitment to it.

Once you have an idea of a preferred kind of therapist, reach out to a mental health organization in your community for referral suggestions. If you are a member of a managed care plan, you can also call their member services hotline for some initial possibilities based on your general preferences.

Finally, with my personal experience and the experiences of my family and friends in the Lost Pines as a touchstone, I offer these thoughts in the hope that they will be helpful and comforting to you if you are suffering because of a great loss:

- Whether or not you are in therapy, write down your feelings and experiences. You can do this through a journal or diary or a memoir intended only for yourself. Putting your thoughts in writing will help organize and clarify them. Later they will be a reminder of what you learned and why. Some people do this with a blog, but it can be dangerous to pour out your feelings online when they are still flowing from you like lava. If you're going to share them with the public, it's probably better to let them cool first. If I had started a blog in the weeks after the fire, I have no doubt I would regret online content that would outlive me.

- A life-changing event will amplify your emotions in good and bad ways. To avoid hurts that might never heal, be quick to apologize when you do wrong, and equally quick to forgive when you are wronged.

- Even though almost everyone hates to accept help with simple daily tasks, doing so will make your journey a little easier.

- Be aware of the stages of grief: it will help you make sense of what you're experiencing, especially if you're angry or resentful.

- Be prepared for guilt and regret. When I think back on the months immediately after the fire, I am amazed at how often I was pulled down by self-blame and a feeling of shame because there were many others worse off than us. If someone had told me straightforwardly and compassionately that this was a natural response to a catastrophic event, I might have been able to deal with these cancerous emotions in a better way.

- Cultivate gratitude and savor its healing effects. I don't believe anyone can tell you what you should be grateful for. But if you have anyone you love, and who loves you in return, you have a seed. If you can see or hear beauty anywhere around you, you have a seed. The fact that you are alive is a seed.

ACKNOWLEDGMENTS

I was privileged to have three discerning readers without whom I couldn't have written this book.

Ross Ramsey gave me the initial push to write *Hail of Fire*, and he stayed with me through three major rewrites. A splendid writer and editor himself, he encouraged, mentored, and—when necessary—criticized. To keep my spirits up, we shared some laughs over our respective R-rated experiences with the Texas legislature.

Denise Gamino, a first-rate journalist and eagle-eyed editor, took my raggedy first draft and helped me shape it into something that I could build on. She was like those guys pouring the foundation wall of our new house. She redirected me in a not-too-hot and not-too-cold way at a time when a cruel word might have been fatal to the effort. She provided the solid foundation for everything that came afterward.

Janice Shay is a multitalented woman whose days are mainly spent on the visuals of the book world. But she did two things for which I can never repay her. She provided brilliant editorial feedback at a critical moment. And she introduced me to the wonderful people at Trinity University Press, a small group of professionals who immediately won me over with their passion for what I had written and with their obvious skills in the publishing world.

Thanks are also due to Cynthia Pence, who provided helpful feedback.

I am grateful to Amanda Hartfield, one of Amelia's high school classmates who has embarked on an auspicious photography career. In addition to the pictures she took of me, she visually documented the devastated area around the Bastrop State Park toad pond where I used to take my daughters. Her work unmistakably shows what the fire did and what nature's talents for resurrection will face in the coming decades.

Several individuals helped in tangible and important ways during our one-year stay in Austin, and I thank each of them: Mary Jane Moran, Colette Bellville, and Chris Claiborne.

Four months after we moved into our new home, Dan Welcher—my neighbor and friend and music composer extraordinaire—gave me something that only he could give. I will treasure it, and play it, for the rest of my life.

In the weeks immediately after the fire, my consulting clients—especially Ilene Baylinson, Jan Ruff, Sherry Matthews, Wardaleen Belvin, Fred Knapp, and Rich Robleto—gave me the time and space I needed to begin my recovery. They were kind and patient and supportive. In other words, they were true friends.

Finally, I must pay tribute to the people in Miranda's life outside of her family that have helped bring her to the wonderful place she is in today, doing what she loves—working in a daycare and spending her days around very young children. Holly and I are grateful beyond words to the people who taught and loved her at the Smithville Independent School District and the Bastrop Works vocational program for young adults with disabilities. We also have a lifelong debt to Sharon Heller, a therapist who helped Miranda regain some of her most fundamental skills and who saw in her a radiant, one-of-a-kind soul.